RUSSIAN LAWYERS AND THE SOVIET STATE

Eugene Huskey

RUSSIAN LAWYERS
AND THE SOVIET STATE

The Origins and Development of the Soviet Bar,

1917-1939

PRINCETON UNIVERSITY PRESS

Copyright © 1986 by Princeton University Press
Published by Princeton University Press,
41 William Street, Princeton, New Jersey 08540
In the United Kingdom: Princeton University Press,
Guildford, Surrey

Library of Congress Cataloging in Publication Data
will be found on the last printed page of this book

ISBN 0-691-07706-1

Publication of this book has been aided by a grant from the
Paul Mellon Fund of Princeton University Press

This book has been composed in Linotron Bodoni

Clothbound editions of Princeton University Press books are printed
on acid-free paper, and binding materials are chosen for strength and
durability. Paperbacks, although satisfactory for personal collections,
are not usually suitable for library rebinding

Printed in the United States of America
by Princeton University Press
Princeton, New Jersey

To my family,

all of whom share in this enterprise

Contents

List of Tables

Preface

This is a study of conflict between pre- and postrevolutionary visions of the role of law and the professions in Russia. It seeks to explain how the Bar, a legal institution of the old order dedicated to the representation of individual interests, has been integrated into the Soviet state, whose proclaimed commitment is to the furtherance of collective, or class, interests. The primary focus of the work is on the first two decades of Soviet rule, from the formal abolition of the Russian Bar in 1917 to the end of the 1930s when private legal practice was finally outlawed, when large numbers of young Soviet-trained advocates entered the profession, and when the last vestiges of overt resistance to party and government control of the Bar were eliminated. It was in this period that the Soviet Bar acquired its definitive shape and the major issues of professional development were resolved.

The work began as a doctoral dissertation at the London School of Economics and Political Science, though my concern with the uneasy relationship between lawyers and the Soviet state goes back further, to a thesis written at the University of Essex on the role of defense counsel in the Soviet criminal process. Mary McAuley and Peter Frank of Essex set me to thinking about the politics of the Soviet legal system, and Ivo Lapenna and the late Leonard Schapiro of LSE contributed greatly to my understanding of the relationship between law and politics in the early Soviet period. William Butler of University College, London, introduced me to the intricacies of research on Soviet law. To Peter Reddaway, my dissertation supervisor, I owe a special debt. He was generous with his advice and support, merciless in his insistence on precision and thoroughness, and understanding of the travails of a student working in relatively uncharted waters.

A number of institutions facilitated the research. I gratefully acknowledge the assistance of librarians at the British Library of Political and Economic Science (LSE), the British Library, University College Library, London, the Lenin Library, the Institute of Scientific Information on the Social Sciences, and the Library of Congress. I am indebted to the International Research and Exchanges Board for arranging study for an academic year in Moscow, where much of the information for this work was collected. I would also like to thank the Kennan Institute for Advanced Russian Studies for a short-term grant that enabled me to complete the library research in this country.

Peter Solomon and Sally Ewing kindly read the manuscript and offered comments based on their own research in Soviet legal development. Janet Martinez, my wife, was there throughout to read drafts, to assist in the research, and to listen and respond to my incessant musings about the world of Soviet lawyers. Her enthusiasm never flagged as we moved from place to place in search of the answers.

RUSSIAN LAWYERS AND THE SOVIET STATE

Introduction

When the Bolsheviks assumed power in October 1917, they inherited intact from the old regime an established Bar that in the last decades of tsarist rule had occupied a prominent place in the Russian intelligentsia. But like all segments of the creative and professional intelligentsia, the members of the Bar—known in Russia as advocates[1]—were an inheritance that the new regime accepted with ambivalence. As the educated elite of the country, the intelligentsia was essential to the Bolshevik program of transforming Russia into a modern industrial state. However, as specialists whose social backgrounds and professional activities were associated with the old ruling circles, they posed a

[1] The advocate is the member of the legal community who offers legal services to individuals and organizations. This may consist of oral advice, the preparation of legal documents, the representation of parties in civil suits, or criminal defense. In terms of his functional responsibility he could be compared to the American attorney-at-law, whose legal practice encompasses activities that in England are divided between barristers and solicitors.

The term *advocate* (*advokat*) was in popular use throughout the period from 1864 to 1939, but it was not until 1939 that it entered official parlance. Instead of exclusively following the official designation through all its twists—from private and sworn advocates (*chastnye i prisiazhnye poverennye*) in the prerevolutionary period to legal representatives (*pravozastupniki*) in the years of the Civil War and defenders (*zashchitniki*) in the period from 1922 to 1939—I have elected to use the popular term interchangeably with the official designation of the moment.

The reader familiar with the Russian language will note that in a few footnotes from the 1922 to 1939 period the term *ChKZ* figures in the title of articles. This is yet another term for advocate, which stands for *chleny kollegii zashchitnikov* [members of the college of defenders]. Advocates were often referred to in the interwar years as "chekaze."

threat to the party's monopoly of political power. Furthermore, they could not be relied upon to faithfully implement revolutionary economic and social policies.

The Soviet response to this dilemma was to exploit the talents of the old intelligentsia over the short term while pursuing a long-term policy of establishing a compliant Soviet elite. The new elite gradually took shape as a result of periodic purges of segments of the old intelligentsia, policies of coercion and persuasion directed at the remainder of this group, and the education of a new generation of young Soviet specialists. The changes in personnel were accompanied by equally extensive institutional reforms, which affected both the professional associations of specialists and the institutions in which they worked. In some cases these changes involved the alteration of existing institutions; in others, the creation of new ones. The process of elite transformation also affected the work of specialist groups. The traditional functions of the intelligentsia were modified to accord with the new goals and methods of Soviet policies. This brought significant changes to the form and content of specialists' labor.

Although the formation of a politically reliable and professionally competent elite was an acknowledged goal of Soviet policy, there was considerable disagreement in governing circles over the methods and tempo of policy implementation. For this reason the early years of Soviet rule were characterized by a marked inconsistency in approach to elite transformation. Official policy shifted back and forth in response to changing conditions in the country and to realignments of political forces within the Communist party.[2] At times it became difficult to

[2] Originally known as the Russian Social-Democratic Labor party (Bolshevik), the party was renamed the Russian Communist party (Bolshevik) in 1918. It would later drop the label Bolshevik and replace Russian with All-Union to indicate the multinational character of the organization. The terms Bolshevik and Communist will therefore be used interchangeably.

It should also be noted that in this work the term Soviet state encompasses both the Communist party and the government. This definition of the state, which is broader than that employed in much Western literature on the Soviet Union, highlights the underlying unity of political authority in the Soviet Union and makes it possible to draw distinctions between the state and society.

identify an official line, as competing factions in the party and government pursued varied policies toward the specialists. It was only in the 1930s, when Stalinism emerged triumphant, that a single approach was adopted and carried through to its conclusion.

By the end of the 1930s all specialist groups—from artists and academicians to engineers and lawyers—had been subordinated to Soviet rule. But the procedures employed in this operation varied considerably from one specialist group to the next. Policy directives of the highest party bodies provided only broad guidelines on elite transformation, which were then translated into specific policies for each group. Thus, although all segments of the creative and professional elite were subject to the same general currents in Soviet political and social development, each specialist group traveled along a distinct path to incorporation into the Soviet system.

The aim of this study is to closely examine the development of one specialist group, the Bar, from its origins in the prerevolutionary period until its absorption into the Soviet order in the late 1930s. The Bar's development was given shape by two lines of conflict that lie at the heart of this analysis. The first was between the advocates and the state. Jealous of their professional traditions and institutional autonomy and unreservedly hostile to Soviet power, the advocates in the wake of revolution sought to preserve the old methods of corporate government and legal practice. The young Soviet state, however, rejected the premise of an "apolitical" profession on which the lawyers' claim to independence and the maintenance of legal tradition rested. For the Bolsheviks, laws and legal institutions were instruments of the ruling class. It followed, therefore, that advocates and other legal personnel, who were seen to represent the interests of the bourgeoisie before the Revolution, would now be called on to serve the proletarian state.

In the first two decades of Bolshevik rule the state employed numerous methods to break the resistance of the advocates to Soviet power and to integrate the profession into the emerging legal order of state socialism. This study examines in detail the sovietization of the Bar's personnel, the evolution of a system of supervision over the advocates by government institutions, and the penetration of the profession by the Communist party. Reluctant to direct scarce talent into an institution so closely linked to the old order, the Communist party encountered stiff resistance from advocates in the 1920s when its members, a small minority in the Bar, first sought to gain control over the profession's governing organs. This spirit of opposition in the Bar continued throughout the interwar period.

The conflict between the advocates and the Soviet state was sustained by disputes among political and legal officials over the appropriate role of the lawyer in a socialist legal system. This second line of conflict, located within the Soviet state itself, prevented the development and implementation of a consistent policy on the Bar. Some officials, confident of the imminent demise of law, evinced little sympathy for the continued existence of the Bar; others proved more tolerant, whether for reasons of legitimation, judicial efficiency, or social control. The debate over the future of the Bar continued without resolution until the emergence of a Stalinist orthodoxy in the 1930s, when it was decided that a Western-style Bar, with at least the appearance of independence, was necessary in the Soviet system.

As legal policy makers struggled to carve out a place for the Bar in Soviet society, the profession's membership, organization, and functions in the legal system underwent important changes. These changes, which are chronicled throughout the interwar period, marked a departure from prerevolutionary patterns of behavior but often fell short of the transformations in personnel, institutions, and legal practice desired by the Soviet state. The unsuccessful attempt by the state to collectivize the Bar exemplifies the distance that frequently separated policy from practice.

One of the most important elements of the Bar's transformation was the development of a new approach to the practice of law. At stake was not only the means of providing legal services to the population but also the relationship between lawyer and client. In the following pages the reform of legal practice is illustrated primarily through an examination of the role of the advocate in criminal cases. Criminal defense places in sharpest relief the conflict between the profession and the state and between the advocate as representative of the individual interests of the client and as representative of the collective interests of socialist society.

On one level this is a history of the formative years of an institution that has received little attention from Soviet as well as Western writers.[3] But it has not been possible to write a history of the Soviet Bar without addressing the broader questions raised by Soviet legal development, such as the paradoxical growth of both law and terror in the era of the Great Purges. Whereas traditional scholarship on the Stalin period has understood the emphasis on law in the late 1930s as window dressing

[3] The groundbreaking work of John Hazard, *Settling Disputes in Soviet Society: The Formative Years of Soviet Legal Institutions* (New York, 1960), provides an extremely useful account of legislation affecting the Bar and other legal institutions in the first decade of Bolshevik rule. The book is less valuable, however, as a history of the Bar in this period because of its often uncritical approach to the impact of legislative acts on the law in practice.

The only other treatment in English of the formative years of the Soviet Bar is to be found in a section of Samuel Kucherov's *The Organs of Soviet Administration of Justice* (Leiden, 1970). Although reaching rather different conclusions from Professor Hazard on the role of the advocate under Soviet socialism, Kucherov, like Hazard, relies almost exclusively on legislative reforms to illustrate developments within the Bar. An overview of the institutional history of the Bar is provided in A. Bilinsky, *Die Organisation der sowjetischen Anwaltschaft* (West Berlin, n.d.).

In the Soviet Union a large number of books and articles devoted to the formation of the Bar were published before World War II. Among the most important of these are M. Shalamov, *Istoriia sovetskoi advokatury* (Moscow, 1939); M. Kozhevnikov, *Sovetskaia advokatura* (Moscow, 1939); E. Rivlin, *Sovetskaia advokatura* (Moscow, 1926); A. Tager, "Sovetskaia advokatura za 20 let," *Sotsialisticheskaia zakonnost'*, no. 11 (1937), p. 16; M. Ravich, "Sovetskaia zashchita," *Sovetskaia iustitsiia*, no. 7 (1937), p. 31.

In the postwar period there has been no monograph-length general study of the development of the Soviet Bar published in the Soviet Union. Recently, however, several books and dissertations have appeared on the formative years of the profession in some of the non-Russian union republics. See, for example, G. Sarkisiants, *Advokatura sovetskogo Uzbekistana* (Tashkent, 1972); I. Martinovich, *Advokatura v BSSR* (Minsk, 1973); M. Mumin, "Sozdanie i razvitie advokatury v Uzbekistane" (*Kandidat* dissertation, Tashkent, 1975); B. Durdyev, "Organizatsiia i razvitie sovetskoi advokatury v Turkmenistane" (*Kandidat* dissertation, Ashkhabad, 1974).

for the terror, this study views the movement toward the stability of law as a fundamental and permanent reorientation in Soviet legal development. The new respectability accorded to the legal system in the 1930s represented not a political tactic of the moment but rather a long-awaited resolution of disputes on the nature of law in Soviet society. The issue, therefore, was not the law being used as a façade for the terror but the legal system being used alongside, and ultimately in place of, the terror as a mechanism of repression and social control. Under Stalin the struggle between the two approaches to social control remained inconclusive. In the late 1930s, for example, open, exemplary repression by the courts, championed by the Procurator-General Vyshinsky, coexisted with secret, summary justice by extraordinary institutions, favored by Ezhov, the head of the People's Commissariat of Internal Affairs, the NKVD. Only after Stalin's death did the Soviet leadership commit itself to the dismantling of the mechanism of mass terror.

This view of the relationship between law and terror under Stalin is supported by a reperiodization of Soviet legal development. The study shows that the shift toward the stability of law began as early as 1932 and not, as widely believed, in 1936, the year that witnessed both the enactment of the Stalin Constitution and the launching of the Great Purges. In general, the periods of early Soviet legal development, around which the book's chapters are organized, swing back and forth from legal nihilism to legal revival. But they do not respect the divisions between the years of Leninist and Stalinist rule. The picture of Soviet legal development presented here illustrates that the juxtaposition of a benign legal system under Lenin with a harsh and repressive Stalinist legal order is unjustified.[4]

In part an interpretation of the legal revolution that accompanied the introduction of state socialism in Russia, this study

---

[4] It is not only Soviet scholars who seek to portray Soviet legal development in such terms. In a new preface to *Settling Disputes in Soviet Society*, Professor Hazard speaks of the return of contemporary legal policy makers after the "Stalinist aberration" to the "humanism" of the Leninist legal system. Preface to the Octagon Edition (New York, 1978).

is also designed to contribute to an understanding of elite trans-formation in early Soviet history. The Bar was influenced by the political and social processes that transformed the entire Russian intelligentsia in the interwar period, though the effects on the advocates were often less immediate and less far-reaching than on other professional groups. With the exception of the years of radical experimentation during the Civil War, the advocates enjoyed a surprising degree of continuity in legal practice and corporate self-government. Indeed, I will argue that Soviet advocates were not only the last major segment of the intelligentsia to be integrated into the new order but that this integration was, and remains, less complete than in other professional groups.[5] This is explained by the predominance of prerevolutionary personnel in the profession until the end of the 1930s, by the maintenance of a relationship of economic dependence between lawyer and client, which afforded the Bar considerable financial independence from the state, and by the state's preoccupation with the transformation of other specialist groups judged more essential to socialist construction.

Before turning to the advocates in the Soviet period, a few pages will be devoted to their counterparts under the tsarist and Provisional governments. An examination of the origins and development of the Bar in pre-Bolshevik Russia provides a benchmark against which to measure the degree and nature of change in the profession in the Soviet period. In the early years of Soviet

---

[5] Recent studies on the transformation of segments of the creative or professional intelligentsia include L. Graham, *The Soviet Academy of Sciences and the Communist Party, 1927-1932* (Princeton, N.J., 1967); E. Brown, *The Proletarian Episode in Russian Literature, 1928-1932* (New York, 1971); A. Kemp-Welch, "The Origins and Formative Years of the Writers' Union of the USSR, 1932-1936" (London School of Economics and Political Science, University of London, 1976); K. E. Bailes, *Technology and Society under Lenin and Stalin: Origins of the Soviet Technical Intelligentsia, 1917-1941* (Princeton, N.J., 1978); N. Lambert, *The Technical Intelligentsia and the Soviet State* (New York, 1979); S. Fitzpatrick, *Education and Social Mobility in the Soviet Union, 1921-1934* (Cambridge, 1979). We are approaching the point where the empirical literature on professional groups in the interwar period will sustain a general, interpretative work on the formation of the Soviet professional intelligentsia.

rule the majority of advocates had been educated and had practiced under the tsarist system. In order to understand their response to the October Revolution and to the subsequent transformation of the profession it is essential to know something of
the political and legal traditions that characterized the prerevolutionary Bar.

Chapter One

THE EMERGENCE OF A RUSSIAN LEGAL PROFESSION

On the eve of the revolutions of 1917 the legal profession was the product of two distinct currents in Russian legal history, liberal and autocratic.[1] The origins of the profession lay in the autocratic tradition, which dominated legal practice from the first appearance of lawyers in Russian courts in the fifteenth century until the Judicial Reform of 1864. During this period, the functions of legal representatives were narrowly circumscribed. In criminal cases, for example, judges reached their decisions in camera and based them exclusively on a written synopsis of the investigation. Unable to participate directly in court proceedings, the legal representative was restricted to drafting petitions and appeals on behalf of the accused.[2]

Under the autocratic tradition the organizational development of the legal profession was retarded by the state's refusal to allow the formation of a guild or estate of lawyers.[3] Throughout the

---

[1] As John Merryman points out in *The Civil Law Tradition* (Stanford, 1969), pp. 109-119, the unified legal profession familiar to the American lawyer is not present in Continental systems, of which Russia and the Soviet Union are examples. On the Continent the "compartmentalization and immobility" of legal careers produce rigid professional divisions both between private practice and state service and within the state sector itself. In the present work the term legal profession refers to only one segment of the legal community, the private practitioners, or advocates. State legal personnel, such as judges, prosecutors, and investigators, fall outside the scope of this study.

See the research of Brian Levin-Stankevich, "Toward a Study of Professionalization in the Russian Legal Occupations, 1864-1917" (unpublished manuscript, 1982), for an analysis of lawyers in the state sector in the late Imperial period.

[2] E. Vas'kovskii, *Organizatsiia advokatury* (St. Petersburg, 1893), p. 310.

[3] Successive tsars from Peter the Great to Nicholas I were vehemently opposed to the introduction of a Western-style legal profession in Russia. See S. Kucherov, *Courts, Lawyers, and Trials under the Last Three Tsars* (New York, 1953), pp. 113-116, for a selection of tsarist statements on the evils of an estate of lawyers.

pre-Reform period legal representatives were an amorphous group without professional training, organization, or identity. Legal practice was carried on largely by minor state officials in their spare time or in retirement.[4] Familiar with the niceties of bureaucratic language and procedure and occupying relatively unobtrusive positions in the state machinery, the petits fonctionnaires-cum-lawyers were a natural, though poor, substitute for a mature legal profession.

The Judicial Reform of 1864—the embodiment of the liberal tradition in law—attempted to make a decisive break with past policies on the legal profession. The Reform, which sought to introduce elements of a Western-style legal order in Russia, laid the legislative bases for the creation of a competent and self-regulating body of lawyers who would enjoy extensive rights in legal proceedings.[5] But the creation of an estate of lawyers and the redefinition of the lawyer's role in the legal system did not proceed as planned in Reform legislation. The liberal tradition was not sufficiently well-established in Russia to ensure the full implementation of the ambitious program of legal reforms that it had inspired. Defenders of the autocratic tradition, who had been outmaneuvered during the preparation of the Judicial Reform, were strongly represented in government institutions responsible for carrying out the Reform. In many cases they were able to thwart the intent of the liberal reformers by selective implementation of Reform legislation and by the adoption of new laws that did not accord with the principles laid down in the Judicial Reform. Over the last half-century of tsarist rule this tension between liberal and autocratic currents produced a hybrid legal profession that reflected both Western and traditional Russian influences.

The impact of the liberal and autocratic traditions on the prerevolutionary legal profession is clearly evident in the division of lawyers into two distinct branches: the Bar, comprised of sworn

---

[4] E. Vas'kovskii, "Advokatura," in *Sudebnye ustavy 20-go noiabria 1864g. za 50 let* (Petrograd, 1914), pt. 2, p. 251.

[5] See *Uchrezhdeniia sudebnykh ustanovlenii*, arts. 353-406.

advocates (*prisiazhnye poverennye*), and the profession of private advocates (*chastnye poverennye*). From the Judicial Reform of 1864 until the Bolshevik Revolution of 1917 the sworn advocates played the leading role in the Russian legal profession. Created in the image of the Western European professions,[6] the sworn advocates were drawn from the educated and social elite of Russia.[7] For the first time the legal profession became an accepted vocation for the Russian upper classes. The formal requirements for membership in the Bar were very high indeed, especially given the relative backwardness of Russia in this period. Prerequisites for membership included completion of a university-level law course and at least five years of work in a responsible post in the legal system.[8]

Professional associations of sworn advocates existed on the regional level in a loose affiliation with the regional courts, known as palaces of justice (*sudebnye palaty*). By the end of the tsarist period a governing council and general meeting of sworn advocates were operating in each of the fourteen court regions of the Russian Empire. The governing council was responsible for accepting new members into the profession, hearing disciplinary cases, and reaching decisions on other matters of common interest to sworn advocates. The general meeting, which was an assembly of the profession's rank and file, reviewed the activities of the governing council and at regular intervals elected council members. Although palaces of justice in exceptional

---

[6] The drafters of the Judicial Reform of 1864 borrowed freely from Western European professions. The organization of the Bar was inspired by the English and French models, while the fused character of the profession was based on the German example. Vas'kovskii, "Advokatura," pt. 2, pp. 252-256.

[7] Of the initial twenty-six applicants to the Bar in St. Petersburg one was a Doctor of Sciences, one a former lawyer in the commercial court, and the remainder were judges or other officials from state legal institutions. See I. Gessen, *Istoriia russkoi advokatury*, 3 vols. (Moscow, 1914-1916), 1: 142-143.

[8] *Uchrezhdeniia*, art. 354. The educational requirement was waived by the Ministry of Justice during the first five years of the Bar's existence. See "Polozhenie o vvedenii v deistvie sudebnykh ustavov, 19 okt. 1865," cited in K. Arsen'ev, *Zametki o russkoi advokatury (obzor deiatel'nosti s-peterburgskogo soveta prisiazhnykh poverennykh za 1866-74gg)* (St. Petersburg, 1875), pt. 2, p. 1.

cases overturned the decisions of governing councils, the Bar was essentially a self-governing profession.

Included in the Bar was a sizable body of advocates-in-training (*pomoshchniki prisiazhnykh poverennykh*). These university-trained apprentices officially spent five years under the patronage of sworn advocates before becoming eligible to apply for full membership in the profession. Once registered with a patron, however, many advocates-in-training practiced on their own during the apprenticeship period.[9] Approximately two-thirds of new sworn advocates were drawn from the advocates-in-training, with the remainder coming from the bench, the Ministry of Justice, and other state institutions.[10]

The private advocates stood in stark contrast to the Western-style Bar. The private profession, created in 1874,[11] attracted its members from the traditional sources that had supplied legal representatives in the pre-Reform period. Indeed, the first generation of private advocates was composed largely of traditional legal representatives who had continued to practice after the Judicial Reform of 1864.[12] Bringing the traditional legal representatives under government regulation was designed ostensibly to raise their standard of legal practice, though a more important factor in the decision may have been the government's desire to provide a counterweight to the politically conscious Bar.[13]

Unlike the sworn advocates, who could practice in any court in the Russian Empire, the private advocates were restricted to appearing in courts with which they were certified. Each court

[9] Arsen'ev, *Zametki*, pt. 1, p. 38.

[10] M. Gernet, ed., *Istoriia russkoi advokatury*, 3 vols. (Moscow, 1914-1916), 2: 16. The figures cited relate to St. Petersburg in the period from 1873 to 1913.

Although the Bar in Russia and the Soviet Union has drawn a sizable minority of its recruits from among state legal personnel, state legal institutions have not reciprocated. It has been rare for an advocate to leave the Bar for work in the state sector.

[11] The government created the private profession by attaching amendments to Reform legislation governing the Bar. See *Uchrezhdeniia*, arts. 406/1-406/19.

[12] Kucherov, *Courts, Lawyers*, p. 159.

[13] Ibid.

had its own certification procedure, which in some cases involved a written examination.[14] But there were no formal educational or apprenticeship requirements for the private profession, and it was common for courts to admit private advocates with little or no qualifications for legal practice. In general, the state expected little from the private profession. Private advocates, for example, were not obligated, as were the sworn advocates, to accept court-appointed cases.[15]

Legislation governing the private advocates ensured that they remained, in the tradition of the pre-Reform legal representatives, a fragmented group with no professional identity. The complete absence of professional associations of private advocates, together with the immobility imposed on private advocates by the court certification system, kept professional contacts to a minimum. All questions concerning the private profession, including membership and disciplinary matters, were decided in the first instance by individual courts. Broader supervision was exercised by the Ministry of Justice.

In spite of the deep structural divisions within the prerevolutionary legal profession, the functions of advocates varied little from one branch to the next. Most advocates divided their work between litigation, legal counseling, and the drafting of legal documents, though prominent sworn advocates did tend to spend more of their time in court. Litigation was regarded as the essence of legal practice, and advocates competed fiercely for their share of court cases. The less successful advocates had to fall back on inheritance cases and the commercial side of legal practice.[16]

[14] The degree of difficulty posed by the examinations differed considerably from one court to the next. A legal reference book written for private advocates (P. Briunelli, *Poverennye pri zashchite prav* [St. Petersburg, 1914] contains two separate model examinations: an abbreviated version intended for those sitting examinations in provincial areas and a more comprehensive and demanding version used by persons preparing for an examination in a major court center.

[15] Arsen'ev, *Zametki*, pt. 1, p. 53. In areas lacking sworn advocates the court apprentices, and not the private advocates, were appointed to represent defendants without counsel.

[16] Vas'kovskii, "Advokatura," pt. 2, p. 268. The prestige attached to oral advocacy survived the Bolshevik Revolution intact. Unlike contemporary American lawyers,

In prerevolutionary Russia most advocates practiced individually, though it was not uncommon for a successful sworn advocate to engage several apprentices to work in his chambers. While private law firms were virtually unknown, collective legal practice on a small scale did develop, especially from the 1890s onwards, in the form of legal consultation bureaus (*iuridicheskie konsul'tatsii*).[17] These bureaus were often created to serve particular segments of the community, such as the working class, and charged moderate fees, if any at all.

Except in court-appointed cases, when remuneration was given from a common fund, the fees paid to advocates were based on private arrangement with the client. Shortly after the Judicial Reform of 1864, a fee schedule was published by the Ministry of Justice, but it was not binding. It served as a guideline for charges and was applied if a dispute arose between advocate and client.[18] According to one source, virtually all fees privately agreed upon were in the general range of the fee schedule.[19]

The effectiveness of professional legal representation was significantly enhanced after 1864 by procedural changes that were at the heart of the Judicial Reform. Western-style rules of procedure emphasizing oral advocacy and publicity (*publichnost'*) were introduced into the newly created general courts, which

---

for whom courtroom work, particularly in criminal cases, has become less appealing, Soviet advocates continue to give pride of place to litigation. Undoubtedly this is in part because the courtroom has been one of the few forums in Russia and the Soviet Union where individual interests, especially those in conflict with the state, could be openly represented. For an excellent discussion of the prestige attached to lawyers' functions in the United States, see J. Heinz and E. Laumann, *Chicago Lawyers: The Social Structure of the Bar* (New York and Chicago, 1982), pp. 84-134.

[17] A few private law firms were formed in the aftermath of the Judicial Reform of 1864 by traditional legal representatives (*striapchie*) in an attempt to compete from a position of strength with the newly created sworn advocates. See *Istoriia russkoi advokatury*, 1: 144. However, no further reference to these law firms has been found, and it is likely that they were disbanded when the traditional legal representatives were brought under government regulation in 1874.

[18] Arsen'ev, *Zametki*, pt. 1, p. 137.

[19] Ibid., p. 138.

existed at the district (*okruzhnoi*) level and above. In criminal cases within the jurisdiction of these courts, the advocates, though denied access to the preliminary investigation, enjoyed full procedural rights at trial and on appeal. For the first time in Russian history advocates were able to argue before a jury in open court.[20] They were also allowed to consult with an accused person under detention in the period before trial, and in at least one court region the governing council of sworn advocates instructed its members to make use of this right in all cases.[21] Moreover, Reform legislation gave criminal defendants the right to privileged communication with counsel.[22]

The impact of the procedural changes was limited, however. First, although criminal defendants had a right to be represented by legal counsel in all general courts, the scarcity of advocates in many areas frequently left the accused without professional representation. Court practice held that denial of counsel did not in itself constitute grounds for appeal.[23] More importantly, especially after 1889, the liberalization of procedure did not extend to cases heard before the local courts, which resolved the majority of criminal and civil disputes in the last half-century of tsarist rule. Figures from 1910 and 1913 indicate that of the approximately two-and-a-half million criminal cases heard by Russian courts annually (an extraordinary statistic in itself given

[20] Over the period from 1872 to 1912 the level of acquittals in criminal cases without juries varied between 25 and 30 percent; with jury participation the acquittal rate was approximately 40 percent. See table in *Sudebnye ustavy*, pt. 2, p. 360.

[21] A. Nos, ed., *Sbornik materialov otnosiashchikhsia do sosloviia prisiazhnykh poverennykh okruga moskovskoi sudebnoi palaty s 23 aprelia 1866g. po 23 aprelia 1891g.* (Moscow, 1891), p. 180.

[22] *Uchrezhdeniia*, arts. 403 and 566.

[23] G. Fel'dshtein, *Lektsii po ugolovnomu sudoproizvodstvu* (Moscow, 1915), pp. 226-227. Many other procedural guarantees provided by the Judicial Reform were eroded for practical or political reasons in the 1864 to 1917 period, though changes were not always permanent or regressive. In 1892 the rights of the accused were enhanced when the presence of legal counsel was made obligatory in appellate cases heard by the regional courts, the palaces of justice. Five years later advocates were allowed to participate for the first time in the preliminary investigation, having been granted entry in the pretrial stage in cases involving defendants from ten to seventeen years of age. *Sudebnye ustavy*, pt. 1, p. 624.

an adult population of well under 150 million), only 120,000, or about 5 percent, of the cases were heard by the general courts. All but the most serious cases went before local tribunals, which operated without a jury and without the extensive procedural safeguards found in the general courts.[24] Thus, although the old system of class courts was dismantled by the Judicial Reform of 1864, a division between the liberal and autocratic traditions in court procedure remained.

Although the number of advocates in Russia grew at an unprecedented rate in the 1864 to 1917 period, the legal profession was never large enough to satisfy the needs of the population. In 1897 there was one advocate for every 29,800 people. By 1910 the ratio had improved dramatically, to one for every 17,900.[25] However, Russia still lagged well behind the more developed countries of Europe, such as England, which at this time had one lawyer for every 1,684 people.[26]

Another striking characteristic of the prerevolutionary legal profession was its uneven distribution over the empire. A distinct East-West split existed, with the Polish and Ukrainian areas disproportionately well-supplied with advocates. The most neglected regions were central Russia (excluding Moscow), Western Siberia, and Central Asia. Figures from selected court regions show the disparity.

A wide differential in the distribution of advocates also existed along urban-rural lines. To take the most extreme case, in the city of Moscow there was one advocate for every 1,600 persons, whereas in the outlying areas of the Moscow court region—a vast territory covering much of North Central Russia—there was

[24] D. Rodin, "Revoliutsionnye tribunaly v 1920-22gg.," *Vestnik statistiki*, no. 1-3 (1923), p. 160. This important article compares the divisions of the pre- and postrevolutionary court systems into general and local courts and into revolutionary tribunals and people's courts, respectively.

On the distinction between local and general courts, see Kucherov, *Courts, Lawyers*, pp. 43-95; N. Eroshkin, *Istoriia gosudarstvennykh uchrezhdenii dorevoliutsionnoi Rossii* (Moscow, 1983), pp. 235-240; Fel'dshtein, *Lektsii*, pp. 132-166.

[25] *Istoriia russkoi advokatury*, 2: 49.

[26] *Census of England and Wales* (London, 1911), 10: 2, 12.

TABLE 1.1 *THE DISTRIBUTION OF ADVOCATES IN LATE IMPERIAL RUSSIA, 1910*

Court Regions	Persons per Advocate
Warsaw	12,100
Kiev	16,100
Odessa	17,400
Omsk	70,900
Kazan	75,400
Tashkent	128,200

SOURCE: M. Gernet, ed., *Istoriia russkoi advokatury*, 3 vols. (Moscow, 1914-1916), 2: 42.

one advocate for every 55,000 people.[27] To be sure, urban advocates, and particularly those in the Bar, on occasion accepted cases from the more remote areas. Nevertheless, much of the demand in outlying areas for legal advice and for representation in local courts remained unsatisfied by the private and sworn advocates.

In areas where existing legal services were inadequate the gap was often filled by persons practicing law without a certificate, the so-called underground advocates (*podpol'nye advokaty*). The evidence suggests that underground practice was most common in the countryside, where it was likely to be a part-time pursuit of individuals whose sole qualification was their literacy.[28] Underground advocates practiced under constant criticism from the sworn advocates, who decried their lack of professional standards, and from the government, which accused them of inciting the peasants to engage in unnecessary litigation.[29] But the only serious attempt to eliminate underground practice was launched in 1912, and it appeared to have had little impact. Underground legal practice was one of the many intractable problems carried over to the Soviet period.

[27] *Istoriia russkoi advokatury*, 2: 42.
[28] Vas'kovskii, "Advokatura," pt. 2, p. 278.
[29] Vas'kovskii, *Organizatsiia advokatury*, pp. 354-355.

The private and sworn advocates at first competed on the same geographical terrain, but as the Bar grew in size it gradually displaced the private profession from the major court centers of the country. By the end of the tsarist period each branch had a distinct geographical orientation, with the Bar clustered in the larger cities and the private profession dispersed throughout the provinces. In 1914 the four most important judicial centers of the empire—Moscow, Petrograd, Warsaw, and Kiev—contained exactly half of all sworn advocates but only 11.2 percent of private advocates.[30] The greatest concentration of private advocates was in the smaller provincial towns, where 51.5 percent of the private profession practiced. The Bar was represented in these areas by only 6.2 percent of its members.[31] This geographical distribution of advocates indicates that the Bar dominated practice in the regional and national courts while the private profession played the more important role in the local courts. It was only at the district court level, where the two branches were almost evenly represented, that the private and sworn advocates seemed to have been in serious competition.[32]

Membership figures on the legal profession show that the steady rise in the number of sworn advocates in the prerevolutionary period occurred at the expense of the private advocates. Although the private profession, having coopted an existing body of legal representatives, maintained numerical superiority over the Bar until the turn of the century, the total number of private advocates began to decline well before that date.[33] The shift in numerical strength of the private and sworn branches of the legal profession is illustrated in the accompanying tables.

By the end of the tsarist period the private profession seemed on the verge of dying a natural death. But the Bolshevik Revolution interrupted this process. When the Soviet regime began to establish its own legal profession, it brought in considerable numbers of private advocates, especially in the provinces, on

[30] *Istoriia russkoi advokatury*, 2: 57.
[31] Ibid.
[32] Ibid., p. 52.
[33] Ibid., p. 5.

TABLE 1.2 *THE DECLINE OF PRIVATE ADVOCATES*

Year	Number of Private Advocates
1890	3,407
1907	2,662
1913	2,099

SOURCE: M. Gernet, ed., *Istoriia russkoi advokatury*, 3 vols. (Moscow, 1914-1916), 2: 3-5, 57.

TABLE 1.3 *THE GROWTH OF THE RUSSIAN BAR*

Year	Sworn Advocates	Advocates-in-Training	Total
1890	1,830	1,052	2,882
1907	4,286	3,179	7,465
1913	5,658	5,489	11,147

SOURCE: M. Gernet, ed., *Istoriia russkoi advokatury*, 3 vols. (Moscow, 1914-1916), 2: 3-5, 57.

an equal footing with the members of the sworn profession. For the traditionally apolitical private advocates, the creation of the Soviet legal order signified a new beginning as full-fledged members of the legal profession. Because of this the former private advocates constituted a section of the legal profession that was especially malleable to the policies of the Soviet state.

The sworn advocates, on the other hand, were a much more difficult legacy for the Bolsheviks. Unlike the politically inert private profession, the Bar was a socially conscious group of advocates with distinct political loyalties. The mainstream of the profession was firmly committed to the principles of Western liberal democracy. Furthermore, the sworn advocates were jealous defenders of their own institutional interests. Over the period from 1864 to 1917, in spite of persistent attempts by the government to check the development of the legal profession as an intermediary institution in Russian society, the sworn advocates succeeded in establishing and strengthening their professional organizations in all areas of the country. Through these professional institutions the sworn advocates were able to develop traditions of independence from external control, solidarity in the face of attacks from the state, and, especially after 1900, democratic self-government.

The first generation of sworn advocates grew up intellectually in the lively atmosphere of the 1840s and 1850s when ideas imported from Western Europe concerning a political order based on the rule of law were embraced by segments of the young elite.[34] K. Arsen'ev, the chairman of the governing council of St. Petersburg sworn advocates from 1866 to 1874, recounted how he and other young men of his generation formed study circles with the goal of preparing themselves to become the future judges, advocates, and procurators. In these circles they discussed drafts of the Judicial Reform and acted out contemporary trials from Western Europe.[35] For many of this generation the practice of law was a calling and not simply a means of livelihood.

From the mid-1860s until the 1880s the concern of sworn advocates with social justice and the rights of the individual in an autocratic state was expressed primarily through their bold defense of revolutionaries in criminal trials. In defense speeches in political cases the sworn advocates went beyond a purely legal analysis of the issues to expose the iniquities of the autocratic system that gave rise to revolutionary activity. Describing the role of the sworn advocate Alexandrov in the celebrated Vera Zasulich case, an observer of the trial commented: "He did not defend Zasulich, he indicted the entire social order."[36]

By delivering defense speeches in court, the sworn advocates were not simply defending individual revolutionaries, they were acting as critics of the state and, in some cases, as publicists of revolutionary programs on a national scale, since the Russian

[34] On the introduction of Western legal ideas into Russia in this period, see R. Wortman, *The Development of a Russian Legal Consciousness* (Chicago, 1976).

[35] Arsen'ev, *Zametki*, pt. 1, p. 134.

[36] D. Gertsenshtein, "Tridtsat' let tomu nazad," *Byloe*, no. 6 (1907), p. 252, quoted in N. Troitskii, *Tsarizm pod sudom progressivnoi obshchestvennosti 1866-1895* (Moscow, 1979), p. 223. All translations from Russian sources are mine unless otherwise noted.

public was able to follow court proceedings through verbatim transcripts of major trials published in newspapers.[37] The dissemination of advocates' defense speeches to this wider audience was especially worrisome to the tsarist government. Writing in 1878, a police official noted that "the character of defense speeches, besides influencing the outcome of justice in an unfavorable way, engenders fermentation [of ideas] and dissatisfaction in people's minds. It subverts the bases of government authority and perpetuates agitation."[38]

The anger of the government toward the sworn advocates, which had been steadily building since 1871, reached a breaking point in 1878 with the acquittal of Vera Zasulich. At this time the Ministry of Justice invested itself with the power to remove an undesirable sworn advocate from any case, a right that it had previously possessed only with regard to private advocates.[39] In an attempt to further reduce the impact of advocates in sensitive cases the government began to shift the responsibility for the hearing of political trials from the general court system to military courts, which operated without a jury.[40] New restrictions were also imposed on the publication of court proceedings. A circular of the Ministry of Internal Affairs issued in 1879 informed government officials at the local level that in the case of state crimes court transcripts should be "limited, where possible, to a short factual report of the court hearing with the elimination of any extraneous details, especially any tendentious conclusions from the defendant or his counsel."[41]

The first wave of social activism in the sworn profession was

---

[37] During the reforms of the 1860s, Alexander II issued a decree enabling the press to publish transcripts of court cases. S. Kucherov, "The Legal Profession in Pre- and Post-Revolutionary Russia," *American Journal of Comparative Law*, no. 3 (1956), pp. 443, 450.

[38] Troitskii, *Tsarizm pod sudom*, p. 230.

[39] *Istoriia russkoi advokatury*, 1: 236.

[40] N. Troitskii, *Tsarskie sudy protiv revoliutsionnoi Rossii* (Saratov, 1976), pp. 208-209. On military justice in late Imperial Russia, see William C. Fuller, Jr., "Civilians in Russian Military Courts, 1881-1904," *Russian Review*, no. 3 (1982), pp. 288-305.

[41] "K istorii ogranicheniia glasnosti sudoproizvodstva," *Byloe*, no. 4 (1907), p. 230, quoted in Troitskii, *Tsarskie sudy*, p. 210.

dampened by these legal counterreforms and the subsequent general reaction in Russia. Sworn advocates continued to appear in political trials, but the scale and vigor of their participation declined. The profession entered a conservative interlude, during which the commitment to social justice seemed to fade.

The policies of reaction and the downturn in relations between the sworn advocates and the state also had a decided impact on the development of the regional Bar associations. Although the Judicial Reform of 1864 had envisioned the immediate creation of professional organizations of sworn advocates in each of the court regions, the government was in no hurry to implement this legislation. The first governing councils of sworn advocates were formed in St. Petersburg and Moscow in 1866, followed by the Kharkov Council in 1874. But in that year, as part of the legal counterreforms, the Ministry of Justice introduced a temporary moratorium on the creation of governing councils in the remaining court regions. This "temporary" measure remained in force until 1904.

In the regions where governing councils did not exist, sworn advocates, like private advocates, were under the supervision of the palaces of justice and the district courts. But the sworn advocates refused to accept their disenfranchisement. Deprived of officially sanctioned organizations, they formed committees to represent their interests before the courts. These committees were often recognized by the courts, and in some cases they developed into permanent appendages of the courts responsible for a wide range of professional activities. Sworn advocates in some areas established peer tribunals to hear disciplinary cases brought against them, though as a rule disciplinary cases in regions without governing councils were heard by the general courts.[42]

The most serious threat to the organizational bases of the Bar came in the period from 1878 to the 1890s, at the height of

---

[42] For a detailed study of the institutional life of sworn advocates in regions without governing councils, see E. Chernomordik, "Uchrezhdeniia zameniaiushchie sovety prisiazhnykh poverennykh," in *Istoriia russkoi advokatury*, ed. M. Gernet, 3 vols. (Moscow, 1914-1916), 3: 1-63.

reaction in Russia. Alarmed by the effectiveness of sworn advocates as defenders in political cases, the government considered restructuring the profession in order to reduce its autonomy.
Some even suggested abolishing the Bar altogether, though this
never appears to have been seriously discussed at the higher
levels.[43]

In 1890, and again in 1896, government-appointed commissions drew up new legislation on the Bar. The draft laws provided
for closer supervision by the state and, in particular, by the
Procuracy. The Procuracy was to be given the right to protest
any decision of the Bar's governing councils, including membership decisions, to a court for resolution.[44] Furthermore, the
governing councils were to be denied the right to accept into
the profession any applicant suspected of political activities by
the police (*pod nadzorom politsiei*).[45] Although both of the drafts
were submitted to the State Council for final approval, neither
was introduced into law.

With regard to membership selection, the government in this
period did impose limitations on the admission of Jews to the
Bar. On March 3, 1890, a law was adopted setting strict quotas
for entering sworn advocates from non-Christian backgrounds.[46]
After 1889 it also became more difficult for Jews to register as
advocates-in-training, especially in Moscow.[47]

The adoption of discriminatory legislation against the Jews
was a rare instance when the sworn advocates did not unite in
protest against an externally imposed restriction on their authority. Only the St. Petersburg Bar association protested the
measure, which was generally well-received by sworn advocates
in other areas.[48] The willingness to submit to the restriction

[43] *Istoriia russkoi advokatury*, 1: 336.

[44] P. Tager, "Nadzor za organami soslovnogo samoupravleniia prisiazhnykh poverennykh," in *Istoriia russkoi advokatury*, ed. M. Gernet, 3 vols. (Moscow, 1914-
1916), 3: 80.

[45] Ibid., p. 83.

[46] See ibid., 2: 19-22.

[47] Ibid., 1: 291.

[48] Ibid., 2: 97.

appears to have been due to the fear of heightened competition within the profession. From the mid-1880s, the Bar had become something of a haven for Jews unable to find positions in the increasingly hostile state sector. In Moscow, for example, the percentage of Jews among advocates-in-training rose from 3 percent to 17 percent in just two years.[49]

Although restrictions on the admission of Jews into the Bar remained in effect until 1917, they were applied less rigorously after the 1890s. In the last two decades of tsarist rule the Jews comprised a large minority of the profession and were one of its most politically active and professionally distinguished elements. In the words of George Katkov: "In the Kadet Party, in the legal profession, among fellow doctors, the Jews in Russia could feel themselves part of a movement to which they could give their unrestricted allegiance."[50]

In the midst of the reaction of the 1890s a new generation of sworn advocates began to breathe new life into the profession.[51] The young advocates initiated a second wave of activism, more explicitly political in its goals and methods, which continued with undulations until 1917. Unlike the older sworn advocates, the generation of the nineties did not limit itself to courtroom speeches as a means of raising popular consciousness and encouraging social change. Many young advocates organized themselves into groups, such as the Itinerant Club in Moscow, which took legal services to the people.[52] Legal aid centers were set up to help the working class and peasantry, and a few sworn advocates began to devote their services exclusively to the lower classes. In addition, a small circle was formed within the Itinerant Club to represent defendants charged with political crimes.[53]

[49] Ibid., 1: 280.

[50] G. Katkov, *Russia 1917: The February Revolution* (London, 1967), p. 52.

[51] The generation of the nineties was referred to by one sworn advocate as the "second intake" (*vtoroi prizyv*). See B. Gershun, "Vospominaniia advokata," *Novyi zhurnal*, no. 43 (1955), p. 144.

[52] V. Maklakov, *Iz vospominanii*, 3d ed. (New York, 1954), p. 231.

[53] Ibid., p. 233; *Istoriia russkoi advokatury*, 1: 384-390.

The growth of politically active elements within the Bar was rapidly accelerated by the unrest in the country that culminated in the antigovernment uprisings of 1905. The crisis exacerbated the existing divisions in the profession between the reformists and the traditionalists and forced the great uncommitted center of the profession to peel off in support of one group or the other. On November 21, 1904, the St. Petersburg sworn advocates, in an unprecedented move, adopted a resolution calling for a change in the country's political order.[54] A year later they voted to join the general strike as a profession, and young sworn advocates could be seen running through the halls of the courts agitating the court workers to come out on strike.[55] The sworn advocates of Moscow decided against direct participation in the strike, but they did halt work in sympathy.[56]

The events of 1904 and 1905 greatly advanced the politicization of the Bar. The traditionalists' view that lawyers should remain above politics could not be sustained in a revolutionary period. Increasing numbers of sworn advocates affiliated themselves with political parties, and this led to factional activities within the profession, which were often played out at the general meetings. A heightened political awareness among sworn advocates resulted in the further spread of legal consultation bureaus to serve the lower classes and in a higher level of participation by advocates in the self-government of the profession.

Greater involvement of sworn advocates in the affairs of the profession contributed to its democratization. Through their ability to regulate the frequency of general meetings and to set their agenda, the governing councils of the regional Bar associations had previously been able to govern the profession with only limited input from below. But commencing around 1900, power began to be distributed more evenly among the governing council, permanent and ad hoc commissions of sworn advocates, and the general meeting. Final decision-making authority shifted

[54] *Istoriia russkoi advokatury*, 1: 402.

[55] N. Karabchevskii, *Shto glaza moi videli*, 2 vols. (Berlin, 1921), 2: 52.

[56] *Istoriia russkoi advokatury*, 1: 429.

from the governing council to the general meeting, which was summoned more frequently and operated under more open procedure.

The Revolution of 1905 also brought together sworn advocates for the first time on the national level. Two hundred delegates representing all regional Bar associations except those in Siberia met in St. Petersburg in March 1905 as the First All-Russian Congress of Sworn Advocates.[57] The congress resolved to form a national Bar association and to work for the introduction of a democratic, constitutional political system in Russia. The Second Congress, meeting in Moscow in October 1905, was broken up several times by the police but still managed to pass a number of resolutions.[58] After the Second Congress, however, political differences split the national movement in two and led to its eventual demise.

When the political unrest in the country abated, most sworn advocates settled back into the routine of legal practice, but a significant minority remained politically active. In elections to the newly created national legislative body, the Duma, sworn advocates received thirty-six seats, or slightly over 7 percent of the total.[59] This level of representation was out of all proportion to the size of the profession, whose members at this time numbered around four thousand. In the Second, Third, and Fourth Dumas the profession supplied thirty-two, twenty-nine, and twenty-three deputies respectively.[60] The greatest concentration of sworn advocates, both inside the Duma and out, was in the Kadet party.[61]

The already strained relations between the state and the Bar declined even further in the period from 1905 to 1917. As in the 1870s the deterioration was due primarily to the prominent role of sworn advocates as defenders in political trials. Criminal

[57] Ibid., p. 417.

[58] Ibid., p. 419.

[59] Ibid., p. 421.

[60] Ibid.

[61] E. Skripilev, "Karatel'naia politika vremennogo pravitel'stva i apparat ee provedeniia" (Doctoral dissertation, Moscow, 1970), p. 244.

prosecution was a major weapon in the autocracy's last line of defense against revolutionary activity and popular unrest, and the advocates served to dull its effect.

In an effort to intimidate political defenders the state began to repress sworn advocates who represented their clients with vigor in sensitive criminal cases. The freedom of expression that advocates had previously enjoyed in court was no longer respected. Many were arrested, some in open court, and imprisoned or sent into administrative exile for speeches made in defense of their clients.[62] In Warsaw a court expelled an advocate from the Bar for convincing a defendant who had confessed during the preliminary investigation to change his plea at the trial.[63]

The state also impeded the normal functioning of the regional Bar associations. Some general meetings were prevented from taking place by the police,[64] and other forms of harassment were employed to discourage contacts among sworn advocates. In St. Petersburg in 1913 the local procurator ordered sworn advocates to restrict their general meeting to a discussion of the annual report of the governing council and the election of new council members.[65] State interference in the affairs of the Bar was illustrated most vividly by the actions of the authorities in Irkutsk, where the entire governing council of the Bar was arrested and its functions transferred to the district court.[66]

The outbreak of war and the explosion of revolutionary activity in the 1914 to 1917 period brought the Bar as a whole back into the thick of the political battle. In Petrograd revolutionary ideas became increasingly popular among young sworn advocates and the advocates-in-training and, for the first time they penetrated

---

[62] *Istoriia russkoi advokatury*, 1: 488.

[63] Ibid.

[64] Ibid., p. 452.

[65] The regional court later overruled the procurator's action. See ibid., 2: 84.

[66] "Desiatiletie irkutskogo soveta prisiazhnykh poverennykh," *Pravo*, no. 17 (1917), p. 996. Part of the rank and file of the profession was also arrested and tried for political offenses; the remainder of the Irkutsk sworn advocates escaped to other cities or abroad.

the governing council.[67] The political divisions between the generations became acute, with certain elements of the young generation trying to push a reluctant profession into collective action. At one of the frequent and unruly general meetings of the Petrograd Bar held during the war, A. Kerenskii, a leading figure on the left wing of the profession, proposed a resolution committing the sworn advocates to join the protests against the "rotten power" that governed the country. A long debate ensued in which the chairman of the governing council, Karabchevskii, challenged Kerenskii on the necessity of revolution for Russia. After the debate the motion of Kerenskii was defeated by a margin of four to one, illustrating the unwillingness of even the most radical association of sworn advocates, that of Petrograd, to move beyond a reformist approach to social change.[68]

But the resistance of the Bar to revolution proved to be ephemeral. Presented with the February Revolution as an accomplished fact, the profession rallied around the Provisional Government and was propelled almost overnight into a leading role in the Russian political and legal system. Two days after the coup, Kerenskii, the new minister of justice, met with the governing council of the Petrograd Bar to seek its support and to encourage the active participation of the profession in the new government.[69] He received the unqualified endorsement of the council, signaling the beginning of a close association between the Provisional Government and the Bar.

During the nine months of the Provisional Government's existence, the Bar was one of the main sources of talent for the new regime. Including Kerenskii, who became chief minister in July, the profession supplied all five ministers of justice, four of the twenty-two members of the First Department and two of the nine members of the Second Department of the Ruling Sen-

[67] Karabchevskii, *Shto glaza*, p. 27.

[68] Ibid., pp. 64-65.

[69] Ibid., pp. 118-123; *Pravo*, no. 8 (1917), p. 461. Karabchevskii writes that at this meeting Kerenskii began handing out posts in the Ministry of Justice to the members of the governing council.

ate.[70] A steady stream of sworn advocates filled key positions in the judiciary and the Procuracy, replacing many of their former adversaries under the tsarist system.

The scale of the defections from the Bar into government service cannot be determined with precision, but they undoubtedly represented a massive drain of talent, especially in Petrograd and Moscow. Many prominent sworn advocates from the two largest cities were made judges or procurators not only in their own regions but in outlying areas as well. Of the nine members of the Petrograd Bar's governing council serving in February, six had taken jobs in the state sector by the summer.[71] From the rank and file of the profession large numbers of sworn advocates were appointed to posts in local government as civil or militia commissars.[72] The Murav'ev Extraordinary Commission also hired a sizable group of advocates to investigate and prosecute tsarist officials.[73] The state thus became a major employer of sworn advocates, many of whom could not find work in the private sector because of the revolutionary upheavals.

The overthrow of the tsarist system strengthened the institutional bases of the Bar by eliminating the constraints under which it had operated since its inception. The tensions that had prevailed between the profession and the state disappeared, and the regional Bar associations were able to operate de facto as independent institutions after February. In terms of legal practice the benefits of the February Revolution were less obvious. The disruption of the normal functioning of the judiciary significantly reduced the workload of advocates and introduced an element of disorder into the administration of justice. But within this atmosphere the advocates did appear to enjoy enhanced rights in legal proceedings and greater respect from the other participants in court.

The February Revolution was also instrumental in broadening the social base of the Bar. Immediately after the fall of the old

---

[70] *Pravo*, no. 12 (1917), pp. 717-718.
[71] Karabchevskii, *Shto glaza*, p. 125.
[72] Ibid., p. 128.
[73] Ibid.

regime all restrictions on Jewish entrance to the legal profession were lifted. On March 3, 1917, 110 Jews were admitted as sworn advocates in Moscow, and a week later 124 Jews took the oath in Petrograd.[74] Women, who had been forbidden to practice under the tsars, also petitioned to be admitted as sworn advocates, with 45 seeking entrance in Moscow alone.[75] On June 1 the Provisional Government adopted legislation giving women the right to practice law.[76]

It was intended that the changes introduced by the Provisional Government in the aftermath of the February Revolution would be followed by a thorough reform of legislation governing the Bar. The desire of sworn advocates and government alike was to create a Bar that would enjoy the rights promised, but never delivered, by the Judicial Reform of 1864. To prepare the necessary legislation, the Provisional Government formed a drafting subcommittee composed primarily of sworn advocates.[77] The draft of a new law on the Bar provided for the formation of a single, self-governing profession of Russian advocates to include the sworn advocates and their apprentices. A national congress of advocates would meet at least every two years and would select a national governing council. The decrees of the congress, and presumably those of its governing council, would be binding on the advocates throughout the country. As before, governing councils and general meetings would function on the regional level. In addition to the structural reform the draft introduced a number of minor changes that would have improved the operation of professional organizations.[78] The Bolshevik Revolution intervened, however, before the legislation could be adopted.

As in previous periods of revolutionary activity the upheavals between February and October 1917 exposed the political divisions within the profession and transformed the general meetings into forums for political debate. Information on the political

---

[74] *Pravo*, no. 8 (1917), p. 463.
[75] Ibid.
[76] *Pravo*, no. 17 (1917), p. 984.
[77] E. Skripilev, "Karatel'naia politika vremennogo pravitel'stva," p. 237.
[78] Ibid., pp. 237-242.

loyalties of sworn advocates in this period is far from complete, but, as evidenced by public expressions of support, the mass of the profession was solidly behind the Provisional Government. In its composition and in the social and economic interests that it represented the Provisional Government was the natural political ally of all but the most impoverished or revolutionary elements among sworn advocates.[79]

The Bolsheviks and Left Social Revolutionaries had pockets of sympathy, especially among the youth of the profession,[80] but their efforts at agitation among sworn advocates met with little success and in fact may have been counterproductive. Sworn advocates and advocates-in-training representing the two parties of the extreme left did not attempt to nudge the profession over to their way of thinking but to force it with hammer blows. At a general meeting of the Petrograd Bar a recently admitted sworn advocate from the Bolshevik party began his speech by attacking the Bar for its lack of revolutionary fervor and concluded by recommending the abolition of the legal profession in its existing form. In response to this attack Karabchevskii delivered a blistering lecture on the dangers of Bolshevism, which was greeted by a wild, standing ovation from the Petrograd sworn advocates. In a defiant mood the general meeting voted to publish Karabchevskii's speech and to distribute it to all sworn advocates in the country.[81]

[79] In his memoirs Gershun indicates that in the last years of tsarist rule there emerged an advocates' "proletariat"—that is, sworn advocates unable to support themselves adequately because of lack of work. Gershun, "Vospominaniia advokata," p. 135.

[80] Karabchevskii, *Shto glaza*, p. 154.

[81] "Advokatura i sovmestitel'stvo," *Pravo*, no. 16 (1917), pp. 898-902. According to Karabchevskii, after the meeting the local Bolshevik committee issued a directive to vandalize (*razgromit'*) his home in retaliation for his public attack on Bolshevism. Karabchevskii, *Shto glaza*, pp. 154-155.

Chapter Two

THE BAR IN DECLINE: THE RUSSIAN LAWYER IN REVOLUTION AND CIVIL WAR, 1917-1921

In the early autumn of 1917 the Russian Bar appeared to be developing rapidly into a powerful intermediary institution akin to the legal professions in Western European states. But the enhanced position of sworn advocates in the Russian political and legal system was dependent upon the sympathetic policies of the Provisional Government and on the reduced prominence of the state in Russian society, which had facilitated the growth of institutions from below. Once the Provisional Government was swept from the scene by the October Revolution of 1917 the conditions necessary for maintaining the profession along its existing course of development were also removed.

One of the most important changes heralded by the October Revolution was the return to a more traditional relationship between the state and society in Russia. Unlike the Provisional Government, which had signaled a shift away from the pervasive and domineering role of the state in social relations, Lenin was "unconditionally for strong state power and centralization," at least until the old order had been thoroughly transformed.[1] On the question of state power Lenin's revolutionary instincts seem to have taken precedence over the logic of Marxism. Whereas in the summer of 1917 he resurrected the Marxist concept of the "armed people" as the revolutionary replacement for the shattered bourgeois state, by early October he was speaking of the necessity for a proletarian state apparatus more extensive and more centralized than before the Revolution.[2]

[1] V. Lenin, "Can the Bolsheviks Retain State Power," in *Collected Works*, 45 vols. (Moscow, 1960-1970), 26: 116.

[2] Ibid. The attempts to portray Lenin as an enemy of the state are unconvincing. Neil Harding's argument, relying largely on *State and Revolution*, that the Soviet

The gathering of political power into the hands of the state promised to reverse the course of development for intermediary institutions such as the Bar, but the precise implications of the Bolshevik takeover for the legal profession were not immediately clear, even to the new rulers themselves, who came to power without a specific program of legal reforms.[3] The theoretical heritage and the revolutionary experience of the Bolsheviks did ensure, however, that future policy on the Bar, and on the legal system generally, would represent a radical departure from that pursued by the Provisional Government.

Although the Marxist theory of law was at the time in an embryonic state, it did provide the Bolsheviks with a coherent approach to the role of law in society.[4] This approach bore little resemblance to the liberal concept of law that had been gradually taking root in Russia since the Judicial Reform of 1864. Stated simply, Marxists held that in any society, once economic relations reach a certain degree of complexity, a superstructure of laws and legal institutions is erected to regulate economic activity. Because changes in the economy are seen to produce corresponding changes in the legal system, those who control the economy—the ruling class—also control the law. In capitalist society the ruling class is composed of a relatively small group of property owners who manipulate the law and legal institutions to promote their own narrow interests. But with the onset of a socialist revolution the property of the ruling class is expropriated, and the levers of the economy pass to the new proletarian state. Thus, after the revolution law and legal institutions become the instruments of the proletariat to do with as they see fit until such time as economic relations become so routinized that law and even the state itself are no longer nec-

state emerged *in spite of* early Bolshevik theory does not appear to take into account Lenin's revisions of the "commune state" in late 1917. See N. Harding, "Authority, Power, and the State, 1916-1920," in *Authority, Power, and Policy in the USSR*, ed. T. H. Rigby, A. Brown, and P. Reddaway (London, 1983), pp. 38-54.

[3] Stuchka, "Proletarskaia revoliutsiia i sud," *Proletarskaia revoliutsiia i pravo*, no. 1 (1918), p. 1.

[4] The best discussion of Soviet legal thought is still to be found in R. Schlesinger, *Soviet Legal Theory* (London, 1945).

essary and wither away. In Russia in 1917 it fell to the self-appointed vanguard of the working class, the Bolshevik party, to wield the instruments of proletarian rule.

An important implication of Marxist theory was that the law was stripped of its ethical aura. In the Middle Ages, instead of mirroring the material world, law was seen to reflect, or at least approximate, divine justice. When law as a divinely inspired system of rules began to lose its credibility, it sought legitimacy by claiming to be informed by a sense of fairness, or natural justice. By reducing law to an instrument of class rule, the Marxist analysis broke with the centuries-old tradition in which ethical constraints, whether apparent or real, were placed on the legal system. Accepting this analysis, the Bolsheviks viewed law as merely an extension of political power. The formula "revolutionary expediency equals revolutionary legality" expressed the belief of the new regime that laws were just, as long as they served the interests of the revolution.

Legal institutions, in turn, were regarded by the Bolsheviks as inherently political bodies that were at the disposal of a country's rulers. In the words of Lenin: "The court is an organ of power. The liberals sometimes forget this, but it is a sin for a Marxist to do so."[5] In order to create a system of politically reliable legal institutions Lenin argued that a socialist revolution required the destruction of the entire machinery of government. He did not go on, however, to describe the new institutions that would take the place of those destroyed. Nor did he make clear in his writings before October 1917 whether he viewed the Bar as a government institution fated for destruction in a socialist revolution.[6]

The absence of specific theoretical guidelines for policy on the legal profession was counterbalanced by the revolutionary experience of the Bolsheviks, which had a decisive impact on their attitudes towards the advocates. During the years leading up to the October Revolution, the Bolsheviks had extensive

[5] V. Lenin, "The Question of the Bolshevik Leaders Appearing in Court," in *Collected Works*, 25: 174.

[6] V. Lenin, "The State and Revolution," in ibid.

contacts with advocates as defense counsel in political trials, as political opponents representing other parties, most notably the Kadet party, and even as professional colleagues. These associations convinced the revolutionaries that the Bar was an inherently conservative institution, whose members, with few exceptions, were linked professionally, socially, and politically to the ruling class.[7]

A significant number of prominent Bolsheviks had intimate knowledge of the profession, having practiced as advocates under the old regime. P. Krasikov, N. Krestinskii, P. Stuchka, and D. Kurskii were all members of the Bar before the Revolution, as was Lenin himself. After receiving his law degree in St. Petersburg in 1891 at age twenty-one, Lenin worked for a year and a half as an advocate-in-training in his provincial home town of Samara (present-day Kuibyshev), where he applied himself to his new trade with something less than enthusiasm. Working in the chambers of the reform-minded sworn advocate Khardin, Lenin handled a total of ten cases, all petty crimes and all resulting in conviction of the client. As Trotsky suggests, this short, unsuccessful stint in the legal profession probably convinced Lenin of the futility of attacking the problems of Russia's backwardness one case at a time. Larger measures were needed. Beyond this the period of legal practice appeared to have contributed to that "paroxysm of opposition and rage" that Lenin felt toward the liberal intelligentsia in general and the advocates in particular.[8]

The intense hostility of Lenin towards the advocates as a profession stayed with him throughout his life, though it was perhaps never given fuller expression than in a letter he wrote in 1907 to an imprisoned comrade awaiting trial. Advising her on defense tactics and on the proper relationship between lawyer and client, Lenin commented:

---

[7] In his Stalinist novel *Kak zakalialas stal'* (Moscow, 1970), p. 28, N. Ostrovskii offers the advocate Leshchinskii, who fled as Bolshevik forces approached his provincial town in 1918, as the symbol of the old ruling class.

[8] N. Volskii [N. Valentinov], *The Early Years of Lenin* (Ann Arbor, 1969), pp. 146-148; L. Trotsky, *The Young Lenin* (Garden City, N.Y., 1972), pp. 177-180.

One must rule the advocate with an iron hand and keep him in a state of siege, for this intellectual scum often plays dirty. Announce to him ahead of time: "If you, son of a bitch, allow yourself even the slightest indiscretion or political opportunism, . . . then I, the accused, will at once separate myself from you publicly, label you a scoundrel, and state that I reject such a defense."[9]

According to P. Stuchka, who would serve as justice commissar under the new regime, Lenin "was not particularly fond of (*ne osobenno miloval*) jurisprudence and jurists."[10]

Other Bolsheviks were also highly critical of the Bar, though not all were as unequivocally hostile as Lenin. Those who had devoted much time and energy to their careers as advocates seemed especially likely to adopt a more subtle attitude towards the profession, condemning its defense of bourgeois economic interests and its method of internal government while acknowledging the role of certain progressive advocates in assisting revolutionaries in court and in providing legal services to the working class.[11] Because many Bolsheviks who had been associated with the Bar became major contributors to the legal

[9] V. Lenin, "Pis'mo E.D. Stasovoi i tovarishcham v moskovskoi tiur'me," in *Polnoe sobranie sochinenii*, 5th ed. in 55 vols. (Moscow, 1958–), 9:169.

[10] P. Stuchka, *Izbrannye proizvedeniia po marksistsko-leninskoi teorii prava* (Riga, 1964), p. 343.

In this sentiment Lenin was not alone among revolutionaries. During the French Revolution, Danton complained that "[a]ll lawyers are revoltingly aristocratic . . . [and] have arrogated to themselves an exclusive privilege, which is one of the great plagues of the human race." See A. Mathiez, *The French Revolution* (New York, 1964), pp. 229-230. Other revolutionaries have also been "renegades" from the legal profession. Before his revolutionary career Fidel Castro was a law student at the University of Havana.

[11] See the speeches of former advocates at congresses of Soviet jurists held in the first years of Bolshevik rule. *Materialy Narodnogo Komissariata iustitsii*, vypusk 1, Pervyi vserossiiskii s'ezd oblastnykh i gubernskikh komissarov iustitsii (Moscow, 1918); *Materialy Narodnogo Komissariata iustitsii*, vypusk 3, Vtoroi vserossiiskii s'ezd oblastnykh i gubernskikh komissarov iustitsii (Moscow, 1918); *Materialy Narodnogo Komissariata iustitsii*, vypusk 11-12, Tret'ii vserossiiskii s'ezd deiatelei sovetskoi iustitsii (Moscow, 1921).

policy debates in the Soviet period, the differing shades of opinion in this group help to explain the diversity of views after October 1917 on the appropriate course of development for the Soviet profession.

In spite of their differences, however, the Bolsheviks recognized that the highly politicized character of the profession and the nature of its functions in court made the Bar one of the most potent opposition groups within the Russian intelligentsia. Unlike other professional groups, the advocates participated directly in the machinery of state. In the tsarist period, through a vigorous defense of clients charged with political crimes and through reformist or revolutionary propaganda directed at the courtroom audience and beyond, advocates were able to complicate the state's policy of repression and to undermine its legitimacy and authority in the eyes of the public. As the Bolsheviks realized on assuming power, the courtroom tactics that had helped to illuminate and weaken the tsarist system would be employed to challenge the new order.

The task for the new regime was to find a socialist alternative to the Russian Bar. In the first year of the Revolution this search proceeded cautiously. Only as the Civil War deepened in the late summer of 1918 did the central authorities take decisive measures to neutralize the Bar and provide alternative forms of legal representation. This launched a period of experimentation that lasted throughout the Civil War and produced increasingly radical approaches to the legal profession.

The Russian Bar in Year One of the Revolution

The activities of the advocates in the weeks that followed the October Revolution left no doubt about their political loyalties. At a well-attended general meeting of the Petrograd Bar held on November 21, 1917, a month after the fall of the Provisional Government, a resolution condemning the Bolshevik takeover was adopted unanimously (with the abstention of six Internationalists). The Petrograd advocates resolved:

    1) to proclaim forcefully their nonrecognition of the usurpers of authority and to express their outrage concerning the traitorous attempt to tie Russia to a separate peace;

    2) to greet the Constituent Assembly as the sole bearer of supreme authority in the country and to vehemently protest the establishment of a reign of terror over freedom of the individual, of the press, assembly and strikes, unions, the court, and the organs of self-government;

    3) to protest against the arrest of members of the Provisional Government who are the recognized guardians of supreme legal power in the country until the Constituent Assembly [is convened];

    4) to send copies of this resolution to advocates in countries of the Alliance and to express to them our fraternal greetings.

A proposal was then made to send a telegram of support to Kerenskii. After a heated debate the motion was passed by a small majority.[12]

At the same time the governing council of the Bar in Kharkov described the seizure of power by the Bolsheviks as a criminal encroachment on the sovereign rights of the people. The council encouraged everyone to rally to the defense of the Constituent Assembly. Furthermore, it favored outlawing the participation of the Bolsheviks in any future government.[13]

In the initial weeks of Bolshevik rule all branches of the Russian legal community—judges, advocates, and government legal personnel—sought to present a united front against the new regime by withholding their labor from the new legal system. One of the institutions hardest hit by this strike was the Ministry of Justice, renamed the People's Commissariat of Justice by the Bolsheviks. Its functionaries announced a complete work stoppage until the Constituent Assembly was convened. When the new people's commissar of justice, P. Stuchka, arrived at the

---

[12] "U advokatov," *Vek*, November 23, 1917 (old style).

[13] "Rezoliutisiia khar'kovskikh advokatov," *Russkie vedomosti*, November 25, 1917 (old style), p. 6.

ministry, he found an empty building, with only four function-aries present.[14]

At first the advocates' adherence to the boycott was less than complete due to the unwillingness of left-wing advocates to join the walkout. But members of the Bolshevik and Left Social Revolutionary parties practicing as advocates were quickly called to assume posts in the new state institutions. Other left-wing advocates sympathetic to the Revolution also took up responsible positions in the young state, which was desperately short of educated personnel. With the exodus of the left-wing fringe of the profession the Bar was left with a membership that was, almost without exception, hostile to the new regime.

Many of those leaving the Bar were drafted into the People's Commissariat of Justice, where Stuchka appointed five of his six closest lieutenants from among fellow advocates. One of these associates, D. Kurskii, left the Bar in Moscow to become the first head of the administrative section of the Commissariat, which had responsibility for advocates and the courts.[15] But unlike the movement of advocates into state institutions that followed the February Revolution, the post-October exodus placed in positions of political authority advocates who, instead of representing the expressed interests of the profession, were committed to the demise of the Bar in its existing form.

Indeed it was Stuchka who gave the first public indication of policy towards the advocates under Bolshevik rule. In a *Pravda* article on November 10, 1917, the new justice commissar called for the dismantling of the existing Procuracy and the Bar and the transformation of the two organizations into a single public elective institution.[16] These comments sent shock waves through the profession and in Petrograd advocates considered petitioning

[14] *Vek*, November 23, 1917 (old style).

[15] N. Meier, "Sluzhba v komissariate iustitsii i narodnom sude," in *Arkhiv russkoi revoliutsii*, ed. I. Gessen, 22 vols. (Berlin, 1922-1937), 8: 67.

[16] P. Stuchka [K. St.], "Klassovoi ili demokraticheskii sud," *Pravda*, November 10, 1917 (old style), p. 2.

the governing council of the regional Bar association to have Stuchka expelled from the profession.[17]

The worst fears of the advocates were confirmed on November 24 with the adoption of the Decree on the Court.[18] This act, the first legislative step by the Bolsheviks in the creation of a new legal order, formally abolished the Bar, the Procuracy, criminal investigation departments, and virtually the entire court system. But whereas most legal institutions were to be reorganized at once along revolutionary lines, no replacement for the organized profession of advocates was provided by the legislation. Instead, it permitted any individual of good character who enjoyed civil rights to represent persons in court. In effect, the decree opened up legal practice to almost the entire adult population, including the professional advocates of the old regime, while at the same time ordering the closure of the regional Bar associations. Lacking a vision of a socialist Bar, the Bolsheviks felt it necessary at least to be rid of the institutional bases of the existing profession.

In those regions where Soviet power had been firmly established the regional Bar associations were shut almost immediately after the issuance of the decree. In Petrograd a representative of the Investigative Commission of the city's Military-Revolutionary Committee, armed with the necessary papers and a detachment of Red Guards, entered the offices of the governing council of the Petrograd Bar on November 27 and seized the premises. The council's files were also confiscated, though the advocates did manage to spirit away some documents.[19] A few days later the offices of the governing council of Moscow advocates were closed in a similar manner after the

---

[17] "Narodnyi komissar po delam iustitsii," *Svobodnaia rech'*, November 19, 1917 (old style), p. 5.

[18] O sude, *Sobranie uzakonenii*, 1917-1918, art. 150, no. 4.

[19] G. Gamberg, "O zakrytii sudebnykh uchrezhdenii," *Pravda*, December 9, 1917 (old style); "Uprazdnenie bol'shevikami sudebnykh ustanovlenii," *Russkie vedomosti*, November 28, 1917 (old style), p. 4.

executive committee of the city soviet had declared the council dissolved.[20]

The withdrawal of official recognition from the Bar and the eviction of the advocates' leaders from their headquarters did not, however, bring to a halt the activities of the estate. In fact, at least in Petrograd and Moscow the implementation of the decree's provisions on the Bar seemed to have changed little, except the mood within the profession and the venue for the governing council meetings. On December 2, four days after the seizure of its offices, the Petrograd governing council held its regular weekly meeting in a private flat. The usual business of the association was conducted, including the acceptance of several candidates to become advocates-in-training.[21] The following day, on the initiative of the governing council, a crowded extraordinary general meeting of Petrograd advocates took place, as before the Revolution, in the Tenishevskii Academy.[22] During this meeting, government policy towards the profession and the advocates' response to it were discussed. At the same time a general meeting of advocates in Moscow resolved to continue to operate on the basis of the legislation of 1864 and to recognize changes in the legal system only when they were sanctioned by the Constituent Assembly.[23]

The refusal of the advocates to respect Bolshevik legislation abolishing the profession evoked no immediate response from either central or local authorities. In Petrograd the governing council of advocates was able to relocate into new, permanent offices within weeks of the seizure of its former headquarters on the Fontanka.[24] General meetings of the city's advocates continued to be held without interference from the state. In Moscow, too, the governing council of advocates did not cease functioning,

[20] "Ob uprazdnenii suda," *Russkie vedomosti*, December 3, 1917 (old style), p. 6; *Russkie vedomosti*, November 28, 1917 (old style), p. 5.

[21] "Sredi advokatov," *Nash vek*, December 3, 1917 (old style).

[22] "U advokatov," *Nash vek*, December 5, 1917 (old style).

[23] "Sredi advokatov," *Russkie vedomosti*, December 5, 1917 (old style), p. 6.

[24] "V sovete prisiazhnykh poverennykh," *Novyi zhurnal*, no. 43 (1955), p. 149.

though general meetings did not take place after December 1917, reportedly in spite of the absence of external hindrances.[25] The introduction of the Decree on the Court did not, therefore, achieve its objective of eliminating the profession's governing bodies. Instead of marking the end of the organized Bar, the decree ushered in a twilight period of several months during which the old Bar associations continued to function, albeit as increasingly isolated elements in the political and legal system.

The failure of the new regime to act decisively in the suppression of the Bar reflected its uncertainties over the future of the profession in a socialist state. A first, tentative step in the search for a socialist alternative to the Bar was taken on December 19, 1917. On that date the Justice Commissariat directed local soviets to create colleges of accusers and defenders to serve revolutionary tribunals, which were being established in each region (and in cities of over two hundred thousand) to hear cases involving counterrevolutionary crimes or offenses committed by state officials. Entrance to the colleges was to be made on the basis of recommendations from the local soviets. College members, like English barristers, were to be called on to appear in the revolutionary tribunals either as defense counsel or prosecutors.[26]

The idea of a combined, or "fused," profession of lawyers capable of serving either as prosecutors or defenders was soon extended to the newly established regular court system, whose basic units were the people's courts (narodnyie sudy). In early January 1918, the Justice Commissariat, now under the leadership of the Left Social Revolutionary (S-R), Steinberg, drafted legislation that provided for the creation of institutions of accusers and defenders, known as colleges of legal representatives (kollegii pravozastupnikov), to serve the people's courts.[27] This

[25] Zashchita (Vestnik soiuza moskovskikh advokatov), no. 1, August 20, 1918 (Moscow), p. 1.

[26] Instruktsiia o revoliutsionnykh tribunalakh, Sobranie uzakonenii, 1917-1918, art. 170, no. 12.

[27] Dekrety sovetskoi vlasti, 11 vols. (Moscow, 1957-1983), 1: 463.

draft was reviewed twice during January 1918 by the Council of People's Commissars, the Sovnarkom. On each occasion the Sovnarkom chairman, Lenin, introduced significant changes to the text. The amendments desired by Lenin were designed to ensure that professional legal representatives were a smaller, more select, and more carefully supervised group than provided for in the draft of the Justice Commissariat.

Whereas the original draft placed the colleges of legal representatives under the supervision of the courts, mirroring the prerevolutionary pattern, Lenin insisted that they be supervised by the local soviets, whose personnel was politically more reliable. He also objected to the membership provisions in the Commissariat draft. Where the original draft opened up membership in the colleges to any individual who could present a recommendation from a local soviet, Lenin proposed that the soviets be made directly responsible for the selection of legal representatives. Furthermore, he demanded that only the members of the colleges of legal representatives should have the right to accept payment for legal services. Under the Commissariat draft all citizens enjoying civil rights would have retained the right to practice law.[28]

Soviet historians have attributed the variations between the Commissariat draft and the version as corrected by Lenin to a fundamental difference in approach to legal policy between the Bolsheviks and the Left Social Revolutionaries, who held the justice portfolio in the short-lived coalition government from mid-December 1917 to mid-March 1918. It is claimed that I. Steinberg, the Left S-R justice commissar, amended the original draft, which had been prepared by the now subordinate Bolshevik justice official Stuchka, and then presented it to the Sovnarkom as having the unanimous recommendation of the Commissariat. Reportedly, when Stuchka learned of this, he succeeded in re-

[28] Ibid., pp. 464-466; M. Shalamov, *Istoriia sovetskoi advokatury* (Moscow, 1939), p. 21; T. Ulianova "Pervye shagi v sozdanii sovetskoi advokatury," *Vestnik MGU* (Pravo), no. 1 (1971), p. 72.

opening debate on the proposal in the Sovnarkom, which led to the amendments introduced by Lenin during the Sovnarkom sessions of January 16 and 30.[29]

It is indeed true that the Left S-Rs were more willing than the Bolsheviks to accept the legal inheritance from the old regime. Stuchka complained that when the Left S-Rs took over at the Justice Commissariat they attempted to introduce a criminal code based on the 1903 tsarist code.[30] But Bolshevik opinion was far from unanimous on the appropriate course of development for legal institutions. Thus, the policy disagreements that emerged during the drafting of legislation on the advocates and the court system in early 1918 almost certainly reflected differences within the Bolshevik party itself as well as between the Bolsheviks and their coalition partners.

A revised draft on the legal profession, which incorporated Lenin's amendments, was adopted on March 7, 1918, as part of Decree No. 2 on the Court.[31] But the issuance of the new law did not lead to the immediate replacement of the Bar with colleges of legal representatives. Although Decree No. 2 called for the creation of colleges of legal representatives attached to the local soviets, it did not specify the shape that the colleges were to assume, nor did it obligate the local soviets to implement its provisions. The failure of the central authorities to push for the implementation of the new law enabled local soviets, already straining under the weight of central directives and local crises, to postpone setting up the new colleges. In April 1918 local justice commissars from Saratov, Perm, and the Urals reported that in their regions no steps had yet been taken to create colleges

[29] Stuchka, *Izbrannye proizvedenii*, p. 33; TsGAOR SSSR, f. 130, op. 2, d. 1, l. 40, cited in *Istoriia sovetskogo gosudarstva i prava*, 3 vols. (Moscow, 1968), 1: 192; P. Mishunin, *Ocherki istorii sovetskogo ugolovnogo prava 1916-18gg.* (Moscow, 1954), p. 54. See also the account in M. Kozhevnikov, *Istoriia sovetskogo suda 1917-1956* (Moscow, 1957), p. 30, citing TsGAOR, f. 130, op. 26, d. 2, ll. 29, 40.

[30] Stuchka, *Izbrannye proizvedenii*, p. 71; Mishunin, *Ocherki istorii*, p. 54.

[31] O sude (Dekret No. 2) *Sobranie uzakonenii*, 1917-1918, art. 420, no. 26.

of legal representatives. The justice commissars explained that their first priority was to establish prisons and courts.[32]

The delay in implementing the Decree's provisions on legal representatives also reflected the dissatisfaction of legal officials, particularly at the local level, with the tenor of the new legislation. When the First All-Russian Congress of Regional Justice Commissars met in Moscow in April 1918, most of the local legal officials present favored a more radical approach to the legal profession than that indicated in the broadly worded provisions of Decree No. 2 on the Court. Where the decree left unchanged the private fee system under which legal fees were arranged directly with the client, the congress resolved that legal representatives should be placed on a fixed state salary, thereby breaking the bond of economic dependency between the lawyer and his client.[33] The reluctance of the congress to accept the modest reform of the legal profession contained in Decree No. 2 resulted in the reopening of debate on the issue and a de facto moratorium on the creation of colleges of legal representatives.

By the late spring of 1918 it appears that most local soviets had begun grudgingly to organize the colleges, though not along uniform lines. In some areas only prosecutors were drafted into the new institutions.[34] In other regions the colleges were comprised almost entirely of legal defenders, who acted as prosecutors infrequently, and then only in the regional people's courts. But even in cities like Tver, Viatka (present-day Kirov), Saratov, and Petrograd, where most members of the colleges of legal representatives did serve as defenders in court, their numbers were so small that in most cases the public was still turning to the private practitioners of the old regime for legal representation.[35] The Petrograd college, for example, contained no more

[32] *Materialy Narodnogo Komissariata iustitsii,* vypusk 1, pp. 5-6.

[33] Ibid., p. 14.

[34] V. Turin, "Ot kollegii pravozastupnikov do advokatury," *Sovetskaia iustitsiia,* no. 9 (1957), p. 38; *Zashchita,* p. 7; Shalamov, *Istoriia sovetskoi advokatury,* p. 20.

[35] Prilozhenie, *Narodnyi sud, Materialy Narodnogo Komissariata iustitsii,* vypusk

than twenty-two members in a city that before the Revolution had been served by over three thousand advocates.[36]

A resolution of the uncertainties surrounding the legal profession seemed likely as delegates gathered in Moscow in the first week of July 1918 for the Second All-Russian Congress of Regional Justice Commissars. A committee had been appointed to work out a detailed instruction on the colleges of legal representatives that would be presented to the congress for its approval. It was expected that a variant of the model instruction would then be adopted by each local soviet.[37] But the committee, whose members presumably were nominated by the Justice Commissariat in Moscow and reflected the views of its leader Stuchka, prepared a document that conceded little to the demands of the more radical local justice commissars. In the committee proposal advocates retained the right to reach agreement on fees with clients, except when rendering legal services through one of the small number of state-sponsored legal aid centers. The committee plan also provided for the establishment of a governing council in each college to be elected by the college members themselves. Recognizing the similarities between its view of the colleges of legal representatives and the old Bar associations, the committee argued that the positive features of the prerevolutionary profession should not be discarded.[38]

Not unexpectedly, the committee report, whose language and content betrayed the participation of prerevolutionary jurists, received a hostile reception at the congress. Krestinskii, the justice commissar of Petrograd and a member of the Bolshevik Central Committee, led the attack on the report by criticizing the proposed fee system that gave the lawyers "free contact"

---

5 (Moscow, 1918), p. 77; E. Dubkov, "Demokraticheskie osnovy organizatsii sovetskoi advokatury" (*Kandidat* dissertation, Moscow, 1964), pp. 17-18.

[36] "Ot gubernskogo soveta narodnykh sudei," *Izvestiia petrogradskogo soveta*, June 10, 1918, p. 4.

[37] *Materialy Narodnogo Komissariata iustitsii*, vypusk 3, pp. 17, 62.

[38] Ibid., p. 19. The pragmatists of the Justice Commissariat realized that limited state funds prevented the transfer to a system of salaried defenders, at least over the short term.

with clients. The profit motive, it was argued, should not be given an opening in the Soviet system of justice.[39] With the congress seemingly united on this point, the model instruction proposed by the committee was amended to provide for the introduction of a fixed monthly salary for all legal representatives. The major stumbling block to its passage having been removed, the instruction was adopted by a vote of thirty to five.[40]

The acceptance of this measure did not eliminate, however, the uncertainties over policy towards the legal profession. Among the issues left unresolved were how a fully salaried legal profession would be financed from scarce state funds and how the model instruction, which seemed to provide only for an organization of Soviet advocates, could be reconciled with a unified profession of accusers and defenders envisioned by Decree No. 2 on the Court. Furthermore, the instruction passed by the congress was only a recommendation to legislative authorities and not a legislative act in itself. A period of seven weeks elapsed between the end of the congress and the issuance of a formal directive from the center obligating the local soviets to draft defenders into the colleges of legal representatives.

During the first eight months of 1918, while the policy makers vacillated in their approach to the legal profession, the regional Bar associations continued to exist in an atmosphere of relative tolerance. Except in those cities, such as Omsk,[41] where advocates were prominent in armed resistance to Soviet power, the old Bar associations and their governing institutions continued to function, though with a somewhat lower profile and with a less sanguine attitude towards political developments, particularly in the wake of the Bolsheviks' closing of the Constituent Assembly in January 1918. As the new order acquired an air of permanence and the membership of the Bar associations dwindled, the authority of the governing councils of advocates gradually diminished. The councils nonetheless continued to ad-

[39] Ibid., pp. 19-20.
[40] Ibid.
[41] *Materialy Narodnogo Komissariata iustitsii*, vypusk 1, p. 19.

minister the affairs of the estate with a surprising degree of normality. They were not unaffected, of course, by periodic campaigns against remnants of the old regime, but in most areas it appears that until the autumn of 1918 the pressure brought to bear against the advocates was usually psychological in character.[42]

In the spring of 1918, as the untenable position of the old Bar associations in the new legal system became more apparent, groups of advocates in several cities attempted to reach a *modus vivendi* with the authorities by unilaterally creating a new organizational form for the profession, the unions of advocates (*soiuzy advokatov*). The unions were intended to placate the Bolsheviks, whose indecision towards the advocates seemed to open the way for compromise, by breaking formally with the institutional inheritance of the old regime. Although the establishment of the unions of advocates meant the recognition of the new political and legal order, it did not signify the abandonment by its members of their professional traditions. It was, in effect, one final attempt by the advocates to find a place for a Western-style profession in the Soviet system, and it paralleled efforts at cooperation with the new regime being made by elements in other professional groups, such as the engineers, who had been firmly opposed to the Bolsheviks in the wake of the Revolution.[43]

In Moscow the first meeting of the Union of Advocates was summoned on May 2, 1918, by an "initiative group" of concerned advocates. Approximately one hundred fifty advocates attended—an impressive turnout given the uncertainties about the official reaction to the event. After a motion to establish the Moscow Union of Advocates was passed unanimously, the assembly proceeded to adopt a charter for the organization and to elect its governing board. Among the members of the board were

---

[42] An example was the arrest and almost immediate release of three advocates in Moscow. "U advokatov," *Nash vek*, April 20, 1918, p. 3.

[43] K. E. Bailes, *Technology and Society under Lenin and Stalin: Origins of the Soviet Technical Intelligentsia, 1917-1941* (Princeton, N.J., 1978), p. 45.

some of the most prominent names in the prerevolutionary Bar, such as N. Murav'ev and S. Plevako.[44]

One of the first actions of the governing board in Moscow was to appoint a three-man committee to approach the People's Commissariat of Justice with the news of the union's creation and with specific queries about the future role of the advocate in Soviet courts. The committee was at first rebuffed by the justice commissar of Moscow, Schreider. He informed the advocates that "such a union cannot exist, just as a union of angels cannot exist on earth."[45]

After reporting to the governing board, the committee was sent to the national justice commissar, Stuchka, who gave the advocates a more sympathetic hearing. Stuchka informed the committee that the entire question of the advocate's role in Soviet courts was still in the drafting stage. As for the newly created Union of Advocates, he felt that it had every right to exist and he anticipated that the Union would not be hindered in the establishment of local consultation offices for the purpose of legal practice.[46] Stuchka's position clearly contradicted the spirit of Lenin's amendments to Decree No. 2 on the Court, which called for a monopoly of legal practice to be given to those in colleges of legal representatives. It also made apparent the divisions between the moderates in the national Justice Commissariat and the hardliners on legal policy represented by Lenin and the bulk of local justice commissars.

Buoyed by the remarks of Stuchka, the Moscow Union of Advocates worked feverishly over the following weeks to make itself a going concern. At the union's general meeting of June 10, the fourth in six weeks, the advocates adopted a permanent charter as well as detailed rules governing the legal consultation offices. In addition, they decided to organize a Criminal Defense Section that would offer free legal representation to indigents appearing before revolutionary tribunals.[47]

[44] *Zashchita*, p. 3.
[45] Ibid.
[46] Ibid., p. 4.
[47] Ibid., p. 5.

Another appendage to the Union of Advocates set up at this meeting was the Section for the Defense of Russian Interests. In spite of the union's self-declared posture of political neutrality, the section was created to protest the "humiliating conditions" contained in the Brest-Litovsk Treaty with Germany. This action by the advocates was a testimony to the continuing strength of nationalist feelings in their ranks. Although willing to acquiesce to the reforms in social and economic relations, the advocates were as yet unable to reconcile themselves to the disintegration of the empire. The union's journal, published for the first and last time on August 21, 1918, devoted half of its pages to a vituperative polemic against the Brest settlement.[48]

Like the institutional foundations of the legal profession, the traditions of prerevolutionary legal practice died hard. Over the first ten months of Bolshevik rule neither the deprofessionalization of legal practice nor the subsequent provisions for the establishment of colleges of legal representatives succeeded in fundamentally altering the method of delivering legal services to the population. With few exceptions representation in court and legal advice continued to be provided by the private practitioner of the old regime. The one-man law office, usually located in the advocate's home, remained the standard venue for client contact, though collective forms of practice did appear to increase in this period. Besides the local consultation centers operated by the old Bar associations, by the new unions of advocates, or by the state-sponsored colleges of legal representatives, law firms of the Western variety made a brief appearance.[49]

Except for legal services rendered through the legal consultation centers, which charged according to a fixed fee schedule set by the local authorities, advocates' fees were unregulated. This led to harsh criticism by the proponents of a new legal order. An outraged justice official decried the one thousand ruble fee allegedly received by an advocate for filing simple divorce

[48] Ibid., pp. 9-18.
[49] "U advokatov," *Nash vek*, March 14, 1918, p. 4; *Zashchita*, p. 2.

papers. The monthly salary of a people's court judge at this time, it should be noted, was six hundred rubles.[50]

Although a few advocates may have maintained a financially successful practice in the first months after the Revolution, the vast majority were unable to support themselves through private practice. By the spring of 1918 even well-established advocates were reduced to selling their libraries to maintain themselves.[51] In late March the Petrograd Bar association created a labor exchange (*biuro truda*) for its members as well as a mutual assistance fund, which distributed money to the most needy among the advocates and former court officials.[52]

The financial crisis confronting the advocates was due in part to the disruption of court activity following the replacement of the old judiciary with a simplified court system. But more important in this regard was the boycott of Soviet courts imposed on the profession by the Bar's governing councils in the first weeks after the Revolution. Advocates who ignored the boycott were subject to disciplinary measures. In Petrograd in January 1918 the governing council initiated disciplinary proceedings against one of the city's most colorful advocates, Bobrishchev-Pushkin, who had defended a client in a revolutionary tribunal.[53]

As the new regime consolidated its power and the advocates became increasingly desperate for work, the boycott by the profession began to weaken, though not at the same pace in all areas of the country. In Petrograd, where advocates appeared most united in their opposition to the Revolution, the boycott was respected by most advocates well into 1918. In late March the Petrograd governing council rejected by a majority of one a proposal to lift the boycott, though it did exempt from the ban those cases of a "political or literary character" that were heard in the revolutionary tribunals.[54] Under pressure from its criminal

[50] *Materialy Narodnogo Komissariata iustitsii*, vypusk 1, p. 26.

[51] "Kassa vzaimopomoshchi sudebnykh deiatelei," *Nash vek*, March 22, 1918, p. 3.

[52] Ibid.

[53] "V sovete prisiazhnykh poverennykh," *Nash vek*, January 21, 1918, p. 4.

[54] "Vystuplenie advokatov v narodnykh sudakh," *Nash vek*, March 27, 1918, p. 3.

defenders, the governing council in Moscow had completely lifted the boycott on participation in revolutionary tribunals some weeks earlier.[55]

The boycott and the disruptions in the legal system sparked an exodus from the profession that continued throughout the revolutionary and civil war period. Of the more than three thousand advocates working in Moscow before the Revolution, only a quarter of that figure remained in practice by the autumn of 1918. The decline in the number of practitioners in Petrograd was even more rapid.[56]

The first refuge for most advocates appears to have been private enterprises, which employed them as legal consultants or responsible clerical personnel. In the early months of 1917 dozens of advocates were working in one Petrograd enterprise alone.[57] Although the holding of employment outside the profession (*sovmestitel'stvo*) was prohibited under the rules of the Bar, in order to prevent an even more massive reduction in membership the governing councils of the regional Bar associations revoked this prohibition in the case of those working for social or business organizations.[58] The exemption did not extend, however, to advocates employed in state institutions. State employees who did not resign their calling (*zvanie*) were subject to expulsion from the profession. The most prominent advocate expelled for this reason was P. Stuchka.[59]

For the advocates who did remain in private practice in the first year after the Revolution the formal bases of legal proceedings remained largely unaltered, though there were significant changes in the courtroom environment, in state legal personnel, and in the sources of substantive law. Information on

[55] *Zashchita*, p. 2

[56] S. Kobiakov, "Krasnyi sud: vpechatleniia zashchitnika v revoliutsionnykh tribunalakh," in *Arkhiv russkoi revoliutsii*, ed. I. Gessen, 22 vols. (Berlin, 1922-1937), 7: 249.

[57] Turin, "Ot kollegii pravozastupnikov do advokatury," p. 38.

[58] "Sovmestitel'stvo u advokatov," *Russkie vedomosti*, December 6, 1917 (old style), p. 6.

[59] "V sovete prisiazhnykh poverennykh," *Nash vek*, January 21, 1918, p. 4.

the character of legal proceedings in this period is incomplete, but it does appear that the liberal reforms in criminal procedure introduced under the Provisional Government were respected by many Soviet courts until well into the Civil War. Advocates retained, for example, at least the formal right to participate in the pretrial investigation and, according to one contemporary observer, were even permitted to attend the investigator's inter- rogation of witnesses.[60] Although minor criminal trials were held in the local people's courts, where decisions were rendered by a three-man panel consisting of a professional judge and two lay assessors, more serious criminal cases, such as murder, were tried in regional people's courts (*okruzhnye narodnye sudy*) or the revolutionary tribunals, which gave the advocate the oppor- tunity to argue before a jury.[61] Even though attempts were made by the Bolsheviks, especially in the revolutionary tribunals, to pack the juries with reliable members of the laboring classes, Soviet jurors were not always immune to the legendary oratorical skills of the Russian advocate. One former advocate described a revolutionary tribunal, composed primarily of old women re- cently drafted into the party, that was moved to tears by the defense speech of the advocate.[62]

There was, to be sure, a general decline in respect for pro- cedural guarantees and a concomitant weakening of the advo- cate's ability to effectively represent the interests of his client. But the defense speeches of advocates were still vigorous and often uncompromising. To the chagrin of the Bolsheviks, Russian advocates continued their prerevolutionary tradition of criticizing the political order as a means of shifting responsibility away from the accused and onto the state. In the celebrated case of the Union of Trade and Industry, the advocates strongly attacked the Cheka, comparing its provocations to the intrigues of the tsarist *okhrana*. Their defense speeches were not interrupted

[60] O sude (Dekret No. 2), art. 21; Kobiakov, "Krasnyi sud," p. 272; *Materialy Narodnogo Komissariata iustitsii*, vypusk 2 (Moscow, 1918), p. 39.

[61] O sude (Dekret No. 2), art. 3; Dekret o revoliutsionnykh tribunalakh, *Sobranie uzakonenii*, 1917-1918, art. 50, no. 4.

[62] Kobiakov, "Krasnyi sud," p. 248.

once by the judges.[63] Although some judges were less generous towards the advocates, a policy of mass intimidation was not employed in this period to force the advocates to abandon their traditional methods of court defense.

THE CIVIL WAR AND THE RISING TIDE OF LEGAL NIHILISM

In the late summer of 1918 a new phase in the Revolution, and in the development of the Bar, was ushered in. Over the first eight months of 1918 vocal opposition against the regime had turned to armed resistance, with the formation of anti-Bolshevik military forces on the periphery, the abortive uprising of the Left Social Revolutionaries, the assassinations of the prominent Bolsheviks Volodarskii and Uritskii, and a near successful attempt on the life of Lenin. This last event, which took place on August 30, 1918, was followed a week later by the Red Terror, a declaration formalizing the hardening of Bolshevik policy begun several weeks earlier.[64] In theory directed against counterrevolutionaries, the Red Terror was in fact a campaign against all those who refused to support Bolshevik power.[65]

The introduction of the Red Terror and the deepening Civil War had far-reaching effects on the legal system, especially on punitive policy (*karatel'naia politika*). Primary responsibility for the investigation and trial of criminal cases shifted from the ordinary courts and investigative units to extraordinary legal institutions, such as the Cheka and the revolutionary tribunals,

[63] Ibid., p. 260; *Iz istorii VChK* (Moscow, 1958), p. 141.

The advocates were also willing to make personal appeals to the political leadership for leniency towards their clients. In "The Case of the Provocateurs" the defenders arranged a personal audience with Sverdlov in the Metropol Hotel following the conviction of their clients. The chairman of VTsIK did not intercede, however, and the death sentences were carried out. See *Zashchita*, p. 8.

[64] O krasnom terrore, *Sobranie uzakonenii*, 1917-1918, art. 710, no. 65.

[65] When an appeal was made by Moscow advocates on the conviction of Menshevik workers in the city of Tiumen, the chief state prosecutor N. Krylenko reportedly replied: "We must execute not only the guilty. Execution of the innocent will impress the masses even more." I. Steinberg, *In the Workshop of the Revolution* (London, 1955), pp. 226-227.

both of which had been assuming an increasingly important role in the legal system since their creation at the end of 1917. The traditional bourgeois concerns for norms in law and procedure, which had informed Soviet legal proceedings to a considerable degree during the first year of the Revolution, were now being abandoned in the interests of preserving the infant state.

This reorientation of legal policy in the late summer of 1918 signaled the end of the atmosphere of relative tolerance in which the Russian Bar had functioned since October 1917. Given the continuing efforts of advocates to maintain independent associations, it was regarded as essential to eliminate the institutional remnants of the prerevolutionary profession. Over the period from August to late September 1918 all remaining Bar associations and unions of advocates in Bolshevik-held territory were permanently closed, and private practitioners were effectively banned from the courts.[66] Thus, the range of policy options on the legal profession was narrowed, though serious disagreements remained over the appropriate socialist alternative to the Bar.

The failure of the Justice Commissariat to adopt a consistent policy exacerbated the long-standing divisions among local legal officials over the correct approach to legal representation. Whether due to the low priority attached to the question of professional legal representation, to the continuing divisions among central policy makers on the issue, or to the lack of coordination between center and periphery characteristic of the young Soviet state, local authorities received virtually no guidance on the provision of legal services to the population. At a local conference of justice workers in Saratov held on August 22, 1918, an official complained that the recently established colleges of legal representatives in the area found it "difficult to work because of the inadequate information from the Justice Commissariat."[67]

This situation gave full rein to local initiative, resulting in

[66] B. Gerschun, "Russland," in J. Magnus, *Die Rechtsanwaltschaft* (Berlin, 1926), p. 230.

[67] *Narodnyi sud, Materialy Narodnogo Komissariata iustitsii*, vypusk 5, p. 8.

the proliferation of competing policies on the legal profession. In Petrograd, for example, the local people's courts proposed to introduce a system of labor service (*trudovaia povinnost'*) for court defense—a proposal that proved to be two years ahead of its time. Beginning with the September court session, the people's courts planned to summon as defenders advocates or other jurists on the basis of paid labor duty: "The defender will be chosen from among citizen-jurists whose pasts are beyond reproach. Party membership will not be required. Payment to defenders will be made on the same basis as that to expert witnesses." This measure, appearing in *Petrogradskaia Pravda* on August 24, was an attempt to circumvent the problem of finding a professional organization for defenders appropriate to a socialist society.[68]

But before the Petrograd experiment could be put into effect, the Sovnarkom issued a decree directing local authorities to create a single, organized profession of defenders within the framework of the state-sponsored colleges of legal representatives.[69] This long-awaited signal from the center was followed immediately by supplementary legislation at the local level. On August 26 and 28, respectively, the regional soviets in Petrograd and Moscow issued detailed instructions setting out the structure and basic rules of operation for the colleges in their areas.[70] Over the following weeks legislation on local colleges of legal representatives was adopted by other regional soviets throughout the territory controlled by the Bolsheviks.[71]

Inspired by Decree No. 2 on the Court and by the model instruction on colleges of legal representatives passed by the

---

[68] "Advokatskaia povinnost'," *Petrogradskaia pravda*, August 24, 1918, p. 3. The idea of compulsory labor service for advocates appears to have been first advanced by Stuchka in the spring of 1918. See "U advokatov," *Nash vek*, April 20, 1918, p. 3.

[69] B. Gershun, "Vospominaniia advokata," p. 150.

[70] "Kollegiia pravozastupnikov v predelakh soiuza kommun severnoi oblasti," *Petrogradskaia pravda*, August 27, 1918, p. 4; "Postanovlenie presizidiuma mossoveta rabochikh i krasnoarmeiskikh deputatov ot 28-go avgusta o kollegii pravozastupnikov," *Izvestiia VTsIK*, September 3, 1918, p. 6.

[71] *Narodny sud*, pp. 24, 33, 60-62.

Second Congress of Justice Commissars, the legislation adopted by local soviets was similar in many respects. All local legislation, for example, provided that only college members could practice law, though close relatives of a litigant or designated state officials were permitted to appear in court as unpaid representatives. This monopoly over legal practice granted to the colleges of legal representatives was supplemented by detailed legislation that imposed deadlines beyond which the traditional private practitioner could not accept new cases. Local soviets were united therefore in calling a halt to legal practice outside the framework of the new colleges.[72]

But the locally adopted instructions on the colleges of legal representatives differed on a number of important issues. Perhaps the most fundamental disagreement among local soviets concerned the method of payment of legal representatives. In Petrograd members of the college of legal representatives were placed on a fixed salary equal to that of a people's court judge. The earning of outside income was strictly prohibited.[73] In Moscow, on the other hand, the local soviet, which appeared to be more in tune with the moderate leadership of Stuchka at the Justice Commissariat, adopted a system of remuneration that prevented money from changing hands between lawyer and client but nonetheless maintained much of the financial incentive of private practice. Clients paid their fees into the college's central fund on the basis of a set fee schedule and these earnings were in turn disbursed to the members of the college according to a formula that took into account the number of cases handled and their complexity.[74]

---

[72] "Kollegiia pravozastupnikov v predelakh soiuza kommun severnoi oblasti," p. 4; "Postanovlenie prezidiuma mossoveta," p. 6.

[73] "Kollegiia pravozastupnikov v predelakh soiuza kommun severnoi oblasti," p. 4; "Postanovlenie prezidiuma mossoveta," p. 6.

[74] "Postanovlenie prezidiuma mossoveta," p. 6. Although the payment systems in Moscow and Petrograd appear to have served as models for many other colleges, local soviets in some areas adopted their own systems of remuneration. The legal representatives in Tim, for example, charged according to a fee schedule but received payment directly from clients. In justifying this approach, which he regarded as temporary, the local justice commissar noted that the local soviet had found both

Local soviets were also divided over the degree of self-government that the colleges of legal representatives should enjoy. Here again Petrograd stood out as the proponent of an "administrative" approach. In Moscow, although the formal responsibility for selection and dismissal of college members rested with the local soviet, the college did have the right to reject new members if it gave just cause (*pravo motivirovannogo otvoda*). Furthermore, it was allowed to recommend to the local soviet candidates for membership in the college.[75] None of these rights was accorded to the college in Petrograd, where membership questions were solely the province of the local soviet.[76]

The relative liberalism of the Moscow legislation was evident on a number of other issues. Whereas in Moscow advocates of the old regime had the right to complete cases arising before September 1, 1918, in Petrograd the advocates were to cease activity at once, except in cases for the disabled assumed before March 7, 1918—the date when Decree No. 2 on the Court was passed into law. Furthermore, instead of having all their cases assigned by the college administration or the court, as in Petrograd, legal representatives in Moscow were able to accept cases directly from clients. Finally, the local soviet in Moscow inserted a conscience clause into its instruction that enabled legal representatives, who were occasionally called on to prosecute cases, to excuse themselves from acting as prosecutors in criminal cases, if, having studied the case materials, they disagreed with the bases of the prosecution.[77]

The differences in the legislation of the Petrograd and Moscow soviets led to quite distinct paths of development for the colleges

---

the Petrograd and Moscow models wanting—the former because of its failure to encourage productivity and the latter because of its complexity, *Narodyi sud*, p. 20. The same system was used in Saratov where, according to Kurskii, college members received clients just as before the Revolution. D. Kurskii, "O edinom narodnom sude," *Izbrannye stat'i i rechi* (Moscow, 1958), p. 57.

[75] "Postanovlenie prezidiuma mossoveta," p. 6.

[76] "Kollegiia pravozastupnikov v predelakh soiuza kommun severnoi oblasti," p. 4.

[77] "Postanovlenie prezidiuma mossoveta," p. 6.

of legal representatives in the two cities, at least over the short term. By providing the college in their area with a more traditional constitution, the local authorities in Moscow clearly hoped to draw into the institution large numbers of advocates whose presence would legitimize the college in certain quarters and ensure the exploitation of a considerable reservoir of trained legal personnel. As anticipated there appears to have been a transfer en masse of members of the old Bar into the new college of legal representatives in Moscow. Within a few months of its creation the Moscow college had eight hundred members, almost all of whom were former advocates or court officials.[78]

In the autumn of 1918 the Moscow college functioned in many ways like the prerevolutionary Bar association. The internal affairs of the profession were run by a twelve-man governing council elected by the rank and file of the college. The governing council established the internal rules of conduct for the profession and heard disciplinary cases arising from complaints on the behavior of legal representatives. Besides recommending to the local soviet candidates for membership in the college, the governing council actively used its right of challenge to prevent soviet-sponsored Bolshevik party members from entering the profession. This provoked heated exchanges between the legal department of the local soviet, responsible for the supervision of the college, and the governing council of the college and undoubtedly contributed to the hardening of official policy toward the legal representatives in the ensuing months.[79]

In Petrograd the local authorities were not prepared to compromise with the former advocates to secure their entrance into the new institutions. When the policy of the local soviet became apparent in late August, the governing council of the Petrograd Bar, whose headquarters had been closed earlier in the month, decided at a clandestine meeting to "die a noble death" rather than negotiate with the authorities on their terms.[80] There re-

[78] Kobiakov, "Krasnyi sud," p. 249.
[79] Ibid.
[80] Gershun, "Vospominaniia advokata," p. 151.

mained, however, a small group among the Petrograd advocates that hoped to achieve an amicable transfer of the membership of the Bar into the colleges of legal representatives. Headed by the flamboyant advocate Bobrishchev-Pushkin, this "initiative group," along with some members of the mainstream of the profession, summoned the final meeting of advocates in Petrograd to discuss the question of membership in the new Soviet institution. With the advocates assembled on September 20 in the City Duma building, Bobrishchev-Pushkin proposed that the estate transfer en masse into the regional college of legal representatives. After the suggestion was debated at length, A. Isaev, a liberal and one of the pillars of the Petrograd profession, offered a counter-proposal which provided that the decision to enter the college should be a matter for the individual, and not the collective, conscience. This was passed by an overwhelming majority.[81]

The distinct histories of the colleges of legal representatives in Moscow and Petrograd in the autumn of 1918 illustrate the care that must be taken in describing general developments in the profession in this period. Legal policy making was still very much a local affair. Although a network of colleges with similar structural characteristics was created throughout Bolshevik-held territory, the method of remuneration, the degree of self-government, and the venue for legal practice differed from one college to the next. These differences, in turn, determined the quality and quantity of persons drawn into the colleges and, to some extent, the character of legal services provided to the local population.

But no sooner had the colleges of legal representatives begun to establish themselves than a new shift took place in legal policy. On November 30, 1918, the All-Russian Central Executive Committee (VTsIK) adopted the Law on the People's Court, which superseded existing legislation on the courts and on the legal profession.[82] Drafted by the new national justice

[81] Ibid., p. 152.
[82] O narodnom sude RSFSR (Polozhenie), *Sobranie uzakonenii*, 1917-1918, art. 889, no. 85.

commissar, Kurskii, who had replaced the more moderate and assertive Stuchka, the law reflected the desire for a simplified and uniform legal system that could more effectively carry out the punitive policy of the state.[83]

Under the new legislation the colleges of legal representatives were to be replaced by the even more awkwardly labeled colleges of accusers, defenders, and representatives in civil cases (*kollegii obvinitelei, zashchitnikov, i predstavitelei storon po grazhdanskim delam*)—a misleading name change since college members were to be called on only rarely to appear as prosecutors. The members of the new colleges were to be salaried state functionaries hired by the local soviets and paid at the same rate as people's court judges. Clients were still to be charged a fee, but this was to be paid into the account of the Justice Commissariat, from whose budget salaries would be met.[84]

In order to further impersonalize the relationship between lawyer and client, the Law on the People's Court stipulated that citizens could no longer turn to a specific lawyer for help. In both civil and criminal cases requests for legal assistance had to be made through the college administration or the court, which then appointed the lawyer. In addition, representatives in civil suits were assigned to argue a citizen's case only when the college administration felt the complaint, or its defense, to be justified.[85] The state was thereby ruling on the validity of a case before it had been put before the court.

On the question of collegial self-government the law was vir-

---

[83] J. Hazard, *Settling Disputes in Soviet Society: The Formative Years of Soviet Legal Institutions* (New York, 1960), pp. 57-59. In his discussion of the Law on the People's Court, Professor Hazard describes Justice Commissar Kurskii as the architect of the new approach to the court system, whereas it appears that he was simply its draftsman. Contemporary descriptions of Kurskii show him to have been a meek and cautious man surrounded by more aggressive political and legal figures, such as N. Krylenko, who Kobiakov maintains was the main inspirer of the Soviet system of justice in this period. Kobiakov, "Krasnyi sud," p. 250; Meier, "Sluzhba v komissariate iustitsii i narodnom sude," p. 68.

[84] O narodnon sude RSFSR.

[85] Ibid. Refusal to accept a case could, however, be appealed by citizens to a court.

tually silent. In the last line of the section on the legal profession it was stated that a governing council would be selected by the members of the college for a one-year term. But except for its responsibilities relating to the distribution of work among college members, the powers of the council were not specified.[86]

The provisions of the law on the colleges of accusers and defenders represented a considerable victory for the left wing of the legal establishment. The concessions to the bourgeois legal tradition that had been apparent in the formation of colleges of legal representatives in Moscow and other cities were now withdrawn, and the stage was set for the transfer to a uniform, state socialist system of legal representation. This reform in legal policy reflected the general tendency of the authorities to rely increasingly on centralist solutions to policy problems in the conditions of civil war.

Like earlier reforms of the legal profession, the provisions of the Law on the People's Court were introduced with some delay. Begun in Moscow on January 2, 1919, the transfer to the new system was not completed in the city until March 1, 1919.[87] Reform came even later to many colleges in outlying areas, especially in regions under siege by White forces. The transformation of the colleges was not carried out in Turkestan, for example, until May 6, 1919.[88]

One of the most significant effects of the reform was the drastic diminution in the size of the profession. Having assumed responsibility for the financing of the colleges, the state appeared committed to keeping their membership at a minimal level. In Moscow a ceiling of two hundred members was placed on the regional college, which had contained four times that number at the begining of 1919. As it happened, only sixty persons were drafted into the new college of accusers and defenders.[89] Thus,

[86] Ibid.

[87] Dubkov, "Demokraticheskie osnovy organizatsii sovetskoi advokatury," p. 26; Kobiakov, "Krasnyi sud," p. 249.

[88] M. Mumin, "Sozdanie i razvitie advokatury v Uzbekistane" (*Kandidat* dissertation, Tashkent, 1975), p. 31.

[89] Kobiakov, "Krasnyi sud," p. 249.

over a period of fifteen months, from the October Revolution until March 1919, the number of practicing defenders in Moscow decreased from over three thousand to one hundred.[90]

The decline in the number of legal practitioners meant that during the Civil War professional legal representation was available to only a very small proportion of the population. Most of those unable to obtain the services of a college member simply did without legal assistance, but some turned to the so-called underground advocates (*podpol'nye advokaty*) for help. The underground advocates, whose activities were to trouble Soviet legal officials as they had tsarist officials before them, were often minor government functionaries practicing law clandestinely on a part-time basis. Unable to appear in courts after the summer of 1918, they composed legal documents such as civil pleadings and criminal appeals for their clients. It appears that during the Civil War the ranks of the underground advocates were swelled with former members of the Bar who were struggling to survive under the new regime.[91]

Just as the deepening Civil War reduced the number of professional defenders, it further diminished the scope of their participation in legal proceedings. This was particularly evident in criminal cases. From the end of 1918 defenders were, with few exceptions, excluded from the pretrial stage of the criminal process.[92] At the trial itself the participation of the defender became a contingent, and not an absolute, right. If under Decree No. 2 on the Court the presence of an advocate was permitted in all criminal cases heard in the people's courts, the Law on the People's Court of November 1918 gave the judges the right to prevent the defender from representing a client in court, except in the relatively few cases when a state prosecutor was present or when the case was being heard by a six-man jury.[93]

---

[90] M. Gernet, ed., *Istoriia russkoi advokatury*, 3 vols. (Moscow, 1914-1916), 2: 3-5.

[91] E. Rivlin, *Sovetskaia advokatura* (Moscow, 1926), p. 36.

[92] Tsypkin, *Pravo na zashchitu* (Saratov, 1959), pp. 1,294-1,295, cited in V. Stremovskii, *Uchastniki predvaritel'nogo sledstviia v sovetskom ugolovnom protsesse* (Rostov, 1966), pp. 158-159.

[93] O narodnom sude RSFSR, art. 43.

Another result of the movement to simplify the legal system was the abolition of the regional people's courts,[94] in which serious criminal cases were tried before a jury. These courts, which were staffed largely by trained jurists from the old regime, had built a reputation for adherence to traditional procedural norms. Shortly after their formation in the spring of 1918 they were referred to as an oasis of justice by a non-Bolshevik paper.[95] With their dismantling, the defender was deprived of an institution that had given him the fullest rein for defense activities.

The effectiveness of the defender in representing the accused in criminal cases was further diminished by the expanded jurisdiction of extraordinary tribunals in this period. These institutions were at the cutting edge of Bolshevik repressive policy, as illustrated by the over six thousand persons executed in 1920 alone on the basis of tribunal verdicts.[96] Although the revolutionary tribunals established at the regional, and later national, level are perhaps the best known of these institutions, there also existed military revolutionary tribunals, railway tribunals, and special sessions of the people's courts—the latter created to hear in closed session the overflow from the regional revolutionary tribunals.[97]

Since the secret police, the Cheka, assumed primary responsibility for criminal investigation in cases heard by extraordinary tribunals, there was little opportunity for defenders to participate at the pretrial stage in sensitive criminal cases.[98] Indeed, in many cases investigated by the Cheka repression was applied on the spot without the niceties of a formal legal hearing. Of

---

[94] Ibid., art. 1.

[95] "Oazis pravosudiia," *Nash vek*, May 1, 1918, p. 3.

[96] D. Rodin, "Revoliutsionnye tribunaly v 1920-22 gg.," *Vestnik statistiki*, no. 1-3 (1923), p. 170.

[97] See Kozhevnikov, *Istoriia sovetskogo suda*, pp. 68-115.

[98] G. Leggett, *The Cheka—Lenin's Political Police* (Oxford, 1981), pp. 146-147. In some areas the Cheka was the only functioning legal institution. See the letter to Kurskii in which the Vitebsk Party Committee notified the Commissariat that it was having to cease activities of local legal institutions because all their personnel had been mobilized by the party. *Perepiski sekretariata TsK RKP (b) s mestnymi partiinymi organizatsiiami*, 8 vols. (Moscow, 1957-1974), 7: 311-312.

those serving time in labor camps in 1919 and 1920, over one-half were there as a result of administrative, and not judicial, action (*napravleno tuda v administrativnom poriadke*). In the cases that were sent to trial on the basis of a Cheka investigation, although the defender was permitted by law to appear with the permission of the judge, in practice his presence was even less likely than in the ordinary people's courts. Virtually all cases in the revolutionary tribunals in this period were heard without benefit of prosecutor or defender. At the Fourth Congress of Revolutionary Tribunals it was agreed by the delegates that a full-fledged trial with the participation of the sides should be reserved for exceptional cases only.[99]

The legal obscurantism evident in the movement away from formalized norms and procedures was due in considerable measure to the educational backgrounds of cadres staffing the revolutionary tribunals. Of the judges in the revolutionary tribunals 83 percent had no more than a primary education and only 4 percent had received a university-level degree. In contrast, approximately 20 percent of the people's court judges were university-educated jurists from the old regime. Members of the revolutionary tribunals were selected, therefore, almost solely on the basis of their political loyalty. Over 99 percent were members of the Communist party, whereas party membership among people's court judges was only 29 percent.[100] When revolutionary tribunals composed of relatively well-educated members were compared with those whose members were without higher education, it was found that the conviction percentage was considerably higher in the latter and the degree of punishment more severe.[101] Thus, the harshness of Soviet justice in

[99] Rivlin, *Sovetskaia advokatura*, pp. 24-25; V. Kuritsyn, *Perekhod k nepu i revoliutsionnaia zakonnost'* (Moscow, 1972), p. 107. The decisions of revolutionary tribunals and people's courts accounted for only 27.8 and 16.4 percent, respectively, of all confinements in labor camps. See Kuritsyn, *Perekhod k nepu i revoliutsionnaia zakonnost*, p. 107.

[100] Tarnovskii, "Lichnyi sostav i repressiia revtribunalov," *Ezhenedel'nik sovetskoi iustitsii*, no. 11 (1922), p. 6.

[101] Ibid.

this period reflected not only the new ideology of the Bolsheviks and the life and death struggle of the Civil War but also the promotion of untrained cadres into responsible legal positions. This resulted in a kind of mob justice (*samosud*) in the service of the state.

In the relatively few cases when the defender was admitted to the trial—whether in the ordinary court system or in the extraordinary tribunals—his ability to influence the outcome of the case was severely limited. No longer could he be assured that the procedural guarantees that he had previously enjoyed would be respected. The rules on court procedure of 1864, which had remained applicable in the first year of the Revolution except when they contradicted existing decrees or a judge's revolutionary legal consciousness, were abolished outright by the Law on the People's Court. Thereafter, judges were guided in the determination of court procedure only by the scant Soviet decrees on the subject and their own revolutionary legal consciousness.[102]

It cannot have been often that the application of revolutionary legal consciousness, whether on substantive or procedural law, worked to the advantage of the defense. Judges were under increasing pressure from the political authorities to place the interests of the state above all other considerations. The court was assigned to the front line in the campaign to preserve the young and vulnerable Soviet state through mass repression. According to Kozlovskii, a former advocate and a moderate member of the Board of the Justice Commissariat: "The court is no more and no less than . . . an organ of the dictatorship. Forget the illusions about the independence of courts, and so forth. This is bourgeois rubbish."[103] For the judges, most of whom by this time were reliable Soviet cadres, the crisis conditions and the explicit signals received from the political authorities encouraged a harsher approach to judicial decision making than had been followed in the first year of the Revolution.

[102] O narodnom sude RSFSR, art. 22.
[103] *Materialy Narodnogo Komissariata iustitsii*, vypusk 11-12, p. 80.

In addition to the reforms in the organization, financing, and procedural position of legal defenders during the Civil War, an attempt was made to redefine the relationship between the lawyer and his client and thereby the method of defense to be employed by the professional representative in the courtroom. For legal policy makers, especially those holding more left-wing views, the posture of the legal defender as servant of the client seemed inappropriate in Soviet courts.[104] Although ideas about the proper approach to court defense were as yet ill-defined, the predominant view among legal authorities was that the "one-sided approach" to legal defense characteristic of bourgeois court proceedings could not be justified in a socialist state, whose institutions represented the interests of the working masses. It was expected that the defender, no longer tied financially to the client, would adopt a more objective position in legal proceedings.[105]

The first step in the development of a new approach to legal defense was taken in November 1918 with the publication of the Law on the People's Court. The opening line of the section on the legal profession noted that legal representatives existed "to aid the court in the most complete illumination of all the circumstances relating to the defendant."[106] But growing expectations among legal officials that the defender's proper role was solely as an aide to the court, and not as the representative of the interests of the client, did not bring a corresponding change in the defenders' behavior in the courtroom. Most members of the colleges of accusers and defenders, having been educated and socialized professionally under the tsarist legal system, still regarded the criminal process as a conflict between two sides—the prosecution and the defense. This traditional approach to criminal defense required the defense counsel to represent as vigorously as possible the interests of the defendant.

[104] Ibid., p. 10.
[105] Ibid.
[106] O narodnom sude RSFSR, art. 40.

THE DEMISE OF AN ORGANIZED PROFESSION OF DEFENDERS

As the Civil War in Russia drew to a close, renewed efforts were made to formulate a distinctly socialist policy on professional legal representation. The reshaping of Bolshevik policy on the advocates in this period was due in part to increasing uncertainty about the necessity of professional legal representation in a socialist society. The summary character of legal proceedings in the atmosphere of civil war made unnecessary the presence in court of prosecutors and defenders, and therefore the continued existence of institutions to house them appeared to some superfluous. Moreover, in the relatively few cases when the sides did participate the defender's behavior in court did not, in the eyes of many judges, serve the interests of the state.[107]

Operating outside of direct party supervision, the colleges were also vulnerable to accusations of misconduct. During the Civil War, justice officials in Petrograd reported that all the members of the local college of accusers and defenders except one were arrested and convicted for accepting payment from clients in addition to their state salary. Indeed, the system of control over the colleges' internal affairs was not sufficiently developed to ensure the maintenance of strict discipline of the members. The local soviets gave little attention to the colleges, and local party organizations appeared to ignore them altogether. There is no evidence of primary party organizations existing among defenders in the period from 1918 to 1920. Educated party members were in great demand and could not be spared for an institution that was not engaged directly in socialist construction.[108]

[107] *Chetvertii vserossiiskii s'ezd deiatelei sovetskoi iustitsii* (Moscow, 1922), pp. 5-10; Kuritsyn, *Perekhod k nepu i revoliutsionnaia zakonnost'*, p. 118.

[108] Rivlin, *Sovetskaia advokatura*, pp. 21-22; *Materialy Narodnogo Komissariata iustitsii*, vypusk 11-12.

Statistics compiled from thirty-two regions (*gubernii*) of Russia for 1921 list 195 consultants, only 4 of whom were Communist party members or candidate members. Narodnyi Komissariat iustitsii, *Otchet IX vserossiiskomu s'ezdu sovetov* (Moscow, 1921), p. 28.

Despite the shortcomings perceived by the state in the colleges of accusers and defenders, the system might have limped along had it not been for developments outside the legal system in the method of organizing labor. The free labor market, which prevailed throughout the first year of Soviet power, had been replaced in large measure during the Civil War in order to guarantee the production and distribution of material for the war effort. Those who were not mobilized directly into the armed forces were obligated to perform labor service, usually according to their skill or profession. Although originally conceived as a temporary measure to see the country through the economic crises of the war period, the idea of "the permanent and unlimited conscription of labor by the state" began to be advanced as the apotheosis of labor organization in a socialist society.[109] Thus, as reconstruction approached, the state prepared to transfer the militarized labor system begun under war communism onto a civilian economy.

The signal for the replacement of the colleges of accusers and defenders with a form of labor service appears to have been given by Lenin personally.[110] In *Left-Wing Communism: An Infantile Disorder* Lenin wrote that "in Russia we abolished, and rightly so, the old bourgeois Bar. But it is now reappearing in our midst in the form of 'soviet' legal representatives."[111] On May 11, 1920, as Lenin's book was being prepared for the printers, the first step was taken in the transfer to a system of labor conscription for lawyers with the issuing of a decree by the Sovnarkom "On the Registration of Persons with a Higher Legal Education."[112] The decree called on all trained jurists of

---

The issue of party members joining institutions of defenders in large numbers did not arise until 1922, when it sparked considerable controversy and debate within the party.

[109] E. H. Carr, *The Bolshevik Revolution, 1917-1923*, 3 vols. (London, 1950-1953), 2: 216.

[110] Dubkov, "Demokraticheskie osnovy organizatsii sovetskoi advokatury," p. 32.

[111] Lenin, "Detskaia bolezn'—levizny v kommunizme," in *Polnoe sobranie sochinenii*, 41: 101.

[112] "Postanovlenie SNK o registratsii lits s vysshim iuridicheskim obrazovaniem," in *Dekrety sovetskoi vlasti*, 8: 181-184.

the old regime, of whom the vast majority were advocates, to register at once with the local soviets or face prosecution.

The plan to transfer to a system of labor conscription for lawyers was confirmed at the Third All-Russian Congress of Justice Workers held in Moscow from June 25 to 29, 1920. In a report setting out proposed amendments to the Law on the People's Court, an official of the Justice Commissariat, Cherliunchakevich, argued that the experiment with the colleges of accusers and defenders had been unsuccessful. Echoing the words of Lenin, he noted that "instead of an institution of legal representatives there has continued to exist an institution of advocates of the bourgeois order." The Justice Commissariat proposed, therefore, to amend the relevant sections of the Law on the People's Court in order to replace the colleges of accusers and defenders with a system that periodically assigned jurists working in private or government institutions to cases on the basis of obligatory labor service. This meant the abolition of an organized profession of defenders.[113]

This nihilist approach to the legal profession was not, however, without critics from the more moderate wing of the legal community. In debate following the official report a number of delegates openly opposed the amendments of the Justice Commissariat on the legal profession. One delegate chastised the Justice Commissariat for smearing the legal defenders, who, he felt, had done admirable work over the preceding two years. He challenged the Commissariat to support its portrayal of the colleges with concrete evidence.[114] Although many others were less supportive of the existing state of affairs in the profession, they nonetheless believed that an organized institution of legal defenders in some form was essential. Of the twelve delegates participating in the debate, eight favored the retention of institutions of legal defenders, three delegates—all members of the Board of the Justice Commissariat—supported the dismantling of the colleges, and one delegate suggested a compromise be-

[113] *Materialy Narodnogo Komissariata iustitsii*, vypusk 11-12, p. 5.
[114] Ibid., p. 12.

tween the two positions. But despite vocal opposition, the resolution of the Commissariat incorporating the amendments on the legal profession was adopted by the congress.[115]

Unlike its position at the Second Congress of Regional Justice Commissars in mid-1918, the Justice Commissariat now appeared to move ahead of the local justice workers in the advocacy of more radical reforms in the legal system. This was due in part to the changing political complexion of the Commissariat itself. The composition of the Board of the Justice Commissariat had become increasingly left-wing during the Civil War with the inclusion of such outspoken legal nihilists as Krasikov. In this case, however, the Commissariat may have been acting as much out of financial as political considerations in its new policy on the legal profession. At a time when the financial burden of the Commissariat was particularly heavy, the elimination of the colleges of accusers and defenders must have been a relatively painless method of trimming expenditures.

The attacks on the colleges of accusers and defenders made by Lenin and the officials of the Justice Commissariat were followed by the rapid elimination of the colleges over the summer of 1920, even though the amendments to the Law on the People's Court had not yet been formally enacted by the government. In a letter of August 26, 1920, proposing the amendments to the presidium of VTsIK, Kurskii noted that the liquidation of the colleges had already begun at the local level. It is therefore likely that the colleges of accusers and defenders ceased to exist well before the amendments to the Law on the People's Court were finally enacted by VTsIK on October 21, 1920.[116]

Having dismantled the colleges, however, the legal authorities did little to ensure the timely and effective transfer to a system of labor service. Whether due to the impracticality of the labor

---

[115] Ibid., p. 8.

[116] I. Sukharev, "Organizatsiia i deiatel'nost' advokatury SSSR" (*Kandidat* dissertation, Moscow, 1973), p. 16; Polozhenie o narodnom sude RSFSR, *Sobranie uzakonenii*, 1920, art. 407, no. 83. The law was followed a month later by a supplementary instruction on the legal profession. Instruktsiia ob organizatsii obvineniia i zashchity na sude, *Sobranie uzakonenii*, 1920, art. 543, no. 151.

service system or the early shift in the general political climate away from the concept of labor conscription, no sustained effort was made by legal officials either at the local or national level to involve the mass of eligible jurists in the provision of legal services to the population. A major stumbling block to the reform was the failure to provide incentives to the employers of trained legal personnel to release their specialists for periods of labor service. The justice departments of local soviets, which had the responsibility for conscripting jurists in their areas and for assigning them to cases,[117] appear to have had little influence over the enterprises and government institutions employing legal personnel. Thus, many departments did not even bother to compile lists of jurists, while those that did received a poor response from jurists eligible for labor services.[118]

Unable to enlist the cooperation of jurists or their institutional employers, the justice departments were themselves forced to assume the responsibility for the provision of legal services to the population. Acting on instructions from the Justice Commissariat in Moscow, local justice departments began to establish sections of full-time paid consultants (*konsul'tatsionnye podotdely*) at the end of 1920. Their sole function was the extension of legal aid to the public.[119] According to a recent Soviet source, the overwhelming majority of cases defended in court in this period were argued by these consultants.[120] In effect, then, the colleges of accusers and defenders were forsaken not for a system of labor service but for a new, though less developed, state Bar.

[117] GAORSS MO, f. 2,359, op. 1, l. 12, cited in Dubkov, "Demokraticheskie osnovy organizatsii sovetskoi advokatury," p. 36.

[118] A. Tager, "O prokurature i advokature, obvenenii i zashchite," *Pravo i zhizn'*, no. 8-9 (1927), p. 60.

[119] N. Kuchemko, *Ukreplenie sotsialisticheskoi zakonnosti v Sibiri v pervye gody nepa (1921-1923)* (Novosibirsk, 1981), p. 146.

[120] A. Tager, "Sovetskaia advokatura za 20 let," *Sotsialisticheskaia zakonnost'*, no. 11 (1937), p. 69. Like the membership of the colleges of accusers and defenders, the justice department consultants were drawn almost exclusively from the ranks of prerevolutionary jurists. Kurskii sanctioned the employment of some former college members as consultants "until such time as the defense has been placed on the new bases." Kurskii, *Izbrannye stat'i i rechi*, p. 67.

Employing only 650 defenders nationwide, the consultation sections provided little more than token legal assistance to Soviet citizens.[121] In Omsk, for example, legal officials estimated that 85 consultants were required to render legal services to the local population, though only 10 were hired by the local justice department.[122] Because of their small numbers the consultants were limited primarily to providing routine legal aid to the public, either in the form of oral advice or assistance in the preparation of complaints, appeals, and other legal documents. Consultants did not argue civil cases at all, and they were present only rarely in criminal proceedings.[123]

An uncommon sight in criminal trials, the defender was excluded altogether from the preliminary investigation during this period. With the replacement of the old investigation commissions by the single criminal investigator in October 1920 the defender was prohibited by law from participating in the criminal process before the issuing of the indictment—a measure justified on the grounds of protecting the inexperienced investigator from the shrewd bourgeois lawyer. The introduction of the amended Law on the People's Court also marked the end of the jury system in Russia. Serious criminal cases were tried thereafter by the more easily controlled three-man bench, usually consisting of a professional judge and two lay assessors.[124]

These reforms were a devastating blow to criminal defense. By eliminating the jury trial, the legislation of October 1920 increased the relative importance of the investigation in the criminal process. At the same time the new law ensured that the investigation would be less thorough and balanced by removing it from judicial oversight and by excluding counsel from investigative proceedings.[125] Through such reductions in the

[121] *Otchet IX vserossiiskomu s'ezdu sovetov*, p. 28.

[122] Kuchemko, *Ukreplenie sotsialisticheskoi zakonnosti v Sibiri*, p. 147.

[123] Dubkov, "Demokraticheskie osnovy organizatsii sovetskoi advokatury," p. 35.

[124] Polozhenie o narodnom sude RSFSR (1920); V. Poznanskii, "K voprosu ob uchastii zashchitnika v stadii predvaritel'nogo rassledovaniia," in *Uchenye vypuski khar'kovskogo iuridicheskogo instituta*, vypusk 2 (1949), p. 121.

[125] The reader familiar only with the common law tradition should be reminded that criminal procedure in Russia before 1920 closely followed the inquisitorial

defender's formal rights in the legal process, and through the direct subordination of state legal personnel to political authority, the concept of legal defense was all but extinguished. Only the remnants of the adversary process and the professions to which it gave rise remained in Soviet Russia at the end of the Civil War.

During the Revolution and Civil War, the legitimacy of direct political intervention in judicial decision making implicit in the Leninist approach to law was firmly embedded in the Soviet legal consciousness. Nowhere was this erosion of the boundaries between law and politics more apparent than at the center. In February 1922, Lenin, angered by reports of widespread swindling, wrote a harsh letter to the deputy finance commissar criticizing the justice commissar, Kurskii, who supervised the courts: "Is our justice commissar sleeping? What is needed here is a number of exemplary cases with the application of the strictest punishment."[126] This approach to law as an unmediated instrument of state power combined with the vulnerability of the Soviet state in the first years of its existence to produce a legal system that had little need for a trained profession of legal

---

system found in Continental Europe. In this system the investigation is not an adversarial procedure with prosecution and defense engaged in the finding of fact but rather a theoretically objective inquiry, usually conducted by state investigators under court supervision. Because of the independent nature of the investigation the trial itself is often a less protracted and less important stage of the process than in common law countries. Although adversarial relations are present between prosecution and defense at the trial, the contest between the sides is somewhat constrained in comparison with common law systems by the more active role assumed by the judge. An excellent introduction to Continental criminal procedure can be found in J. Merryman, *The Civil Law Tradition* (Stanford, 1969). On the origins of the inquisitorial process, see J. Langbein, *Prosecuting Crime in the Renaissance* (Cambridge, Mass., 1974).

The beginnings of the divergence of Russian and Soviet procedure from the modern Continental model can be traced to 1920, when the Soviet state abandoned both direct judicial control of the investigation and the right to counsel at the investigative stage.

[126] Lenin, "Pis'mo zamestiteliu Narkomfina," in *Polnoe sobranie sochinenii*, 54: 160. See also Leggett, *The Cheka*, pp. 346-347.

defenders. Thus, the developments in the legal profession in this period reflected the desire not only to neutralize the opposition-minded Bar of the old regime but also to replace it with a minimalist profession of legal representatives, in terms of both numbers and functions.

By the time of the introduction of Lenin's New Economic Policy (NEP) in early 1921, a thorough transformation of the Russian legal profession had occurred. The rising tide of legal nihilism during the Civil War prevailed over the efforts of moderate state legal personnel and the advocates themselves to preserve what Stuchka would call the "cultural achievement" of the traditional profession.[127] The prerevolutionary Bar, which had been a large and well-organized institution playing a central role in the legal system, was eliminated and replaced by a small number of state consultants who were almost totally excluded from the Soviet courtroom. From a profession of some 13,000 advocates in 1917, the number of full-time professional legal representatives dwindled to around 650 by 1921.[128]

The new regime clearly succeeded in neutralizing the Bar as an institution. But what of the advocates themselves? According to one estimate, between 1,500 and 2,000 sworn advocates, or approximately 15 percent of the profession, emigrated.[129] Of this group, a small number settled in the newly formed states that had been on the periphery of the Russian Empire, such as Poland and Latvia, though most moved to Western Europe or North America. Councils of sworn advocates were set up in Paris, Brussels, Berlin, and New York and functioned as social clubs for a number of years.[130]

Some advocates, of course, died over the four years that separated the October Revolution from the introduction of NEP. The level of natural attrition was heightened considerably by the widespread starvation of the Civil War. Advocates, like other

---

[127] "Reforma sovetskogo ugolovnogo protsessa," *Revoliutsiia prava*, no. 1 (1928), pp. 120-121.

[128] *Istoriia russkoi advokatury*, 2: 3-5.

[129] Gerschun, "Russland," p. 231.

[130] Ibid.

members of the Russian intelligentsia, were struggling to find the means for survival. According to a Petrograd sworn advocate who lived through the period, the advocates fared better than the former judges, who were less adaptable, but nonetheless many members of the Bar died of starvation and disease.[131] Other advocates were killed in the terror of the Revolution and the Civil War. Perhaps the first victim of the Revolution from the profession was an advocate in Tashkent, who was killed by a mob (*samosud*) in the early days of the Bolshevik uprising in that city.[132]

If one assumes that the level of attrition equaled the level of emigration in the Bar, then 9,000 to 10,000 former members of the profession remained in Russia in 1921, a group that was on the whole slightly younger, less financially successful, and less conservative than those who departed. Of the sworn advocates and advocates-in-training remaining in the country, only about 225 were employed as consultants in local justice departments in 1921. Approximately 70 private advocates also worked as consultants.[133] Thus, on the eve of NEP the vast majority of former advocates were engaged in different work from that which they had done before the Revolution.

Some of these advocates held other legal positions. Besides consultants there were approximately 340 sworn advocates and advocates-in-training and 200 private advocates working in various capacities in local justice departments or in judicial institutions.[134] Of the 3,000 people's judges in 1921, for example, about 175 were former advocates.[135] Advocates were also to be found in the People's Commissariat of Justice in Moscow (though

---

[131] Meier, "Sluzhba v komissariate iustitsii i narodnom sude," p. 86.

[132] "Stolichnaia advokatura i politicheskii moment," *Nash vek*, December 19, 1917. Among the advocates killed by the Cheka was A. Vilenkov, a liberal and former counsel for the British Embassy, who was executed in 1919. Steinberg, *In the Workshop of the Revolution*, p. 163.

[133] *Otchet IX vserossiiskomu s'ezdu sovetov*, p. 28.

[134] Ibid.

[135] Ibid.

the number in this institution was relatively small) and in other political posts throughout the new Soviet government.

An exact accounting of the remaining 8,000 to 9,000 members of the prerevolutionary Bar is not possible, but it appears that a large percentage of these advocates found employment as legal consultants in economic enterprises and government agencies. According to one source, the labor service system was introduced in 1920 to fully exploit the talents of advocates who were "hiding" in institutions and enterprises.[136] Many other advocates, however, must have taken menial jobs outside the legal system and perhaps have supplemented their incomes with underground legal practice.

Although the first four years of Bolshevik rule witnessed the breaking up of the old Bar and the dispersal of its membership, it failed to produce a viable replacement, either in terms of organization or personnel, for the bourgeois profession of advocates. After numerous experiments with this segment of the prerevolutionary elite, legal policy makers abandoned their search for a radical alternative to the Bar. When the new conditions under NEP brought the revival of a Western-style institution of defenders, many former advocates, ever conscious of the traditions and identity of their estate, emerged from the professional wilderness to resume their first calling.

[136] N. Levin, "Zashchita v sovetskom ugolovnom protsesse (v formal'nom smysle)" (*Kandidat* dissertation, Leningrad, 1946), p. 112.

Chapter Three

THE BAR RESTORED, 1922-1927

To this point there has been only one
approach to law: whatever stands in the way
of strengthening Soviet power must be
destroyed. But now times have changed.
Our great task is to force the population to
respect law.

—*M. Kalinin*[1]

Russia emerged from the Revolution and Civil War an exhausted
and devastated nation. The young Bolshevik regime had succeeded in consolidating its military and political position in the
country, but in so doing it laid waste to the economy and eroded
its social bases of support. Not only did thousands of the Communist party's most loyal adherents die in fighting for the Revolution, the working class itself, which gave the Bolsheviks the
theoretical justification and the human material with which to
govern, was severely depleted. The number of workers declined
from 2.6 million in 1913 to under 1.2 million in 1921.[2]

The years of deprivation and mass repression also undermined
the legitimacy of the new regime in the population at large and,
in some cases, even among its own supporters. The short-lived,
anti-Bolshevik mutiny among Kronstadt sailors, who four years
earlier had helped to bring the Bolsheviks to power, became a
symbol of the precariousness of the regime's hold on the nation.
Thus, in March 1921, with the economy in shambles and the

---

[1] *Vserossiiskii s'ezd deiatelei sovetskoi iustitsii, IV* (Moscow, 1922), p. 95.

[2] *Izmeneniia sotsial'noi struktury sovetskogo obshchestva 1921—seredina 30-kh
godov* (Moscow, 1979), p. 23. The figures represent *rabochie tsenzovoi pro-
myshlennosti.*

population on the verge of massive civil unrest, Lenin announced a retreat from the policies of the civil war period. In their place he proclaimed the New Economic Policy, which called for the reintroduction of capitalist elements in the economy and a curtailment of mass repression.

A fundamental reappraisal of legal policy followed the introduction of NEP. The legal system in place at the end of the Civil War not only lacked support among the masses, it also was not equipped to provide the stability in legal relations essential to the expansion of private economic activity. What was needed was a legal order with sufficient traditional elements to guarantee its effectiveness and legitimacy in the conditions of NEP without endangering the foundations of state socialism laid in the first four years of Bolshevik rule. The process of creating such a legal order began in late 1921 and involved the partial rehabilitation of legal theories, institutions, and personnel of the old regime. Among the institutions resurrected was the Bar.

The Rebirth of an Organized Profession of Defenders

The need for a new approach to the legal profession became increasingly evident in the first months of the New Economic Policy. With the extension of the capitalist economic sector legal relationships grew more numerous and complex and caused increasing demand for legal advice and representation. The skeletal profession of consultants attached to local justice departments was clearly incapable of meeting these needs, and already the underground practice of law, traditional in the Russian countryside, was beginning to take hold in the cities. For Justice Commissar Kurskii the choice was clear. "Either we create a profession of advocates under our control, or a private profession will take over."[3]

The rebirth of a profession of legal defenders was also essential to restore the confidence of the masses in the legal system. Although the popular view of advocates in Russia was not flat-

---

[3] *Vserossiiskii s'ezd* . . . , *IV*, p. 13.

tering, it did recognize the importance of professional representation in legal proceedings. After the widespread and often arbitrary repression of the Civil War had undermined the legitimacy of all legal institutions, the restoration of an institution of professional defenders was one means of assuring the population that a more equitable legal system was being created under NEP. In the words of an official from the Justice Commissariat: "We introduced court defense in order to arouse in the worker-peasant masses undivided loyalty to the courts and to guarantee complete respect towards them."[4]

In addition, the reshaping of policy toward the legal profession reflected the growing concern of the Soviet government with its image abroad. As the revolutionary regime began trade negotiations with the capitalist powers in 1921, it realized the importance of putting a legal face on the new social order. Besides specific safeguards for foreign persons and property in Russia, the creation of a stable, more traditional legal system would instill confidence in the revolutionary regime among its new trading partners. Speaking of the reform introduced in the areas of procedural guarantees and legal representation, a Sovnarkom official commented: "This is one of the trumps that we are using on the bourgeoisie at the Genoa Conference."[5]

The reform of the legal profession was first proposed publicly at the Fourth All-Russian Congress of Justice Workers held in Moscow in late January 1922.[6] Among the items on the agenda

---

[4] Ia. Brandenburgskii, "Revoliutsionnaia zakonnost', prokuratura, i advokatura," *Sovetskoe pravo*, no. 1 (1922), p. 7.

[5] *Vserossiiskii s'ezd . . . , IV*, p. 136.

[6] Five hundred twenty-six delegates were in attendance at this first justice congress since the end of the Civil War. Virtually all delegates were local justice workers, with 53 from regional justice departments, 54 from the regional courts, 49 from the revolutionary tribunals at the regional level, 37 representing corrective labor establishments, 52 from district-level justice departments, 22 from military revolutionary tribunals, 23 from transport revolutionary tribunals, and 67 from the justice apparatus of autonomous republics. The center was represented by only 11 delegates from the People's Commissariat of Justice and 6 judges from the Supreme Tribunal attached to VTsIK. Of the 374 voting delegates, 278 were Communist party members. Ibid., p. 14.

this produced perhaps the greatest degree of controversy and division among the delegates, most of whom were local justice officials. During the extensive debate on the legal profession, a vocal minority of the delegates protested the proposed resurrection of an institution of advocates "from the archival dust." For this left-wing, or nihilist, group of justice workers it was not the moment to reintroduce the adversary process into Soviet court proceedings. They argued that the presence of defenders representing only the interests of individuals would weaken the repressive capacity of the people's court at a time when it was being called on to assume the functions previously carried out among the population by the Cheka and the Red Army.[7]

This position may indeed have received more support had the delegates not been made aware of the commitment of the political leadership to reform. Not only did the official *rapporteur*, Cherliunchakevich, propose the formation of a profession of defenders and an enhancement of the defender's role in the legal system, but in a statement to the congress intended to stifle opposition the chairman informed the delegates that the question of reestablishing an institution of defenders had already been decided by the Sovnarkom. This was used to justify a decree of the congress presidium denying corapporteur status to the spokesman for the legal nihilists, even though he had collected the requisite number of signatures among the delegates.[8]

A majority of congress delegates agreed to support the return to a more traditional policy on the legal profession, but there remained serious disagreements over the extent to which a new organization of defenders should be modeled on the prerevolutionary profession. As in the debates of 1918 a major area of dispute concerned the source of the advocate's income. In the official report Cherliunchakevich outlined a system wherein defenders would receive payment directly from the client.[9] This was fiercely criticized by some for reintroducing a relationship

[7] Ibid., p. 128.
[8] Ibid., p. 122.
[9] Ibid., p. 129.

of economic dependency between the lawyer and his client. Warning of the consequences of such a policy, one delegate counseled: "The advocate is like a talking machine. He continues to operate as long as you drop money in him."[10] It was feared that in the conditions of NEP the defenders would become the servants of a resurgent capitalist class.

Another point of contention concerned the character of state supervision of the institution of defenders. In keeping with Lenin's amendment to Decree No. 2 on the Court, the official report proposed that the new colleges of defenders be attached to and supervised by the local soviets.[11] In an unexpected intervention from the dais N. Krylenko asked the congress to amend the provisions so that the new regional courts, of which he was prime sponsor, would assume supervisory responsibilities over the Bar. Although the amendment enjoyed considerable support, it was defeated by a vote of the delegates.[12]

In addition to illustrating the divisions within the legal community on policy toward professional legal representatives the proceedings of the congress provide insight into the considerations of the political leadership in reshaping policy on the legal profession along more traditional lines. In justifying the volteface on the legal profession to delegates the national officials at the congress emphasized the necessity of a temporary retreat from a socialist institution of defenders in order to meet the requirements of NEP. Responding to criticism that the new policy was not ideologically orthodox, Krylenko argued that "being a true Marxist means realizing what is possible in given historical circumstances."[13] Thus, the idea of a state institution of defenders was not abandoned as the ultimate goal of Soviet legal policy. It was simply declared inappropriate "in our conditions of capitalist encirclement and a half-capitalist economy."[14] The immediate need was to suppress the underground Bar, and this

[10] Ibid., p. 130.
[11] Ibid., pp. 124-125.
[12] Ibid., pp. 132-138.
[13] Ibid., p. 132.
[14] Ibid., p. 135.

meant the creation of a profession "sufficiently autonomous to attract the old sworn advocates and to have the trust of the masses."[15]

The history of legislation on the legal profession in this period indicates that it was the central political leadership that was the most insistent on resurrecting the traditional elements of the Bar. In fact, the People's Commissariat of Justice, which was responsible for drafting the legislation on the legal profession, had to be pushed by the Sovnarkom before it produced a draft that was inspired sufficiently by the prerevolutionary model to satisfy the political authorities.[16] Evidently acting on the instructions of the Sovnarkom, the Justice Commissariat prepared a "Draft Decree on the Bar" in late 1921 (the term Bar, *advokatura*, had previously been used in official sources only to refer to the prerevolutionary or bourgeois legal profession). This draft provided, among other things, that clients make contact with lawyers only through legal consultation bureaus and that charges for all manner of legal services be made according to an established fee schedule.[17] These restrictive provisions were rejected by a committee of the Sovnarkom, known as the Little Sovnarkom, which amended the draft to give the defenders the right to receive clients at home. In civil cases the application of the fee schedule was upheld, but in criminal cases the lawyer was to be free to settle on a fee by private arrangement. The Sovnarkom apparatus also went much further than the Justice Commissariat in strengthening the independence of the new institutions of defenders.[18]

It appears that the Little Sovnarkom played the primary role in shaping legislation on the legal profession at the beginning of NEP. Unlike in previous reforms of the profession, Lenin, as Sovnarkom chairman, seems on this occasion to have been an altogether passive actor in the policy-making process. Soviet

[15] Ibid., p. 125.
[16] Ibid., p. 123.
[17] Ibid., pp. 123-127; "Iz deiatel'nosti Narkomiusta," *Ezhenedel'nik sovetskoi iustitsii*, no. 1 (1922), p. 11.
[18] "O professional'noi advokature," *Izvestiia*, May 10, 1922, p. 2.

historians of the subject, searching desperately for the imprint of the *vozhd'* on legislation affecting the advocates, have come up only with a minor amendment by Lenin, which exempted law professors from the ban on state employees joining the new colleges of defenders.[19] This intervention reportedly occurred after Lenin received a letter from the rector of a Siberian university proposing such an exemption.[20]

The devolution of policy-making responsibility from the Sovnarkom to the Little Sovnarkom on the issue of the restoration of the Bar would certainly be in keeping with the tendency, documented by T. H. Rigby,[21] for the Sovnarkom in this period to restrict itself to discussing only the most pressing issues of national policy, except where less important questions generated divisions in the Little Sovnarkom. In those cases the dispute was elevated to the Sovnarkom for resolution. According to an official in the Sovnarkom apparatus, the Little Sovnarkom acted unanimously in approving a draft on the legal profession prior to the Fourth Congress of Justice Workers.[22]

Although the role of institutions in shaping policy toward the Bar can be documented, at least in rough outline, the political forces influencing policy are much less clear. Very little can be said with certainty except that, barring the opposition of Krylenko to placing the colleges of defenders under the supervision of local soviets, there is no available evidence of significant disagreements among the legal policy makers in Moscow on the decision to return to a more traditional legal profession. The divisions among local justice officials at the Fourth Congress of Justice Workers do not appear to have been reflected at the

---

[19] "Polozhenie o kollegii zashchitnikov," *Ezhenedel'nik sovetskoi iustitsii*, no. 24-25 (1922), p. 28.

[20] "Pis'mo V. I. Leninu," *Novyi mir*, no. 4 (1970), pp. 191-192. It is likely that Lenin's absence from full-time work due to illness in the period from December 1921 to March 1922 prevented him from contributing significantly to the debate on the Bar.

[21] T. H. Rigby, *Lenin's Government: Sovnarkom 1917-1922* (Cambridge, 1979), pp. 190-191.

[22] *Vserossiiskii s'ezd* . . . , *IV*, p. 135.

center, whether due to tighter party discipline imposed in the wake of NEP, to the greater degree of pragmatism among national leaders, or to the lack of importance attached to policy relating to a legal institution representing individual interests.

Unlike earlier debates on the legal profession under Bolshevik rule, the policy-making process at the beginning of NEP was influenced considerably by the ideas and activities of respected jurists from the old regime. Bourgeois legal theories appeared, thinly-veiled, on the pages of Soviet legal journals, and members of the prerevolutionary legal establishment were summoned to participate in the drafting of legal codes under the supervision of loyal Soviet cadres.[23] Krylenko complained that in drafting the 1922 Code of Criminal Procedure, which set out the role of the defense in criminal cases, he was kept busy preventing two bourgeois specialists in the drafting commission from simply rewriting the 1864 statutes.[24] Commenting on the draft decree of the Bar, which had emerged from a Sovnarkom commission headed by the prerevolutionary jurist Marenville, a delegate to the Fourth Congress of Justice Workers stated: "I do not know what advocate worked out the draft, but I do know that I see no protection of workers' interests in it."[25] In fact, an "initiative group" of former advocates did participate directly in the drafting of the legislation on the new colleges of defenders.[26]

Many former advocates were heartened by the new direction

[23] Prerevolutionary jurists contributed most frequently to the journals *Pravo i zhizn'*, edited by A. Vinaver, M. Gernet, and A. Trainin, and *Sovetskoe pravo*, the journal of the Institute of Soviet Law. For a ten-month period in 1926 the advocates published their own journal, *Revoliutsionnaia zakonnost'*, through the profession's cooperative publishing house "Pravovaia zashchita." *Revoliutsionnaia zakonnost'* ceased publication without warning after the Fifteenth Party Conference in October 1926.

[24] "Doklad N. Krylenko," *Revoliutsiia prava*, no. 1 (1928), p. 104.

[25] *Vserossiiskii s'ezd* . . . , *IV*, p. 134. The speaker, Diakonov, though not an advocate himself, became a presidium member of the Moscow college of defenders during NEP.

[26] *Otchet prezidiuma moskovskoi gubernskoi kollegii zashchitnikov za 3-i otchetnyi period (1 okt. 1923 po 1 aprelia 1924)* (Moscow, 1924), p. 25. Hereafter cited as *Tretii otchet.*

of policy on the profession. N. Murav'ev, a prominent sworn advocate before the Revolution and a member of the newly created Juridical Society, welcomed what he perceived as the state's new willingness to be guided by pragmatic, and not ideological, considerations.[27] Other advocates, however, while praising the independence to be granted to them, continued to press for a complete rehabilitation of the prerevolutionary profession. Proposals to create a Bar completely independent of the state were contained in letters to the Justice Commissariat and in drafts of legislation on the legal profession submitted to regional conferences of jurists. A Soviet historian who has had access to the archives of the period claims that elements in the old intelligentsia saw in the emerging Soviet Bar an instrument of "legal opposition" to Soviet power.[28]

But in spite of the assertion by Cherliunchakevich that "in essence the draft [law on the Bar] envisions the creation of the former governing councils of sworn advocates," a number of restrictions on the autonomy of the profession remained in the legislation, including the right of government supervisory institutions to veto new members of the Bar.[29] These restrictions were criticized by advocates—seemingly oblivious of the character of Soviet rule—on the grounds that a professional organization should not be subject to political control.[30] Whatever softening up of the profession may have been achieved during the Revolution and the Civil War, once an opening presented itself, the advocates attempted to exploit it by pushing for the most complete regeneration possible of the foundations of the prerevolutionary Bar.[31]

---

[27] "O professional'noi advokature," p. 2.

[28] Ibid. V. Kuritsyn, *Perekhod k nepu i revoliutsionnaia zakonnost'* (Moscow, 1972), p. 116. On May 10, 1922, *Izvestia* published a letter submitted by a group of advocates who sought the creation of an independent Bar. One of the signatories was Maliantovich, a former sworn advocate and a justice minister in the Provisional Government. V. Kuritsyn, "Stanovlenie sovetskoi advokatury," *Sovetskoe gosudarstvo i pravo*, no. 7 (1971), p. 115.

[29] "O professional'noi advokature," p. 2.

[30] Ibid.

[31] This attitude was also evident among other professional groups. University

The groundwork for the reform of the profession was contained in three major legislative acts adopted in 1922, which were subject to only minor modifications—primarily through the issuance of substatutory (*podzakonnye*) acts—in the five remaining years of NEP.[32] On May 25 and 26, 1922, the All-Russian Central Executive Committee adopted a new Code of Criminal Procedure for the Russian Soviet Federated Socialist Republic (RSFSR), to take effect on July 1, and a Statute on the Bar, which was an amended version of the draft statute circulated by the People's Commissariat of Justice in January 1922.[33] Whereas the Code of Criminal Procedure contained detailed provisions on the role of the defender in criminal proceedings, the Statute on the Bar only laid out the contours of the organization and functions of the new Bar associations, to be known as colleges of defenders. The more detailed Statute on the College of Defenders was issued six weeks later, on July 5, 1922, by the People's Commissariat of Justice.[34]

The decision to adopt legislation on the colleges of defenders in two stages was evidently an attempt to prevent the more controversial elements of the reform from being discussed in the relatively open forum of VTsIK. As it was, the Statute on the Bar produced considerable disagreement at the VTsIK session, where members were highly critical of the virtual monopoly of legal practice to be given to the Bar. In fact, they amended the relevant article to allow any citizen to defend in court, and it

---

professors, for example, pushed for the establishment of their own autonomous professional organization at the beginning of NEP. S. Fitzpatrick, *Education and Social Mobility in the Soviet Union, 1921-1934* (Cambridge, 1979), p. 75.

[32] *Podzakonnye akty* are directives issued by the executive organs of the Soviet government, which included in this period the Council of People's Commissars (Sovnarkom) and its subordinate institutions (e.g., the People's Commissariat of Justice). Although these directives have the force of law, they often remain unpublished and restricted to internal use of the bureaucracy. See D. Loeber, "Legal Rules 'For Internal Use Only,' " *International and Comparative Law Quarterly* (1970), p. 70.

[33] Ugolovno-protsessual'nyi kodeks RSFSR, *Sobranie uzakonenii* (1922), art. 230, no. 20-21; Polozhenie ob advokature, *Sobranie uzakonenii* (1922), art. 425, no. 36.

[34] "Polozhenie o kollegii zashchitnikov," pp. 27-29.

was only with great difficulty that Krylenko and Brandenburgskii managed to introduce the qualifying phrase that the right of representation for nonadvocates was subject to approval by the court.[35]

The new body of legislation on the Bar, in place by mid-summer of 1922, provided for the formation of a college of defenders in each region of the country.[36] No provision was made for a national Bar association. The colleges were to be formally attached to the regional people's courts, and responsibility for supervising the affairs of the profession was to be divided among the courts, the soviet executive committee (*ispolkom*), and the Procuracy at the regional level. The decision to shift supervisory responsibility away from the regional justice departments and toward the courts and the Procuracy was a late amendment to the Statute on the College of Defenders. It followed the establishment of a centralized Procuracy within the Commissariat of Justice and the installation of Krylenko as the senior procurator of the RSFSR.[37] Thus, the proposal of Krylenko to attach the colleges of defenders to the courts, voted down six months earlier at the Fourth Congress of Soviet Justice Workers, was finally incorporated into legislation on the legal profession.

The formal supervisory powers of state institutions vis-à-vis the colleges of defenders were spelled out in considerable detail. Perhaps the most important element of external supervision concerned the selection and dismissal of college members. The initial membership of the colleges of defenders was to be selected by the executive committee of the regional soviet, after which the direct responsibility for admitting members passed to the colleges' own presidia. The supervisory organs, however, retained the right in law to veto new members within one month of their acceptance by the presidium and to overturn the decisions of the presidium to reject candidates.[38]

---

[35] M. Isaev, *Podpol'naia advokatura* (Moscow, 1924), pp. 14-15.

[36] "Polozhenie o kollegii zashchitnikov," p. 27.

[37] "Itogi s'ezda deiatelei iustitsii," *Ezhenedel'nik sovetskoi iustitsii*, no. 6 (1922), p. 2.

[38] "Polozhenie o kollegii zashchitnikov," p. 28.

In addition to the rights of intervention in personnel questions government organs were given general supervisory responsibility over the colleges of defenders. The legislation was careful to provide supervisory institutions with the means by which the internal affairs of the colleges could be monitored. Transcripts of all meetings in the colleges, whether involving the rank and file, the presidium, or the internal disciplinary tribunal, were to be sent without delay to the regional court or Procuracy. Furthermore, the presidium was obligated to present reports twice yearly to the regional courts on the activities of the college.[39] The legislation did not stipulate, however, the methods by which supervisory institutions would influence the colleges when their behavior did not conform to expectations.

These powers of government oversight notwithstanding, the degree of autonomy given to the colleges was, at least on paper, quite considerable. As in the prerevolutionary profession the affairs of the regional colleges were to be administered by a presidium that would be elected periodically by a general meeting of the entire college. In addition to its power to select and dismiss college members the presidium had a wide range of other responsibilities, including the hearing of disciplinary cases involving defenders and the organization and operation of legal consultation bureaus to serve the workers and peasants.[40]

The new legislation restored to defenders the right to receive clients at home, but at the same time it obligated them to participate in legal consultation bureaus, which were regarded by the political authorities as a more effective and ideologically acceptable venue for delivering legal services to the masses. In not specifying the degree of participation expected in the consultation bureaus, however, the legislation seemed to recognize that for the foreseeable future the defender's private office would remain the primary point of contact between the lawyer and his client.[41]

[39] Ibid.
[40] Ibid.
[41] Ibid.

The fee system was also based on prerevolutionary practice, though with a number of important exceptions. While the charges for legal services were determined "as a general rule, by mutual agreement between the individual client and the member of the college of defenders," fees for certain groups were set by law.[42] Individuals recognized as indigent by a court could not be charged for legal services by a defender. Furthermore, workers in state or private enterprises and employees (*sluzhashchie*) of state institutions were charged according to an established fee system, whether the legal services were rendered through an advocate's private office or a consultation bureau.[43]

Although private legal practice was largely unregulated by legislation, policy makers did attempt to establish some potential for supervision. As a means of monitoring private practice under NEP, defenders were obligated by law to keep detailed records of cases assumed. Information on all aspects of the case, from the legal documents prepared to the financial transactions between lawyer and client, were to be recorded in diaries (*knigi dlia zapisi del*) that were subject to inspection by the college presidium.[44]

The functions of the defender in the legal system remained essentially the same: to represent clients in civil and criminal cases, to offer oral and written advice, and to prepare legal documents. But the system in which the defenders practiced did change in the first months of NEP. The institutions and procedures that shaped the advocate's working environment were reformed along more traditional lines. The new emphasis on law as an instrument of state policy held the promise of a return of the advocate from the periphery to the center of the legal system.

---

[42] "Taksa oplaty zashchitnika rabochimi gosudarstvennykh i chastnykh predpriiatii i sluzhashchimi sovetskikh uchrezhdenii," *Ezhenedel'nik sovetskoi iustitsii*, no. 24-25 (1922), p. 29.

[43] Ibid.; "Polozhenie o kollegii zashchitnikov," pp. 28-29.

[44] *Otchet o deiatel'nosti prezidiuma leningradskoi gubernskoi kollegii zashchitnikov po ugolovnym i grazhdanskim delam pri leningradskom gubsude za chetyre polugodiia (s 15 marta 1923 po 1 aprelia 1925)* (Leningrad, 1925), p. 63.

The Emergence of a Soviet Bar

The adoption of legislation on the legal profession in the summer of 1922 was followed immediately by the submission of large numbers of applications for membership in the new colleges of legal defenders. In Moscow officials in the justice department of the regional soviet had compiled a preliminary list of college members by the first week in August.[45] The initial intake of defenders into the Moscow college continued until October 8, 1922, when a presidium was elected by the first general meeting of Moscow defenders.[46] At that time direct responsibility for the day-to-day administration of college affairs passed from the regional soviet to the college's presidium. In the months that followed this pattern was repeated throughout the country, and by the end of 1923 it appears that colleges of defenders were functioning in most regions.[47]

A large majority of the members of the new colleges came from the ranks of so-called bourgeois specialists—members of the professional class trained under tsarist rule. Although this was the expressed intent of official policy, it created conditions within the colleges that were highly undesirable from the regime's point of view. Not only did the reform of the legal profession resurrect an important group traditionally hostile to Communist rule, it also created for this group insitutions that enjoyed a considerable degree of organizational independence.

The apparent retreat in the process of transforming the advocates reflected a new recognition by the political leadership that a competent Soviet legal intelligentsia could not be created by pursuing the nihilistic policies of the civil war period.[48] The

---

[45] Ia. Brandenburgskii, "Kommunisty i kollegii zashchitnikov," *Pravda*, August 8, 1922, p. 1.

[46] "Kollegii zashchitnikov," *Ezhenedel'nik sovetskoi iustitsii*, no. 36 (1922), p. 22.

[47] The subsequent creation of new colleges took place as a result of the division of administrative regions into smaller units.

[48] The conciliatory attitude toward the advocates followed at least two years after

human material of the old regime had to be relied on, at least until a new generation of Soviet specialists began to emerge. In the interim, however, the utmost care had to be taken to ensure that sufficient political control was exercised over the bourgeois specialists. In 1922, writing on government functionaries, Lenin outlined the new approach to elite transformation:

> [T]here are hundreds of thousands of old officials who came over to us from the Tsar and former bourgeois society and who, sometimes consciously, sometimes unconsciously, work against us. Nothing can be done here in a short space of time, that is clear. Many years of hard work will be required to improve the machine, to reform it, and to enlist new forces.[49]

Thus, while the Soviet state under NEP resolved to exploit the talents of elites not openly hostile to the new order over the short term, it embarked on a long-term policy of creating institutions and cadres of a Soviet type.

As applied to the Bar, this policy had three major goals: first, to sovietize the membership of the profession through the purging of its most intractable elements, through the reeducation of the remaining bourgeois specialists, and through the gradual infusion of Soviet-trained personnel; second, to transform the self-governing colleges of defenders into compliant instruments of state rule through the establishment of an effective mechanism of external supervision by government institutions and through the placing of Communist party members in leadership positions within the colleges; and, finally, to redefine the role of legal representation so that the functions of the defenders could not

---

a similar policy was introduced toward the technical experts, such as engineers and agronomists. See K. E. Bailes, *Technology and Society under Lenin and Stalin: Origins of the Soviet Technical Intelligentsia, 1917-1941* (Princeton, N.J., 1978), p. 51.

[49] V. Lenin, *Socheneniia*, 27: 353, cited in M. Fainsod, "Bureaucracy and Modernization: The Russian and Soviet Case," in *Bureaucracy and Political Development*, ed. J. LaPalombara, 2d ed. (Princeton, N.J., 1967), p. 250.

be employed to challenge or undermine the power and authority of the state.

The pursuit of these goals, however, was constrained during NEP by the desire to maintain the confidence of the masses, and the advocates themselves, in the new profession. To rely too heavily on coercion, rather than persuasion, in transforming the profession might stiffen the resistance of the defenders at a time when their social composition and relative organizational autonomy made them especially difficult to subordinate to party rule. Furthermore, to proceed too rapidly with the process of *Gleichschaltung* would alienate lawyer and client and result in the growth of an underground Bar outside of state control. Thus, the development of the legal profession from 1922 to 1927 reflected the tensions between the desire to establish a distinctly Soviet Bar and a recognition of the limits to such a policy imposed by the conditions of NEP.

The Membership of the Colleges of Defenders

The formation of the colleges of defenders in the second year of NEP resulted in the return of a considerable number of advocates to their traditional metier. But the continuity in cadres between the prerevolutionary profession and the new Soviet colleges was by no means complete. Not only was the Soviet Bar considerably smaller than its prerevolutionary counterpart, especially in the first years of NEP, it also contained many prerevolutionary jurists from other tsarist institutions as well as some individuals without legal training or experience. This was therefore a new profession, albeit one that accepted much of the inheritance from the old regime.

It is not possible to provide on a national scale a precise picture of the backgrounds of new entrants into the colleges of defenders. Reliable figures are available, however, from certain regions, with the Moscow college offering the most complete information on its membership. In April 1923, at the end of its first six months of operation, the college of defenders in Moscow was composed of 449 members, 322 of whom had worked in the prerevolutinary Bar as sworn advocates or advocates-in-training. Seven had practiced as private advocates before the Revolution. The remaining members of the Moscow college appear to have been divided almost evenly between qualified jurists associated with other prerevolutionary legal institutions and Communist party "promoted workers" (vydvizhentsy) with little or no legal education.[50]

At the end of its first year the Leningrad college of defenders was comprised of 281 members, 256 of whom were jurists from the old regime. Of the remaining 25 defenders, 4 were workers and 21 had other nonlegal occupational backgrounds.[51] Since the figures for Leningrad do not break down the prerevolutionary jurists into their constituent groups of judges, procurators, and advocates, an exact determination of the number of former advocates among the new entrants to the college cannot be made. From a comparison of the list of practicing advocates in 1915 with the list of college members in 1923, it is known that 103 advocates (out of 1,750) working in the city at the beginning of World War I joined the Leningrad college of defenders.[52] But the total number of prerevolutionary advocates is almost certainly well above that figure, given the numerous additions to the profession during the war and the migration of prerevolutionary advocates from other areas into Petrograd from 1915 to 1923.

Information from other regions also fails to delineate the former advocates from other prerevolutionary jurists entering the colleges of defenders. It is clear, however, that in most regions the overwhelming majority of defenders had worked as qualified jurists in the tsarist legal system. Figures from the RSFSR for

---

[50] *Otchet prezidiuma moskovskoi gubernskoi kollegii zashchitnikov za pervoe polugodie (s 8 okt. 1922 po 1 aprelia 1923)* (Moscow, 1923), pp. 5-12. Hereafter cited as *Pervyi otchet.*

[51] "Godovshchina petrogradskoi kollegii zashchitnikov," *Rabochii sud*, no. 10 (1923), p. 43.

[52] *Ves Petrograd* (Petrograd, 1915), pp. 728-767; *Ves Petrograd* (Petrograd, 1924), pp. 341-343.

1923 indicate that approximately 75 percent of all entrants to the colleges had received a higher legal education in tsarist institutions.[53] The major exception to this pattern was in Central Asia. In Turkestan no more than one-quarter of the defenders were qualified jurists from the old regime.[54]

In spite of the large numbers of applications for membership to the colleges (the Moscow college had 1,000 in its first six months of existence),[55] the size of the Soviet Bar was kept very modest in the first phase of NEP. This was evidently intended to prevent the influx en masse of prerevolutionary jurists into the profession, which would have greatly complicated the process of assimilating the bourgeois specialists. In Moscow and Leningrad the membership of the colleges of defenders in 1923 was only 15 to 20 percent of the size of the prerevolutionary Bar in those cities.[56] Over the RSFSR as a whole the number of defenders in 1923 reached 2,800, or approximately 25 percent of the prerevolutionary total.[57]

During the remaining years of NEP, the membership of the colleges of defenders expanded rapidly. From 1923 to 1927 an additional 2,000 members were admitted to the Bar in RSFSR alone.[58] Although the rapid growth of the colleges was stimulated by the increasing demand for legal services, it would not have been possible without the acquiescence of the political authorities who were empowered by law to set a membership ceiling for each college. After successive liberal increases in the ceiling were approved by the local officials directly responsible for the supervision of the profession, a decision was taken in 1926 by

---

[53] Ia. Brandenburgskii, "K voprosu ob iuridicheskoi pomoshchi naseleniiu," *Ezhenedel'nik sovetskoi iustitsii*, no. 7-8 (1924), pp. 147-148.

[54] B. Durdyev, "Organizatsiia i razvitie sovetskoi advokatury v Turkmenistane" (*Kandidat* dissertation, Ashkhabad, 1974), p. 70.

[55] *Pervyi otchet*, p. 11.

[56] Ibid., p. 12; "Godovshchina petrogradskoi kollegii zashchitnikov," in *Istoriia russkoi advokatury*, ed. M. Gernet, 3 vols. (Moscow, 1914-1916), 2: 3-5.

[57] Brandenburgskii, "K voprosu," p. 147.

[58] P. Topalov, "K voprosu o reorganizatsii kollegii zashchitnikov," *Proletarskii sud*, no. 8 (1928), p. 8.

central policy makers to remove the restrictions altogether on the number of defenders to be admitted to the colleges.[59]

The increase in the size of the Bar was most pronounced in the larger cities, which were witnessing a massive influx of new inhabitants in the middle years of NEP to more than offset their depopulation in the civil war period. In Moscow the college of defenders increased its membership from 320 in 1922 to over 1,200 in 1927.[60] Over the same period the membership of the Leningrad college grew from 201 to almost 600.[61] In Kiev, too, the college underwent a significant expansion, and by 1927 it contained over 300 defenders.[62]

Not all areas benefited from this expansion. Central Asia in particular lagged well behind the rest of the country. In 1926 the official yearbook *All-Central Asia (Vsia Srednaia Aziia)* reported only 112 advocates registered in this vast territory, with almost half that number concentrated in the city of Tashkent. At least eight regions of Central Asia, including the Kirgiz Autonomous Oblast', were without advocates. With the authorities as yet unwilling to lower professional standards for advocates or to engage in the education of a new generation of Soviet defenders, the wide disparity in the geographical distribution of advocates inherited from the old order remained intact.[63]

Despite the massive infusion of new cadres into the Bar in most areas of the country during NEP, the changes in the social composition of the profession desired by the regime were not achieved. In fact, very little progress appears to have been made in sovietizing the membership of the colleges, as the vast majority

[59] M. Shalamov, *Istoriia sovetskoi advokatury* (Moscow, 1939), p. 49.

[60] Topalov, "K voprosu," p. 8. The college contained 1,205 members in 1927, but a significant minority of those advocates lived in surrounding *uezdy*.

[61] *Ves Leningrad* (Leningrad, 1928), pp. 400-405. This figure refers only to urban advocates.

[62] "God raboty kievskoi kollegii zashchitnikov," *Vestnik sovetskoi iustitsii*, no. 6-7 (1927), p. 235. Two hundred and twenty of this number lived in Kiev proper.

[63] *Vsia Srednaia Aziia na 1926* (Tashkent, 1926), pp. 433-437, 614-615, 660, 674. By 1929 Kirgizia had thirty-one advocates. *Iuridicheskii kalendar' na 1929g.* (Moscow, 1929), p. 388.

TABLE 3.1 *MEMBERSHIP IN THE SOVIET BAR IN 1927: RSFSR AND SELECTED REGIONS*

	Number of Advocates
RSFSR	4,696
Moscow	1,206
Leningrad	583
Kiev	300
Khar'kov	222
Voronezh	124
Tver	107
Vinnits	92
Kamenets-Podol'sk	71
Tashkent	67
Kherson	66
Novgorod	54
Moghilev-Podol'sk	51
Orenburg	37
Iakutsk	6
Murmansk	5

SOURCE: P. Topalov, "K voprosu o reorganizatsii kollegii zashchitnikov," *Proletarskii sud*, no. 8 (1928), p. 8; *Ves Leningrad* (Leningrad, 1928), pp. 350-354; "God raboty kievskoi kollegii zashchitnikov," *Vestnik sovetskoi iustitsii*, no. 6-7 (1927), p. 235; "V khar'kovskoi kollegii zashchitnikov," *Vestnik sovetskoi iustitsii*, no. 15 (1927), p. 534; "Po kollegiiam zashchitnikov," *Ezhenedel'nik sovetskoi iustitsii*, no. 10 (1927), p. 294; A. Baranov, "Deiatel'nost' kollegii zashchitnikov tverskoi gubernii za 1926," *Rabochii sud*, no. 19 (1927), p. 1,519; "V vinnitsskoi kollegii zashchitnikov," *Vestnik sovetskoi iustitsii*, no. 6-7 (1927), p. 236; "V kamenets-podol'skoi kollegii zashchitnikov," *Vestnik sovetskoi iustitsii*, no. 15 (1927), p. 534; M. Mumin, "Sozdanie i razvitie advokatury v Uzbekistane" (*Kandidat* dissertation, Tashkent, 1975), p. 66; "V khersonskoi kollegii zashchitnikov," *Vestnik sovetskoi iustitsii*, no. 3 (1927), p. 105; "V novgorodskoi kollegii zashchitnikov," *Rabochii sud*, no. 8 (1927), p. 737; "Deiatel'nost' mogilev-podol'skoi kollegii zashchitnikov," *Vestnik sovetskoi iustitsii*, no. 17 (1927), p. 600; "Kollegii zashchitnikov v iakutskoi ASSR," *Ezhenedel'nik sovetskoi iustitsii*, no. 11 (1927), p. 327; "V murmanskoi kollegii zashchitnikov," *Rabochii sud*, no. 4 (1928), p. 371.

of new members continued to come from the prerevolutionary intelligentsia. In 1926 approximately 70 percent of the profession in the RSFSR had received a higher education before the Revolution.[64] Even as late as 1928, 80 percent of the members of the Leningrad college were described as *intelligenty*.[65]

Although the colleges remained dominated by the bourgeois specialists, the percentage of workers and peasants in the profession did increase over NEP. Each of these two social groups was forced into the colleges by the political authorities to serve a particular purpose. The workers were introduced into the rank and file of the colleges to strengthen the *noyau* of defenders who could be depended on to place the interests of the party and state above those of the profession. Undoubtedly the state would have preferred to introduce professionally competent as well as politically reliable cadres into the Bar, but it was still too early to contemplate the entrance of sizable elements from a Soviet legal intelligentsia. Having abolished the faculties of law in the aftermath of the Revolution, the new regime began to establish

TABLE 3.2 *THE SOCIAL BACKGROUNDS OF LENINGRAD ADVOCATES*

	1924	1925	1929
Worker/craftsman	5	13	53
Peasant	22	27	80
Tradesman (*meshchane*)	123	131	
Employee (*sluzhashchie*)	66	71	562 (*intelligenty*)
Professional	64	73	
Gentry	9	10	

SOURCES: *Otchet o deiatel'nosti prezidiuma leningradskoi gubernskoi kollegii za-shchitnikov po ugolovnym i grazhdanskim delam pri leningradskom gubsude za chetyre polugodiia* (Leningrad, 1925), p. 13; "Otchet leningradskogo oblastnogo suda," *Rabochii sud*, no. 3-4 (1929), p. 253.

[64] A. Elokhovskii, "Lichnyi sostav i rabota chlenov kollegii zashchitnikov v RSFSR za 1925 g.," *Revoliutsionnaia zakonnost'*, no. 15-18 (1926), p. 77.
[65] "Otchet leningradskogo oblastnogo suda," *Rabochii sud*, no. 3-4 (1929), p. 253.

Soviet legal education only in the mid-1920s. The small number of jurists who were graduated from Soviet universities during NEP were channeled into state legal institutions, which were desperately short of trained personnel.[66] Therefore workers with no formal legal training, but possessing party or trade union credentials, had to be relied on to augment the regime's narrow base of support in the colleges of defenders.

By the end of NEP the working-class component in the colleges still comprised only a small minority of the profession. In the RSFSR in 1926, the latest date for which statistics are available, workers made up slightly less than 10 percent of the Bar.[67] This proportion was significantly lower in some areas, such as Leningrad, where workers accounted for less than 5 percent of the college's membership in 1928.[68]

The peasants represented a more numerous element in the Bar, though they played no significant political role in the profession. In 1924, following the "Face to the Countryside" campaign launched by the party, pressure began to be exerted on the highly urbanized colleges of defenders to extend legal services to the rural areas, in part as a means of legitimizing the new Soviet legal order among the peasants.[69] As Kalinin reasoned, the adoption of land decisions by seemingly neutral legal institutions would prove a great advantage over the civil war system, where decisions were made by overtly political bodies.[70] In addition, officials were concerned about restricting the activities of the underground advocates, some of whom, it was feared, were former Social Revolutionaries intent on undermining Soviet power in the countryside.[71]

[66] Fitzpatrick, *Education and Social Mobility*, pp. 72-73.

[67] Elokhovskii, "Lichnyi sostav," p. 77.

[68] "Otchet leningradskogo oblastnogo," p. 253.

[69] "Ob okazanii iuridicheskoi pomoshchi naseleniiu," Tsirkuliar no. 61 Narodnogo Komissariata iustitsii, *Ezhenedel'nik sovetskoi iustitsii*, no. 18 (1924), p. 436.

[70] *Vserossiiskii s'ezd . . .*, IV, p. 97.

[71] P. Erypalov, "Podpol'naia advokatura v derevne," *Ezhenedel'nik sovetskoi iustitsii*, no. 36 (1922), p. 4.

Various attempts were made to relocate urban defenders in the countryside, either on a short-term or a permanent basis, but the resistance by the rank and file to relocation efforts was fierce. Those defenders who did move to the villages usually had so much difficulty in establishing a financially viable practice and in adapting to the rural life style that they returned to the cities within a short period.[72] Unable to direct urban advocates to the countryside in significant numbers, the colleges opted instead for a policy of accepting the more literate members of the peasantry into the Bar to serve the rural areas. Because the peasants had no formal training, their entrance into the profession in effect divided the colleges into urban and rural components, with differing qualifications, social backgrounds, and professional standards for each group. Although the urban advocates far outnumbered their peasant colleagues, the peasant-defender did become an increasingly common sight in the countryside in the later years of NEP. The peasant component of the Bar at the end of NEP ranged from 12 percent in the Leningrad college of defenders to 26 percent in the Novosibirsk college.[73] Over the RSFSR as a whole the peasants comprised slightly under 19 percent of the profession at the beginning of 1926.[74]

Of all the social groups, perhaps the greatest beneficiaries of the rapid growth of the Bar during NEP were the Jews. The absence of official statistics on the ethnic composition of the profession prevents an exact determination of the Jewish component of the Bar, but the lists of advocates published in city directories of the period reveal a disproportionately high percentage of Jews in certain colleges. Jews appear to have accounted for between 45 percent and 50 percent of the mem-

[72] The Bar did not send advocates to the countryside voluntarily. Government supervisory institutions refused to approve the entry of new urban members into the profession until the Bar had made a serious effort to recruit defenders for work in the countryside. See *Otchet prezidiuma novosibirskoi kollegii zashchitnikov za 1926g.* (Novosibirsk, 1927), p. 8.

[73] Ibid., p. 9; *Otchet o deiatel'nosti prezidiuma leningradskoi*, p. 13.

[74] Elokhovskii, "Lichnyi sostav," p. 77.

bership of the Leningrad college of defenders in 1927.[75] In 1925 an estimated 300, or approximately 40 percent, of the 776 members of the Moscow college were Jewish.[76] The major Ukrainian colleges also contained a high percentage of Jews,[77] and in Baku 16 percent of the regional college was Jewish in 1928.[78]

The creation of a Soviet Bar under NEP provided an opportunity for legal practice to the large reservoir of Jews trained in the law but unable to freely pursue their careers under the old regime. Those Jewish jurists who under tsarist rule were either excluded from the legal profession altogether or made to accept lower-level positions in legal institutions were now able to compete on an equal basis with non-Jews for places in the colleges of defenders.

The strong Jewish representation in the Bar appears to have had no clearly ascertainable effects on the development of the profession during NEP. Certainly, there is no indication that the political authorities, whether at the local or national level, even took note of the ethnic composition of the colleges in this period. But it is important to recognize the heavy concentration of Jews in the early Soviet Bar not only because of its subsequent effects on relations between the state and the profession, especially in the last years of Stalin's rule, but also because of the likelihood that Jewish advocates brought a somewhat less hostile, or at least more ambivalent, attitude toward the regime than other jurists inherited from the prerevolutionary period. Viewed from the perspective of NEP, the accession to power of the Bolsheviks appeared to guarantee a continuation of the policy of nondiscrimination toward the Jews that had been launched by the

[75] *Ves Leningrad*, pp. 400-405. These percentages and the following ones from Moscow are conservative estimates. Because the lists provided first name and patronymic, as well as surname, the margin of error should not be too great.

[76] *Vsia Moskva* (Moscow, 1926), pp. 140-149.

[77] See, for example, *Ves Kharkiv* (Kharkov, 1928), pp. 42-45.

[78] A. Abdullaev, "Iz istorii advokatury azerbaidzhanskoi SSR (1927-1930gg)," in *Trudy* (NII pravovoi zashchity: Baku, 1970), p. 13. Abdullaev identifies 34 of the 208 college members as Jews, evidently relying on archival sources for this information.

February Revolution. Whatever their misgivings about the character of Soviet power, Jewish advocates were probably more conscious than their Russian colleagues of the alternatives to Bolshevik rule. [79]

While the dominance of prerevolutionary cadres in the Soviet Bar at the end of NEP cannot have pleased those officials responsible for legal policy, the infusion of bourgeois specialists continued over the period for two reasons. First, the transformation of the Bar enjoyed a relatively low priority on the political agenda. This meant not only that the oversight of the profession was less rigorous than that of other groups, such as the writers, but also that no concerted effort was made to provide competent, reliable cadres to replace the specialists from the old regime. To have forcibly introduced unqualified cadres en masse into the colleges would have undermined the authority and practical value of the profession.

Second, unlike most other members of the professional elite, the advocates were chosen by their regional professional associations—the colleges—and not directly by the state. [80] Although the autonomy of the colleges was gradually reduced over NEP, due to increasing party dominance on the presidia and heightened external supervision by government institutions, the Bar's leadership remained responsive to the demands of the rank and file, especially when those demands were made by a unified membership. Thus, under the conditions of NEP, a radical shift in cadres policy to alter the composition of the colleges in favor of untrained workers and peasants would have brought vigorous resistance from the profession.

Because of the lack of success in cadres policy it was espe-

[79] It is perhaps noteworthy that Jews entering the Bar during NEP often had relatives already in the colleges. In 1927, for example, there were fifteen Jewish families represented by two or more college members in Leningrad (most of these were identified by matching surnames and addresses, though a few were matched on the basis of identical surnames and patronymics). See *Ves Leningrad*, pp. 400-405. Thus began an association that would continue over subsequent decades.

[80] In this sense they differed from technical specialists, virtually all of whom were employed by the end of NEP in government institutions or enterprises.

cially important for the regime to prevent the colleges of defenders from developing into intermediary institutions dominated by members of the prerevolutionary intelligentsia. The danger of a hostile professional organization operating outside of party and government control was indeed foreseen by the political and legal authorities responsible for the formation of the Bar at the beginning of NEP. While the Soviet state was willing to grant to the profession "certain freedoms" (*nekotorye svobody*), it was not prepared "to tolerate any attempt to organize a state within a state in the Soviet Republic."[81] In order to prevent the transformation of the colleges "into corporations in the style of the old estates of sworn advocates,"[82] the party began placing its own members in the colleges shortly after their formation in an attempt to gain control of the profession from the inside. This policy was only adopted, however, after serious debates within the party on the appropriateness of directing scarce party cadres into a suspect profession.

Communist Party Penetration of the Profession

In the summer of 1922 the justice department of the Moscow regional soviet, while compiling a list of members for the new colleges of defenders, came upon several requests for membership from Communists applying on their own initiative. The local justice officials immediately referred these requests to party organs to determine if the acceptance of Communists in an institution so closely linked to the old regime was admissable.[83] This sparked a national debate within the party on what role, if any, Communists should play in the colleges of defenders.

The controversy assumed a public character on August 8, 1922, when Ia. Brandenburgskii, the Sorbonne-educated head of the judicial institutions department of the People's Commissariat of Justice, contributed a front-page discussion article on

[81] Ia. Brandenburgskii, "Revoliutsionnaia zakonnost' na 3-i sessii VTsIK," *Ezhenedel'nik sovetskoi iustitsii*, no. 18 (1922), p. 1.

[82] Ibid.

[83] Brandenburgskii, "Kommunisty," p. 1.

the subject to *Pravda*.[84] Brandenburgskii argued that it was essential for Communist party members to enter the Bar in order to exercise internal control over the profession and to be available for those sensitive cases where only Communists should defend in court. This position, which appeared to reflect the view of most legal officials in the government, was vehemently attacked five days later by M. Andres in another discussion article in *Pravda*.[85] Andres represented the considerable body of opinion in the party which held that scarce party cadres should not be wasted on an institution that had no future in a socialist state. Communists, he argued, should take their places at the "commanding heights of revolutionary legality" where their role was "to discuss and decide, and not to illuminate or obfuscate, cases." He conceded that once government legal institutions were filled with Communists it would be possible to consider directing party members into the colleges of defenders, but by that time the Bar might well have passed like "a bad dream."[86]

This latter stance was supported by P. Krasikov, deputy people's commissar of justice and a long-standing party leader. In a *Pravda* article of late August 1922 Krasikov counseled against the entrance of Communists into an organization that was in the service of the bourgeoisie.[87] Although not proposing a formal ban on Communists joining the profession, he did suggest that any party member entering a college of defenders should be treated by his party cell "as an extremely suspect person, and, in any event, as unreliable." Furthermore, if a party organization did grant permission for one of its members to join the Bar, it should restrict his practice to specific trials or to work in particular legal consultation bureaus.[88]

Following the article by Krasikov, the debate was transferred

[84] Ibid.
[85] M. Andres, "Kommunisty v kollegii zashchitnikov," *Pravda*, August 13, 1922, p. 1.
[86] Ibid.
[87] P. Krasikov, "O kommunistakh i advokatakh," *Pravda*, August 24, 1922, p. 2.
[88] Ibid.

to the pages of the official legal journal *Ezhenedel'nik sovetskoi iustitsii* [Soviet Justice Weekly].[89] After three months of discussion the party Central Committee settled the dispute with the publication of a circular on November 2, 1922, "On the Entrance of Communists into the College of Defenders."[90] The circular provided that, in view of the dominance of hostile elements in the colleges, party members would be permitted to join the profession only on the following conditions:

1) entering Communists were approved by the regional party committee (*gubkom*) or a higher party organ;
2) individual Communist defenders submitted reports on the activities of the party fraction within their college to the *gubkom*;
3) Communist defenders did not take civil cases in which they were defending bourgeois interests against those of the workers or the state, or criminal cases in which they were defending unhealthy elements such as bribers and rapists;
4) Communist defenders devoted themselves to organizing legal consultation bureaus for the working class.

Furthermore, the party fraction in the colleges of defenders was subordinated directly to the regional party committee and not, as with other primary party organizations, to the lower-level district party committee (*raikom*).[91] Thus, while agreeing in principle to the entrance of Communists into the Bar, the Central Committee served notice to the lower party organizations and to the party rank and file that the flow of Communists into the college of defenders was to be highly restricted. In this respect policy toward the Bar differed fundamentally from that applied

[89] "Iz pechati," *Ezhenedel'nik sovetskoi iustitsii*, no. 29-30 (1922), p. 29; I. Slavin, "Ob uchastii kommunistov v advokature," *Ezhenedel'nik sovetskoi iustitsii*, no. 31-32 (1922), p. 2.

[90] "O vstuplenii kommunistov v kollegii zashchitnikov," Tsirkuliar TsK i RKP no. 97, *Ezhenedel'nik sovetskoi iustitsii*, no. 1 (1923), p. 24.

[91] Ibid.

to other legal institutions, which were being saturated with party cadres in the 1920s.[92]

In the initial stages of NEP, party membership in the Bar was negligible. In Leningrad only 6 of 281 defenders were Communists in 1923.[93] In the same year the colleges in Kaluga and Vladimir, which had 38 and 25 defenders respectively, contained no party members.[94] It appears that other provincial colleges had no more than a handful of Communist defenders.[95]

The Moscow college of defenders provided the sole exception to this pattern. In the capital a sizable group of party members entered the college shortly after its formation in 1922, presumably on the instructions of the regional party committee. By April 1923, 69 defenders, or approximately 20 percent of the college's 449 members, were Communists.[96] The number of party members dropped to 50 in October of that year, but that still represented a far higher level of party saturation than in any other college in the country.[97]

The Moscow college did not serve, however, as a model for increased party penetration of the profession. The middle years of NEP witnessed no significant expansion of party membership in the colleges of defenders. In 1925 the Leningrad college included only 8 Communists among its more than 300 members, while in Kaluga there were still no Communists in a college that

[92] M. Kozhevnikov, *Istoriia sovetskogo suda 1917-1956* (Moscow, 1957), pp. 185-186, and T. H. Rigby, *Communist Party Membership in the USSR, 1917-1967* (Princeton, N.J., 1968), p. 425. Some professional groups, such as village teachers, were also given high priority for party penetration in the mid-1920s. Rigby, *Communist Party Membership*, pp. 55-56.

[93] "Godovshchina petrogradskoi," p. 43.

[94] *Piat' let raboty kaluzhskoi gubernskoi kollegii zashchitnikov (1922-1927)* (Kaluga, 1927), p. 6; "Kollegiia zashchitnikov vo vladimirskoi gubernii," *Ezhenedel'nik sovetskoi iustitsii*, no. 36 (1923), p. 830.

[95] *Otchet prezidiuma novonikolaevskoi gubernskoi kollegii zashchitnikov za vremia s 1 dek. 1924 po 1 noiabria 1925* (Novonikolaevsk, 1925), p. 5; *Sbornik otchetov i rukovodiashchikh postanovlenii prezidiuma kostromskoi gubernskoi kollegii zashchitnikov s 1 avg. 1922 po 1 iiunia 1924* (Kostroma, 1924), p. 14.

[96] *Pervyi otchet*, p. 12.

[97] *Otchet prezidiuma moskovskoi gubernskoi kollegii zashchitnikov za 2-oe polugodie (s 1 aprelia po 1 okt. 1923)* (Moscow, 1924), p. 4. Hereafter cited as *Vtoroi otchet*.

now contained 59 defenders.[98] The following year Communist party and Komsomol members represented only 4.5 percent of the profession nationwide.[99]

Although a modest increase in the number of party members in the Bar did take place in the last two years of NEP, it came at a time when the profession as a whole was undergoing a significant expansion. The Communists therefore continued to account for only a small fraction of Soviet defenders. In the Moscow college, to which almost half of all Communist defenders were affiliated during NEP, the percentage of party members actually declined from 1923 to 1927. While 750 members were added to the college in this period, the size of the Communist component rose by only 30. This meant a reduction in the level of party saturation in the Moscow college from about 20 percent at the beginning of NEP to slightly over 6.5 percent at the end of NEP.[100]

In spite of the party's unwillingness to direct significant numbers of its own cadres into the Bar, it was determined to establish effective internal control of the profession. No sooner had the colleges been formed in 1922 than the meager forces of the party within the profession set out to promote themselves as the rightful claimants to political power in the colleges of defenders. This triggered a fierce struggle for control of the profession's governing organs—a struggle that resulted in only a partial victory for the party during NEP.

During the 1920s, the party groups within the colleges of defenders could not hope to achieve a position of political dominance through strictly democratic means. Vastly outnumbered by nonparty defenders, Communists were not perceived by the rank and file of the profession as the natural leaders of the Bar. In fact, there were strong feelings among many advocates that

[98] *Otchet o deiatel'nosti prezidiuma leningradskoi; Piat' let raboty kaluzhskoi,* p. 6.

[99] Elokhovskii, "Lichnyi sostav," p. 77. This percentage is for the RSFSR and is probably slightly higher than that for other republics.

[100] Topalov, "K voprosu," p. 8; "Pis'mo v redaktsiiu," *Ezhenedel'nik sovetskoii iustitsii,* no. 4 (1927), p. 107.

party members were singularly unqualified to represent the membership on the colleges' governing bodies.[101] This was in part because most Communists accepted into the profession were advocates on paper only. They were usually employed full time in important party and government work and entered the colleges only to assume leadership posts. A. Vyshinsky, who became a leading figure in Soviet legal affairs in the 1930s, served a brief term as a presidium member in the Moscow college of defenders in 1923, even though he spent no time as a practicing defender.[102] It seems that it was only in the Moscow college, with its large group of party *vydvizhentsy*, that Communist advocates actually practiced law. With few exceptions, party members in other colleges were involved with the profession only to the extent of attending the weekly presidium sessions or the periodic general meetings.[103] The party, therefore, directed cadres into the Bar for political, and not legal, activity, a fact resented by much of the profession.

Faced with the prospect of certain defeat in an open election for places on the college presidia, the challenge for party groups was to restrict, and subsequently control outright, the nomination process so that only candidates acceptable to the party would be voted on by the profession's rank and file. The efforts of the party to appropriate the exclusive right to nominate the leaders of the colleges of defenders are vividly illustrated in published accounts of the general meetings of the Leningrad college of defenders in the period from 1922 to 1924.[104]

At the first general meeting of Leningrad advocates, held in September 1922, a single slate of seven presidium candidates was nominated, presumably by the regional soviet that had organized the meeting. The slate of candidates for the seven-man presidium consisted of a majority of nonparty advocates who

---

[101] See, for example, the speech of the nonparty advocate Chlenov to the January 1924 general meeting of Moscow defenders. *Tretii otchet*, pp. 21-27.

[102] *Pervyi otchet*, p. 6.

[103] L. Akhmatov, "Sudebnaia zashchita—Prokuratura," *Vestnik sovetskoi iustitsii*, no. 1 (1927), p. 15.

[104] *Otchet o deiatel'nosti prezidiuma leningradskoi*, pp. 19-87.

enjoyed the confidence of the rank and file of the profession, but it also contained several representatives from the Group of Proletarian Advocates. This fraction within the college was a united front organization composed of the six Communist defenders, unwilling as yet to stand under their own banner, and a slightly larger number of nonparty advocates sympathetic to the Communists. Altogether the group represented approximately 10 percent of the college's membership. Although complaints were voiced over the way in which "unknown" candidates had been recommended to the rank and file, the Leningrad advocates accepted the single, coalition slate of Communist and nonparty defenders.[105] Thus, through the state-controlled nomination process and single-slate voting the Communists managed to secure minority representation on the governing body of the Leningrad college.

After several months in which the freedom of action of the Communist minority on the presidium was restricted by the nonparty majority, a structural reform of the college's governing apparatus was introduced that strengthened the leadership position of the Communists. In April 1923 responsibility for the day-to-day administration of the Leningrad college of defenders was transferred from the presidium to a responsible secretariat (*otvetstvennyi sekretariat*). Of the three presidium members who comprised this body, two were Communists.[106]

The formation of the responsible secretariat in large measure emasculated the presidium. Not only did the secretariat oversee the administration of college affairs, it prepared the agenda for the presidium meetings, thereby controlling the larger body, and it also represented the college before government supervisory institutions.[107] As the majority element in the secretariat, the Communists were able, through a process of institutional leverage, to assume a leading role in the college.

This reform of the Leningrad college had its parallels in other

[105] Ibid., p. 27; I. Segal, "Gruppa levoi advokatury," *Rabochii sud*, no. 6-7 (1925), p. 28.

[106] *Otchet o deiatel'nosti prezidiuma leningradskoi*, p. 7.

[107] Ibid.

colleges throughout the country.[108] Sanctioned neither by legislation nor a vote of the general meetings of the colleges, the formation of responsible secretariats was apparently imposed on the profession by government supervisory institutions acting on the instructions of the central party apparatus. No explicit evidence exists on the method of selecting the secretariat members, but it is clear from the composition of the bodies that supervisory institutions heavily influenced the selection process. Created as a temporary measure to stifle independent tendencies in the profession, the responsible secretariats continued to function in many colleges until the end of NEP.[109]

Although the concentration of decision-making authority in ever fewer hands enhanced the role of the Communists at the leadership level in the colleges, it did little to increase their base of support among rank-and-file defenders. In fact, the manipulation of the profession's governing bodies by a group that could claim little knowledge of legal affairs appears to have heightened opposition to Communist domination in certain quarters. In Leningrad the Group of Proletarian Advocates complained that it had made no progress in carrying out its socio-political tasks in the college because of the hostility of the colleges' rank and file.[110] After the attitudes and behavior of Leningrad advocates had been subjected to severe public criticism by the regional court, a proposal calling for closer ties with judicial organs, improvements in the social composition of the college, and the establishment of proletarian bases of work among the advocates was put forth by a left-wing advocate at a general meeting. Of 184 defenders present, only 7 voted for the motion.[111]

---

[108] *Piat' let raboty kaluzhskoi*, p. 16; *Otchet prezidiuma novosibirskoi*, p. 23; *Pervyi otchet*, p. 17, which published a detailed "Polozhenie o sekretariate prezidiuma kollegii zashchitnikov" setting out the functions of the institution.

[109] In some areas they were disbanded by the middle of NEP. In Kaluga, for example, the presidium reassumed sole responsibility for the internal governing of the college in 1925. *Piat' let raboty kaluzhskoi*, p. 16.

[110] *Otchet o deiatel'nosti prezidiuma leningradskoi*, p. 28.

[111] Ibid., p. 30.

In spite of the oppositionist mood in the Leningrad college, the Communist party fraction decided to withdraw from the Group of Proletarian Advocates and propose its own slate of candidates when new presidium elections were held at a general meeting in June 1923. In the expanded presidium of nine members the Communists asked for a majority of the seats, even though party members accounted for only 2 percent of Leningrad advocates. In the words of the Communist spokesman at the meeting:

> The Communist fraction agrees to enter the presidium at this moment, but only on the condition that it is granted five places and one candidate membership. Only as a majority will it be able to assume responsibility for the work of the presidium. [112]

In justification of this position the spokesman for the party fraction noted that "experience has shown that it is not possible to get by without the participation of Communists."[113]

This statement was clearly intended to remind the advocates that as long as the college resisted party guidance relations with other political and legal institutions, such as the soviets and the courts, would remain strained. Because the Bar was subject to the supervisory authority of these institutions and, perhaps more importantly, because it depended on their good offices for improvement in their living and working conditions, the incentives on a material and psychological level to acquiesce to the demands of the party fraction were very strong indeed. Furthermore, a purge commission had just been created to cleanse the Leningrad college of its politically undesirable elements. With the system of open voting used for presidium elections in Leningrad during NEP, advocates opposing party policy risked expulsion from the profession.[114]

Therefore, after a short recess in the proceedings at the June general meeting, during which the party's demands on presidium representation were discussed, the spokesman for the mass of

[112] Ibid., p. 32.
[113] Ibid.
[114] Ibid., p. 34.

nonparty advocates announced that, "given the objective conditions," the proposal put forth by the Communists would be accepted.[115] It is significant, however, that nonparty advocates retained, for the moment at least, the right to nominate the remaining four members of the presidium as well as one candidate member, none of whom, it appears, belonged to the Group of Proletarian Advocates. In effect, the Communist fraction entered into a coalition—albeit as majority partner—with the genuine representatives of the rank and file of the college.

But this arrangement was regarded as temporary by the Communists. At the next presidium election in the Leningrad college of defenders, held in February 1924, the party fraction attempted to gain complete control over the nominating process. Instead of putting forth a simple majority of nominees for the presidium as it had done previously, the fraction proposed a complete slate of candidates, which included five Communists, two representatives of the Group of Left Advocates (as the Group of Proletarian Advocates had been restyled after the departure of the Communists), and two representatives of the other nonparty advocates. It was expected that this slate would stand unopposed.[116]

The mass of nonparty advocates responded, however, by nominating a complete slate of its own, which also contained both Communist and nonparty advocates. To this move, the Communists replied:

> An abnormal situation has been created. Together with the complete slate of the Communist fraction consisting of nine nominees, an incomplete slate of four persons has been put forward by the nonparty advocates. Two such slates cannot compete one against the other. The nonparty slate is incomplete because the first five candidates on the list, who are members of the Communist fraction, cannot be counted. Nonparty advocates may not include Communists in their slate.[117]

[115] Ibid.
[116] Ibid., p. 43.
[117] Ibid., p. 44.

By forbidding nonparty advocates to nominate party members to the presidium, the Communists asserted their claim to be the only group qualified to recommend candidates for leadership positions in the college. In case the college members were not convinced by the logic of the Communists, they were reminded by the party fraction that although the position of the college vis-à-vis the supervisory institutions had improved somewhat, "it was still far from satisfactory, as evidenced by the purge now in progress."[118]

In spite of the intimidation the college refused to accede to Communist demands for complete control over the nominating process. As a means of undermining the legitimacy of the original Communist slate, the two representatives of the mass of nonparty advocates nominated by the Communists withdrew from the election.[119] The party slate then stood no chance of acceptance by the rank and file of the college.

Realizing the weakness of their position, the Communists proposed postponing the election until the next general meeting. A Communist advocate explained:

As a counterweight to this [Communist] slate, another slate supported by the nonparty mass has been put forward that does not have the requisite political physionomy but that does command, evidently, a majority in the meeting. Faced with the threat of yielding its position, the Communist fraction cannot take part in the elections under such conditions.[120]

Although the deadlock appeared unbreakable, a compromise was reached between party and nonparty leaders during a final recess. The Communist slate was modified, evidently to the detriment of the Group of Left Advocates, to include in the nonparty minority bloc a range of personalities more acceptable to the rank and file of the college. The slate was then put to the vote and accepted.[121]

[118] Ibid.
[119] Ibid., p. 45.
[120] Ibid.
[121] Ibid., pp. 45-46.

Having succeeded by 1924 in reserving for itself the right to propose an official slate for presidium elections, the party was nonetheless limited in its ability to determine the composition of the Leningrad college presidium. Indeed, throughout NEP the balance of political forces in the college ensured that in selecting presidium candidates the party had to consider carefully the preferences of the rank-and-file advocates, at least regarding the nonparty minority bloc on the presidium. Communist leadership of the college was thus constrained by its coalition partners in the presidium and by the threat of a complete withdrawal of support from the college membership.

The accession to power of the Communists in the Leningrad college appears to have been accomplished in a similar manner in colleges throughout the country. In Moscow, where the party fraction accounted for a significant minority of the profession, the published transcripts of the college's general meetings were not as forthright in their descriptions of internal disputes over the leadership questions.[122] But it is clear that the Communists encountered resistance in their efforts to control the nomination process. As in Leningrad, the struggle for the college leadership was waged between more or less organized fractions and involved considerable behind-the-scenes negotiations prior to, and during, presidium elections.

The initial membership of the nine-man Moscow presidium was nominated in the autumn of 1922 on a single, unopposed slate by a Communist defender. The slate, which was approved by a vote of the membership, consisted of five Communists and four nonparty advocates, who represented the Public Bar Group (*gruppa obshchestvennoi advokatury*). The Soviet historian V. Kuritsyn writes that the "Bureau of the Moscow City Party Committee on September 21, 1922, recognized it as absolutely essential (*printsipial'no neobkhodimym*) that Communists comprise a majority of the presidium of the Moscow College of

---

[122] Whereas the Leningrad *otchet* contained large passages evidently taken from the transcripts of the general meetings, the Moscow *otchety* provided a heavily edited synopsis of the meetings with only occasional quotations.

Advocates."[123] Over the next year and a half vacancies on the presidium were divided between candidates put forth by the party fraction and by the Public Bar Group, an organization comprised of prominent bourgeois specialists who openly supported Soviet power.

But at the beginning of 1924 more than one hundred Moscow advocates, disillusioned with the unrepresentativeness of the presidium, coalesced into a fraction known as the New Group to challenge Communist domination of the college leadership. At a general meeting of the college held on January 24, 1924, the New Group complained that the de facto appointment of the presidium by the Communists violated democratic principles.[124] In response to this charge a representative of the Public Bar Group argued that there could be no contradiction between the existing method of elections and democratic principles because "genuine democracy is realized only through the party." Besides, he noted, the New Group was also guilty of attempting to organize the election by carrying on preliminary negotiations on the composition of the presidium with the other fractions before the meeting.[125]

Having established the initial pattern of single-slate nomination, the party was able to coopt the other fractions into participating in this undemocratic procedure. By pushing their claim for presidium representation in caucus, the leaders of the nonparty groups legitimated Communist electoral tactics. While arguing publicly for the internal democratization of the college, the New Group was working behind the scenes to divide the presidium seats evenly among the three major fractions in the college.[126] As it happened a proposal was adopted by the general

---

[123] "Otkrytie deiatel'nosti moskovskoi kollegii zashchitnikov," *Ezhenedel'nik sovetskoi iustitsii*, no. 37-38 (1922), p. 38; *Tretii otchet*, p. 23; Partarkhiv MK i MGK KPSS, f. 3, op. 3, ed. khr. 6, p. 49, cited in Kuritsyn, "Stanovlenie sovetskoi advokatury," p. 116.

[124] *Tretii otchet*, p. 23. It is unclear whether this move by disenchanted Moscow advocates was connected with the news of Lenin's death on January 21, 1924.

[125] Ibid.

[126] Ibid., p. 25.

meeting to divide the four nonparty seats evenly between the New Group and the Public Bar Group, thus leaving the Communist majority in the presidium unchanged.[127] This rebellion of approximately one-quarter of the rank and file in the Moscow college therefore succeeded in slightly eroding the Communist grip on the leadership, but it did nothing to alter the process of leadership selection.

Information on the internal politics of other colleges of defenders under NEP is sketchy. It is known, though, that not all colleges accepted candidates recommended to them, especially when secret balloting was used. In Kostroma the advocates rejected an attempt by a regional justice official, who presided over the initial general meeting of the college and nominated the first presidium, to install an individual on the presidium who was not a college member. This nominee—apparently a party activist—was defeated in a secret ballot, and a write-in candidate was elected in his place.[128] It must be assumed that in the many smaller colleges, where the number of Communist defenders was fewer than the number required to form a majority on the presidium, the leadership of the profession remained in the hands of nonparty advocates.[129]

By the middle years of NEP a pattern had been established in the larger colleges of the RSFSR of Communists controlling the presidium by a majority of one (i.e., five out of nine or four out of seven presidium members were Communists).[130] But this did not apply to the Ukraine. In the Ukrainian colleges the Communists remained a minority group on the presidia throughout NEP.[131] The reasons for the party's evident lack of success

---

[127] Ibid., p. 26.

[128] *Sbornik otchetov . . . prezidiuma kostromskoi*, p. 9.

[129] Because of the state's ability to purge advocates, even those leaders elected by the general meetings could not be assured of remaining on the presidia. For example, two members of the Kostroma presidium were expelled from the college by the regional *ispolkom* in 1927. See ibid., p. 34.

[130] I found no exceptions to this rule in Communist-dominated presidia.

[131] This is based on information from the colleges in Kiev, Kherson, Vinnits, Kharkov, Kamenets-Podol'sk, and Moghilev-Podol'sk. "God raboty kievskoi," p.

in gaining control of the leadership of the Ukrainian profession are unclear, although the consistent level of party representation on college presidia throughout the republic suggests that a decision not to press ahead with attempts of outright domination of the colleges' governing bodies was made by the republican party apparatus, perhaps in response to rebellions against Communist tactics by the profession's rank and file.

Communist successes in penetrating the colleges' leading organs during NEP were, therefore, uneven. Whereas the profession in the Ukraine and the more provincial areas of Russia maintained a nonparty majority on the college presidia, the colleges in Moscow, Leningrad, Omsk, Baku, and other cities were subject to Communist leadership of their governing organs.[132] But the regional variations in the internal politics of the profession may not have been as great as this dichotomy appears to indicate. Although the Communists held a formal majority in certain presidia, their ability to lead the colleges was severely restricted by their unfamiliarity with professional affairs, their lack of contacts with the membership, and their commitments to party and government work outside the profession. Communist presidium members could always be relied on to give their vote when needed, but most had only a passing interest in the business of the college.

The nonparty members of the presidium, who were full-time advocates with an intimate knowledge of the profession and its membership, assumed a significance beyond their minority status on the governing organs. Able to devote themselves wholly to college affairs, the nonparty presidium members appeared to be especially active in administrative work, such as the investigation of disciplinary cases. The record of disciplinary cases

235; "V khersonskoi kollegii zashchitnikov," *Vestnik sovetskoi iustitsii*, no. 3 (1927), p. 105; "V vinnitsskoi kollegii zashchitnikov," *Vestnik sovetskoi iustitsii*, no. 6-7 (1927), p. 236; "V kharkovskoi kollegii zashchitnikov," *Vestnik sovetskoi iustitsii*, no. 15 (1927), p. 534; "Deiatel'nost' mogilev-podolskoi kollegii zashchitnikov," *Vestnik sovetskoi iustitsii*, no. 17 (1927), p. 600.

[132] *Otchet prezidiuma omskoi gubernskoi kollegii zashchitnikov za 1925 god* (Omsk, 1926), p. 5; Abdullaev, "Iz istoriia," p. 17.

heard by the Moscow college's disciplinary commission from 1923 to 1926 indicates that most of the opinions were written by nonparty presidium members.[133] Although the nonparty groups in Communist-dominated presidia could not directly overrule the party fraction on major questions of policy, they were able to play an active role in the leadership of the college.

In considering the degree of party control over the profession during NEP it is also important to note the limits of college government. In this period the presidia of the colleges were primarily concerned with associational activities, such as those relating to membership questions and to the representation of the profession's interests before party and government institutions. Because of the dominance of private practice the professional activities of individual defenders were, for the most part, not subject to presidium scrutiny. The presidium engaged in active oversight of legal practice only with regard to the college-sponsored legal consultation bureaus.[134] Thus, the colleges of defenders under NEP did not have an authority structure that enabled the presidia to closely direct and supervise the everyday behavior of the diffuse mass of college members. Without an effective chain of command operating within the colleges, even the party-dominated presidia could not hope to impose Communist organization and discipline on the profession.

Government Supervision of the Colleges of Defenders

Proceeding hand-in-hand with attempts by the party to establish effective internal control of the Bar was the imposition of a system of external control over the colleges of defenders by government institutions. One of the most important functions of government supervisory institutions during NEP was the softening up of the

[133] *Distsiplinarnoe proizvodstvo za 1926g.* (Moscow, 1926); V. Veger, ed., *Organizatsionnaia rabota i voprosy etiki (s 1 aprelia po 1 oktiabria 1924)* (Moscow, 1924).

[134] The infrequent review of advocates' home-based practice by the presidium normally involved advocates filling out, on a voluntary basis, questionnaires submitted to them by the college.

profession to facilitate the Communist takeover of the colleges' governing bodies.[135] In Leningrad, for example, a presidium election was postponed for two months until a thorough cleansing of the college had been carried out by a purge commission comprised of judges and local soviet officials.[136] A year earlier the executive committee of the regional soviet, complaining that the continued presence of a certain nonparty advocate on the college presidium was "undesirable," adopted a resolution condemning the advocate.[137] In the words of *Rabochii sud* [The Worker's Court], the official journal of the Leningrad regional court, "naturally, it only remained for the newly elected member of the presidium . . . to resign, which he did."[138]

In less cooperative colleges more severe measures were employed by government supervisory institutions to bring the profession into line. Using a well-tried technique from the tsarist period, the regional soviet in Nizhnii Novgorod simply closed down the rebellious local college for several months.[139] Unhappy with an existing college of defenders, the republican justice commissar of Turkmenistan replaced it with a new college and at the same time installed a Communist-dominated presidium.[140] This reportedly occurred in other republics as well.[141]

The power of the state to exclude defenders from the profession was perhaps the most effective method of ensuring that the behavior of defenders, both in the colleges and in the courtroom, remained within desired limits. According to legislation adopted

[135] The restoration of an organized Bar was accompanied by an exemplary purge of a contingent of the more liberal elements in the legal community. In the autumn of 1922 over one hundred "anti-Soviet lawyers, literati, and professors" were deported from the Soviet Union. Fitzpatrick, *Education and Social Mobility*, p. 76.

[136] *Otchet o deiatel'nosti prezidiuma leningradskoi*, p. 35. This occurred prior to the meeting in which Communists first attempted to nominate a complete slate of presidium candidates.

[137] "K V sessii VTsIK," *Rabochii sud*, no. 3-4 (1923), p. 4.

[138] Ibid.

[139] "Konferentsiia chlenov kollegii zashchitnikov moskovskoi gubernii," *Proletarskii sud*, no. 3 (1925), p. 44.

[140] Durdyev, "Organizatsiia i razvitie," p. 77.

[141] Ibid.

at the beginning of NEP, government institutions were empowered to remove undesirable advocates only in the first thirty days after they had been admitted to the college, and then only after justifying their actions.[142] This right of challenge (*pravo otvoda*) was soon expanded in practice, however, as supervisory institutions began to dismiss defenders without explanation and regardless of their length of service in the profession. The law caught up with practice some time later after a Justice Commissariat official noted that the unlimited power of dismissal being exercised by government institutions should be confirmed in legislation.[143]

In any single year during NEP approximately 5 percent of the Bar was expelled by government supervisory bodies,[144] though the intensity of the purges varied significantly by region. In Moscow and Leningrad the turnover of personnel was surprisingly low. Of the advocates who joined the Moscow and Leningrad colleges in 1923, 71 percent and 72 percent, respectively, were still in the profession in those cities in 1929.[145] The colleges hardest hit by purges were in provincial areas. In Kaluga 15 percent of the membership of the regional college was purged from the summer of 1923 to the summer of 1924. After two years of relative quiet another 15 percent of the college was purged from the summer of 1926 to the summer of 1927.[146] In Pskov at the end of 1923 the executive committee of the regional soviet removed twenty-six defenders from a college that almost certainly numbered no more than fifty advocates.[147]

Purges were also particularly severe in the non-Russian areas. In Baku sixty-three members of the newly formed college of

[142] "Polozhenie o kollegii zashchitnikov," p. 28.

[143] "K V sessii," p. 4.

[144] This estimate is based on the yearly statistics on expulsions contained in the various regional *otchety* cited above.

[145] *Vsia Moskva* (Moscow, 1923), pp. 145-151; *Ves Petrograd* (Petrograd, 1923), p. 282; *Iuridicheskii kalendar' na 1929g.* (Moscow, 1929), pp. 306-350.

[146] *Piat' let raboty kaluzhskoi*, p. 6.

[147] "V kollegii zashchitnikov," *Rabochii sud*, no. 12 (1923), p. 37.

defenders were expelled in 1923.[148] Three years later the justice commissar of Azerbaidzhan purged seventy-seven members of the republic's profession. This action was subsequently reversed, however, by the Central Executive Committee of Azerbaidzhan, which formed its own investigating commission to examine the activities of the profession. This commission decided to purge only six advocates.[149] The constant threat of purges raised by the supervisory institutions contributed to the creation of a siege atmosphere in the profession, even in those areas where expulsions were relatively uncommon.

Defenders whose professional activities were perceived as harmful to the Soviet order could also be expelled from the colleges by the profession's own disciplinary tribunals, which were normally composed of presidium members.[150] Most cases came before the colleges' disciplinary tribunals as a result of complaints by clients or other advocates and concerned traditional questions of professional ethics. But a large minority of proceedings were instituted at the prompting of government supervisory institutions, most notably the courts. Of the 137 disciplinary cases heard by the Moscow college in the 1925/1926 accounting year, 42 arose on the basis of judges' complaints.[151]

Considerable use was made of disciplinary proceedings by judges and other government officials to punish the advocates for mistakes of a political character. In a case brought by the Moscow regional procurator, an advocate was punished for, among other things, announcing in court that if his client were placed under detention he, the client, would go on a hunger strike.[152] Political considerations also entered into the resolution of disciplinary cases brought on other grounds. The People's Commissariat of Workers' and Peasants' Inspection (Rabkrin) lodged a complaint against an advocate for accepting a large

---

[148] A. Abdullaev, "Istoriia organizatsii instituta zashchity v azerbaidzhanskoi SSR (1920-1926gg.)," in *Trudy* (NII sudebnoi zashchity: Baku, 1969), p. 46.

[149] Abdullaev, "Iz istorii advokatury," p. 15.

[150] E. Rivlin, *Sovetskaia advokatura* (Moscow, 1926), pp. 103-104.

[151] *Distsiplinarnoe proizvodstvo*, p. 5.

[152] Ibid., p. 57.

amount of tsarist gold currency as payment from a client. After reviewing the background of the defender (he was a Social Revolutionary from 1904 to October 1917), the college disciplinary tribunal decided to exclude him from the profession.[153]

But the disciplinary tribunals were by no means compliant instruments of government institutions in this period, as the following case illustrates. The head of a government department in Moscow protested to the college of defenders because an advocate had uttered the following counterrevolutionary insult in court: "The responsible officials of soviet institutions spend all their time riding around in automobiles and searching out dachas for the summer season." The disciplinary tribunal of the Moscow Bar ruled that, given the truth of the statement, the defender was not subject to disciplinary sanction.[154]

In many other cases brought by government officials the colleges' disciplinary tribunals attempted to protect themselves, and the members of the profession, by finding a defender technically guilty and then imposing only a mild sanction.[155] There were limits, of course, to the leniency that the disciplinary tribunals could show to college members in the face of pressure from the state. Not only could the decisions of a tribunal be reversed on appeal by the regional court,[156] but in some areas the courts suspended the college's own tribunal and temporarily took direct responsibility for the hearing of disciplinary cases against defenders.[157]

Coercion and the threat of coercion were essential elements of supervisory policy that enabled the party and government to maintain adequate control over a profession whose membership and formal autonomy gave it a distinct position among Soviet

---

[153] Veger, ed., *Organizatsionnaia rabota*, pp. 24-25.

[154] Ibid., pp. 50-51.

[155] In general, the disciplinary tribunals appear to have been quite lenient with defenders. Of the 140 cases heard by the Moscow tribunal in the 1925/1926 accounting year, only 4 resulted in suspension or the issuance of a strict reprimand (*strogii vygovor*). See *Distsiplinarnoe proizvodstvo*, p. 6.

[156] "Polozhenie o kollegii zashchitnikov," p. 28.

[157] V. Trapeznikov, "Distsiplinarnaia otvetstvennost' zashchitnikov," *Ezhenedel'-nik sovetskoi iustitsii*, no. 40 (1923), p. 28.

institutions. There were, however, other, more subtle, means employed to direct the profession's behavior into desired channels. Most notable among these was the use of promises of social and economic concessions to the Bar to elicit cooperation with state policies.

When the Bar was established in 1922 it was immediately subjected to a mass of discriminatory legislation. As members of a free profession, advocates were denied social insurance, free medical care, and free education for their children and were forced to pay taxes, rent, and telephone charges at a level significantly higher than the average. Prevented from joining a trade union, the advocates enjoyed few of the public benefits that the new state was beginning to provide.[158] Furthermore, as a suspect element within the legal community, advocates were accorded none of the professional privileges enjoyed by other legal personnel (e.g., the right to submit and receive court documents without queuing with the general public).[159]

Powerless to change these conditions on their own, the colleges of defenders were forced to turn to supervisory institutions, and particularly to the regional soviets, to improve their living and working standards. Government institutions, in turn, agreed to consider the advocates' requests for reform of existing regulations but only on the condition that the profession conform its conduct to the expectations of party and government bodies. Despite constant lobbying by the profession's representatives few concessions were wrung from the state. Although the RSFSR Justice Commissariat reportedly placed proposals that defenders be admitted as trade union members before the central trade union organization VTsSPS, membership was withheld from the profession, as was a recategorization of advocates from members of a free profession to the more desirable state employee status.[160]

---

[158] A. Tseitlin, "Ocherednye zadachi advokatury," *Rabochii sud*, no. 3-4 (1924), p. 139; "O kvartirnoi plate s chlenov kollegii zaschchitnikov," *Rabochii sud*, no. 6-7 (1924), p. 83; A. Tarkopol'skii, "Chleny kollegii zashchitnikov i ikh pravovoe polozhenie," *Proletarskii sud*, no. 3 (1925), pp. 9-11.

[159] *Otchet prezidiuma novosibirskoi*, p. 12.

[160] *Ezhenedel'nik sovetskoi iustitsii*, no. 19-20 (1924), p. 470. Although the VTsSPS ruled in early 1927 that individual advocates could apply to the unions

Thus, legally as well as politically the profession of advocates retained its unfavored position among Soviet institutions.

A primary element in the government's supervision of the Bar was, of course, the regular monitoring of college activities. Courts and soviets at the regional level periodically received detailed oral and written reports on the profession's activities from representatives of the college presidium or its responsible secretariat.[161] These formal reports were supplemented by more informal contacts between college leaders and judges, procurators, and soviet representatives at party and government forums. Officials from supervisory institutions were also able to attend the general meetings and presidium sessions in the colleges of defenders, and it seems that direct observation of the profession's activities became an increasingly frequent occurrence during NEP. In Novonikolaevsk, for example, officials from the local court and Procuracy participated directly in all presidium sessions and general meetings.[162]

Shortcomings discovered in the process of monitoring college activities prompted corrective actions by the state, either in the form of purges or warnings to the presidium or to college members to modify their behavior. The standard of behavior to which the colleges were held varied, however, from one region to the next, as did the means of influencing the profession's activities. Unlike their latter-day counterparts in the USSR, local government institutions in this period did not receive detailed instructions from central authorities outlining a uniform approach to supervisory policy on the Bar.[163] Regional supervisory institutions were

---

"*na obshchikh osnovaniiakh*," the evidence indicates that few, if any, advocates were accepted. "Pravo vstupleniia v profsoiiuz chlenov kollegii zashchitnikov," *Ezhenedel'nik sovetskoi iustitsii*, no. 3 (1927), p. 68. Other minor concessions were made in the areas of telephone charges, rents, and school fees. See Tarkopol'skii, "Chleny kollegii," pp. 9-11.

[161] See, for example, the discussion of a college's *otchet* by the Leningrad regional court. "Plenum leningradskogo gubsuda," *Rabochii sud*, no. 17-18 (1926), p. 1,118.

[162] *Otchet prezidiuma novonikolaevskoi*, p. 4.

[163] There was in fact no all-union justice commissariat until 1936. That date also marked the creation of a separate Bar department (*otdel advokatury*) within the republican justice commissariats. Until that time the advocates were the responsibility of the judicial institutions department in the commissariats.

therefore able, within broad limits, to mold their own relationship with the college of defenders under their control. Whereas some supervisory bodies were quite loose in their oversight of the Bar, others adopted an active, interventionist approach.[164]

The limited coordination that was imposed on the regional supervisory institutions came in the form of occasional circulars published by the republican justice commissariats.[165] These circulars were intended in most instances for the regional courts, which had assumed primary responsibility for the supervision of the Bar by the latter years of NEP. The republican circulars were normally issued to clarify existing legislation or to resolve contentious questions that were not governed by normative enactments. One such directive concerned the distribution and method of payment of court-appointed cases argued by defenders.[166]

Beyond this activity the republican justice commissariats contributed little to the supervision of the colleges of defenders. It is therefore premature to speak of a fully developed, centralized system of government supervision over the advocates during NEP. The chain of command reaching from the political leadership to the individual advocates still lacked two crucial links—a central institution actively coordinating supervisory policy and an intermediary organization within the colleges to connect the presidium with practicing defenders.

Legal Practice under NEP

Although the predominant form of legal practice under NEP was the individual, private practitioner receiving clients at home, the practice of law acquired an increasingly diverse character in this period. Many advocates combined a general legal practice

---

[164] Direct government intervention appeared to be more common in areas where Communist leadership of the colleges was weakest.

[165] Circulars issued by the RSFSR Justice Commissariat tended to act as models for the rest of the country.

[166] "Ob uplate i raspredelenii voznagrazhdenii za zashchitu po naznacheniiu," Tsirkuliar no. 200 Narodnogo Komissariata iustitsii, *Ezhenedel'nik sovetskoi iustitsii*, no. 41 (1925), p. 1,313.

with part-time consulting work for enterprises and organizations. Especially in the latter years of NEP, as the competition for private clients increased, advocates began to devote a larger share of their time to legal work for institutions. In the spring of 1925, 29 percent of Leningrad advocates were receiving the majority of their income from this source, and many of those advocates were among the best paid in the profession.[167] By 1927 consulting work had outstripped private practice as the major source of officially reported income.[168]

With the freedom to contract for private cases and consulting work came two civic obligations imposed on the profession by the regime. The first was the acceptance of court-appointed cases, usually involving criminal defense, that were distributed to the members of the colleges of defenders on a rotational basis. Defenders were entitled by law to be remunerated for most court-appointed cases, though it appears that only token fees were received.[169] More importantly, advocates were expected to be on duty at regular intervals at local legal consultation bureaus, which were operated by the colleges of defenders. A network of consultation bureaus designed to serve the needs of the working masses grew rapidly in urban areas in the early years of NEP, and by 1925 Moscow and Leningrad each boasted over twenty such bureaus.[170] Most of these were neighborhood-based general practice offices, though a few bureaus were established to serve a particular stratum of society, such as women with children, or to advise in certain areas of law.[171]

---

[167] *Otchet o deiatel'nosti prezidiuma leningradskoi*, p. 147.

[168] "V leningradskoi kollegii zashchitnikov," *Rabochii sud*, no. 4 (1928), p. 379.

[169] "Ob uplate," p. 1,313. When possible, fees were collected from the defendants by the college of defenders and placed in a general fund, which was then distributed among advocates on the basis of the number and complexity of cases assumed. The state did not guarantee the fees, however, and therefore it is likely that much of the money owed the profession went uncollected.

[170] *Otchet o deiatel'nosti prezidiuma leningradskoi*, p. 90; I. Glazkov, "Obzor deiatel'nosti iuridicheskikh konsultatsii Moskvy," *Revoliutsionnaia zakonnost'*, no. 1-2 (1926), p. 59.

[171] *Otchet o deiatel'nosti prezidiuma leningradskoi*, p. 90; Glazkov, "Obzor deiatel'nosti," p. 59; "Ob organizatsii iuridicheskoi pomoshchi po voprosam okhrany

Most advocates were reluctant, however, to leave their comfortable and often lucrative home-based practice to spend a shift of several hours in an overcrowded consultation bureau where the pressures of work were great and the financial rewards few. At first only practicing Communist defenders, the more socially conscious nonparty advocates, and beginning advocates could be relied on to serve their shifts, usually two a week, in the consultation bureaus.[172] Gradually, though, the bulk of the profession was drawn into this organized system of legal practice. This was due to the difficulty encountered during the middle years of NEP in establishing a sufficiently large private clientele[173] and to the threat of sanctions for absenteeism. The disciplinary proceedings heard by colleges in the early 1920s included a considerable number of cases brought for failure to provide legal services through the consultation bureaus.[174] By the end of NEP, therefore, virtually the entire profession was offering legal assistance on a part-time basis in the legal consultation bureaus. In Leningrad absenteeism in the bureaus had been reduced to around 10 percent by 1927.[175]

The impression of two systems of legal aid—one operating from the traditional private law office and serving bourgeois elements and the other based on organized consultation bureaus extending aid to the working masses—was encouraged by the authorities. However, this vastly oversimplified the delivery of legal services during NEP. While workers tended to prefer the public consultation bureaus to the alien milieu of the advocate's

---

materinstva i mladenchestva i sotsial'no-pravovoi zashchity detei," Tsirkuliar no. 95 Narodnogo Komissariata iustitsii/no. 128 Narkomzdrava, *Ezhenedel'nik sovetskoi iustitsii*, no. 26 (1924), p. 619.

[172] A. Bilinsky, *Die Organisation der sowjetischen Anwaltschaft* (West Berlin, n.d.), p. 9. The *dezhurstvo* duty was apparently heavier in the smaller provincial colleges and in rural areas.

[173] M. Ravich, "Ideia kollektivizatsii i kollegiia zashchitnikov," *Rabochii sud*, no. 24 (1928), p. 1,751. Only 13 percent of Leningrad advocates were said to have had a constant clientele. *Otchet o deiatel'nosti prezidiuma leningradskoi*, pp. 148, 157.

[174] See Veger, ed., *Organizatsionnaia rabota*, pp. 41-42.

[175] "Rabota iuridicheskikh konsultatsii Leningrada," *Rabochii sud*, no. 13 (1928), p. 991.

private office, the determination of where a citizen would turn for legal assistance depended less on class than on the type of legal problem confronting him.[176]

The legal consultation bureaus were engaged overwhelmingly in offering legal advice on common questions of civil law, such as those concerning family problems and labor disputes. The bureaus were in considerable measure information centers, as indicated by the amount of oral advice given either free of charge or for a nominal fee. Only rarely did citizens turn to the bureaus with problems requiring criminal or civil litigation.[177]

The advocates' private *kabinet*, on the other hand, tended to serve as the point of contact between lawyer and client when the client wanted to secure representation in court or to research a complicated legal issue. To put it simply, during NEP, Soviet citizens turned to the private practitioner when they were really in trouble. In Omsk, although the number of callers (*obrashchaiushchiesia*) to legal consultation bureaus was almost double the number to advocates' home-based practice, ten times as many persons with queries concerning criminal representation were received in the advocates' private offices.[178]

This preference for privately arranged representation in times of difficulty suggests that the public character of the consultation bureaus implied in the popular mind a connection between the state and the profession that would prevent advocates operating within the bureaus from pursuing the most vigorous defense of individual interests. Furthermore, the private offices were more conducive to an open discussion between the lawyer and a criminal defendant, or if he were under detention, his family inter-

---

[176] Shalamov, *Istoriia sovetskoi advokatury*, pp. 47-48. In 1925 the social backgrounds of callers to consultation bureaus and private offices in Omsk broke down as follows:

	Workers	Peasants	Employees	Others
Consultation Bureaus	28.1%	34.6%	18.9%	18.4%
Private Practice	11.7	59.1	14.7	14.5

Otchet prezidiuma omskoi, p. 17.

[177] *Otchet prezidiuma omskoi*, p. 17.

[178] Ibid.

mediary. By turning personally to a defender, and perhaps offering him payment at a level higher than allowed by law, the client hoped to ensure the advocate's undivided interest in the case.[179]

Although legal practice under NEP retained much of its traditional flavor, the economic and social transformations brought about by Soviet rule did begin to reshape the role of the advocates as purveyors of legal services to the population. This was evident in the kinds of cases handled by the profession. With the emergence of a legal order based increasingly on administrative entitlements rather than formal legal rights,[180] the advocates were concerned with a growing number of administrative law questions in their civil practice. In 1925, of the 2,800 callers to Novonikolaevsk consultation bureaus with questions relating to civil practice, over 1,000 sought advice on social security, labor, or housing matters.[181]

Furthermore, the development of a Soviet legal system fundamentally altered the clientele of the Bar. If the prerevolutionary profession served primarily the commercial and propertied elements in Russian society, the Soviet Bar attended to the needs of all social groups within its geographical reach. The formation of a network of legal consultation bureaus and the establishment of local fee schedules with charges graduated according to social category made legal services accessible to even the most needy. In Leningrad, for example, 34 percent of those seeking aid in the city's consultation bureaus in 1924 were unemployed.[182]

In spite of the progress made during NEP in providing legal

[179] Unfortunately, there is little evidence on the frequency with which advocates received payment above that allowed by the fee schedule (mikst). According to A. Mal'ginova, who worked as an advocate in Moscow from 1925 until the 1970s, the acceptance of mikst became a widespread practice only after World War II. Personal interview, Brighton, Massachusetts, January 9, 1984.

[180] This distinction is developed by Sally Ewing in her Ph.D. dissertation, "Social Insurance in Russia and the Soviet Union, 1912-1933: A Study of Legal Form and Administrative Practice," Princeton University, 1984.

[181] Otchet prezidiuma novonikolaevskoi, p. 9.

[182] Shalamov, Istoriia sovetskoi advokatury, p. 48.

services to a broad range of Soviet citizens, opponents of a private Bar criticized the profession for favoring "nonlaboring elements" and wealthy private businessmen, the so-called Nepmen, over the working masses.[183] While this criticism was not justified regarding the profession as a whole, there were areas where advocates, even during duty hours (*dezhurstvo*) at consultation bureaus, spent a disproportionate amount of time serving persons from outside the so-called laboring classes. At the end of NEP, according to one Soviet source, the "private-capitalist sector" accounted for one-third of all work done by Leningrad consultation bureaus.[184]

In certain consultation bureaus workers were indeed underrepresented among those seeking legal assistance. But this appears to have been due to the growth in large urban areas of a network of legal aid centers attached to factories and operated by trade unions. These legal aid centers were created to complement the consultation bureaus by providing legal aid to workers on labor questions. The scope of their activities gradually expanded, however, to include most routine (*bytovye*) legal problems, and by the end of NEP the aid centers were in direct competition with the advocates for the provision of legal services to the proletariat.

Whereas the combination of private law offices, consultation bureaus, and legal aid centers provided most urban residents with accessible and affordable, if somewhat hurried, legal assistance by the end of NEP, the rural population was, as before the Revolution, little served by the organized legal profession. Despite official campaigns to extend legal services to the countryside, the city-oriented Bar barely penetrated even those districts (*uezdy*) contiguous to urban areas. The primary stumbling block was economic. The poverty of the countryside, taken together with the dispersed rural population and the difficulties of transportation, made it virtually impossible for an advocate

---

[183] "Anketa Rabochego Suda," *Rabochii sud*, no. 3 (1928), p. 269.

[184] "Nuzhna li zashchita v sovetskom sude," *Rabochii sud*, no. 11 (1928), pp. 855-856.

to support a family on his earnings. An indication of the financial position of rural advocates is provided in a report of the Kostroma College of Defenders. While advocates in the district center received a modest monthly income of fifty-eight rubles in 1923, the advocates practicing in two of the outlying *uezdy* earned between ten and eleven rubles a month.[185]

The absence of advocates in most rural areas of the USSR during NEP resulted in a thriving underground Bar. Although constant protests were made against these "speculators in law" on the pages of Soviet legal journals, few measures were taken to restrict their activity.[186] According to a knowledgeable advocate writing during the mid-1920s, the relative tolerance that the regime exhibited towards the underground advocates in the countryside was due to their de facto position as watchdogs over the behavior of local party and government officials. The political authorities in Moscow were apparently unwilling to permit legal officials to stamp out the petition writers who kept the center informed of party and government activities in rural areas, where the problem of localism in politics was particularly acute.[187]

If the peasants found it difficult to receive competent advice on legal questions, it was virtually impossible for them to secure a qualified court representative. Because the underground advocates as a rule restricted their activity to composing legal documents, very few individuals appearing before rural courts did so with professional counsel during NEP.[188] But in this

---

[185] *Sbornik otchetov . . . prezidiuma kostromskoi*, p. 23. Whereas urban defenders in the Moscow region reported receiving monthly earnings of 112 to 150 rubles, rural advocates in the region earned on average only 38 rubles a month. Tarkopol'skii, "Chleny kollegii," p. 11.

[186] A. Kirzner, "Iuridicheskaia pomosch' na sele," *Proletarskii sud*, no. 4-5 (1926), p. 9; Kirzner, "Problemy iuridicheskoi pomoshchi derevne," *Proletarskii sud*, no. 8-9 (1925), p. 1.

[187] Rivlin, *Sovetskaia advokatura*, pp. 44-46.

[188] The need for court representation in the countryside was particularly acute, since the peasantry accounted for 56.5 percent of all convictions in the people's courts and 42.2 percent of all convictions at the regional court level. V. Undrevich, "Osnovnye voprosy reformy nashego sudoproizvodstva," *Revoliutsiia prava*, no. 1 (1928), p. 45.

respect civil litigants and criminal defendants in the cities did not fare much better. Despite the greater availability of advocates urban defenders participated in only a small minority of court cases. In Moscow advocates over a six-month period in 1923 participated in 365 court-appointed cases in the regional courts but were assigned to represent defendants only 4 times in the people's courts, which heard over 90 percent of criminal cases.[189] It is likely, therefore, that the laboring poor and the unemployed went without counsel in virtually all ordinary criminal cases during NEP.

Little can be said with certainty concerning the overall frequency of advocates' participation in civil and criminal cases in this period. A Soviet legal historian writing at the end of the 1930s estimated that during NEP more than 70 percent of all cases were heard without advocates.[190] This figure is almost certainly understated. If the load of court cases assumed by advocates in the medium-sized city of Omsk (seventy-three a year per advocate)[191] obtained over the Soviet Union as a whole (where courts heard slightly under four million criminal and civil cases in the accounting year 1926/1927),[192] almost 90 percent of court proceedings would have lacked an advocate.

To what extent the absence of professional representation in Soviet courts was due to the relatively small size of the Bar or to the refusal of judges to admit advocates as counsel is difficult to determine. It is known, though, that the right to legal representation remained contingent, as it had been in the civil war period, on the attitudes of individual judges toward the advocates, in spite of certain procedural guarantees contained in

[189] *Vtoroi otchet*, p. 7. In 1927, 92 percent of all first instance criminal cases were heard in the people's courts, with the remaining 8 percent tried by the regional courts. Reportedly, 4 percent of all trials heard at the regional level involved political cases (i.e., state crimes). "Reforma sovetskogo ugolovnogo protsessa," *Revoliutsiia prava*, no. 2 (1928), p. 70.

[190] Rivlin, *Sovetskaia advokatura*, p. 64.

[191] *Otchet prezidiuma omskoi*, pp. 5, 18.

[192] *God raboty pravitel'stva RSFSR*, Materialy k otchetu pravitel'stva za 1926-1927g. (Moscow, 1928), p. 173. The participation rate is based on an estimated six thousand advocates practicing in 1926.

legislation adopted at the beginning of NEP. In law, only the regional courts, which heard political trials and the most serious criminal cases, had the right to exclude the defender or, having admitted him, to dispense with the defense speech.[193] But in practice these restrictions on legal representation were even more likely to be applied in the people's courts. The people's court judges, who were often *vydvizhentsy* without legal training, were particularly suspicious of, and probably more than a little intimidated by, the well-spoken and urbane advocates.[194] Because the Bar was a suspect profession, the presence of an advocate in court was viewed as a liability by some defendants, who preferred to take their chances without counsel. Indeed, one Leningrad judge reportedly handed out stiffer sentences when defenders were present.[195]

When advocates did participate in criminal cases, their defense activity was usually restricted to the trial stage. Despite proposals by the more reformist elements in the legal community to permit accused persons to be represented by professional counsel in pretrial proceedings, the preliminary investigation remained off-limits to the advocates during NEP.[196] At the appellate stage advocates and underground advocates were active in preparing written appeals in civil and criminal cases, but they appeared in court only rarely.[197] In 1925 oral arguments were offered by advocates in only 4.7 percent of the cases heard by the Criminal Cassation Board of the RSFSR Supreme Court.[198] It appears, however, that the low incidence of oral advocacy in

---

[193] Rivlin, *Sovetskaia advokatura*, p. 39.

[194] According to one observer of the judiciary during NEP, much of the hostility between judges and advocates, which resulted in the suspension of the defenders' formal procedural rights, was explained by class differences. M. Andreev, "Zashchita i sud," *Rabochii sud*, no. 7 (1926), pp. 469-476.

[195] *Distsiplinarnoe proizvodstvo*, p. 48.

[196] Ugolovno-protsessual'nyi kodeks, pp. 310-311.

[197] A. Smirnov, "Podpol'naia advokatura," *Revoliutsionnaia zakonnost'*, no. 15-18 (1926), p. 81. It seems that the underground advocates may have acted frequently as middlemen in the transmission of bribes from clients to judges. Ibid.

[198] "Doklad o rabote ugolovno-kassatsionnoi kollegii za 1925g," *Ezhenedel'nik sovetskoi iustitsii*, no. 3 (1927), p. 73.

appellate cases was due as much to the high cost of retaining counsel in such cases as to court-imposed restrictitons. In those cases where advocates did appear before the Criminal Cassation Board, three-quarters of their clients were from the upper classes.[199]

Although during NEP most advocates continued to employ traditional methods of legal defense learned under tsarist rule, government officials responsible for the oversight of the profession attempted, with varying degrees of commitment, to instill a new approach to legal representation in the bourgeois specialists. In an effort to eliminate prerevolutionary traditions of legal defense, judges frequently subjected defenders to a dressing down in the courtroom for employing improper defense techniques.[200] For more serious violations of courtroom etiquette or the new standards of legal practice (standards usually set, it should be noted, by the judges themselves), judges lodged formal complaints against defenders with their college presidia. In one such case a young Moscow defender was brought before the college's disciplinary tribunal and charged with attempting to confuse the court by using semantic tricks in his defense speech. In view of his youth no formal sanctions were imposed, though he was ordered to work for the next six months under the close supervision of two experienced colleagues.[201]

Judges were particularly important in orienting defenders to the practice of law in the Soviet state since they communicated to the advocates, if only implicitly, their understanding of the role of the professional legal representative in the courtroom. Although defenders received varying, and occasionally contradictory, signals from judges on the appropriate behavior for the defenders in legal proceedings, the approach to law adopted by judges and other legal personnel indicated to the defenders the

[199] Ibid.

[200] M. Andreev, "Zashchita i sud," *Rabochii sud*, no. 7 (1926), pp. 469-473; N. Gribova, "Reforma UPK i rech' zashchitnika v sude," *Rabochii sud*, no. 24 (1928), p. 1,747.

[201] Veger, ed., *Organizatsionnaia rabota*, p. 35.

state's broad expectations regarding the profession's role in the legal system.

This general guidance was supplemented by the staging of show trials, at which defenders were expected to conform their conduct directly to the wishes of the state authorities responsible for organizing the cases. These trials, which became a common occurrence during NEP, were normally heard at factories during visiting sessions of the people's courts.[202] Often conducted between shifts to attract the largest audience possible, the trials were carefully scripted in order to stay within the time allotted and to deliver in the most convincing form the desired political message. Besides campaigning against current social problems, such as pilfering or drunkenness at the factory, the show trials sought to heighten the respect of the masses for the judicial system and to instruct legal personnel in the correct approach to courtroom behavior in cases of political significance. To the participating defender, and to the profession at large, the show trials indicated that a vigorous defense of clients' interests would not be tolerated when cases assumed an exemplary character.[203]

The effort to mold the human material from the old regime into members of a Soviet professional elite also involved the enlisting of defenders in the campaign to publicize the new legal order among the masses. Defenders were expected to articulate and legitimate state interests by giving public lectures as legal propagandists. This attempt at mass mobilization of the profession, which would at once popularize the legal system and alter the attitudes of the defenders themselves, appears to have been somewhat successful in terms of the level of participation by

---

[202] Epifanov, "O pokazatel'nykh protsessakh," *Rabochii sud*, no. 19-20 (1925), p. 829. In the Krasnopresnenskii district of Moscow, thirty-two such trials were staged in 1926 alone. See "Otchet o rabote narsuda krasno-presnenskogo raiona goroda Moskvy," *Proletarskii sud*, no. 1-2 (1927), p. 22.

On the trial of the Social Revolutionaries in 1922, which attracted worldwide attention, see M. Jansen, *A Show Trial under Lenin* (The Hague, 1982).

[203] A clear example of state pressure on advocates to play a supporting role in such cases occurred in Moscow in 1926 when, on the eve of a show trial, the prosecutor warned the advocate that it would be unseemly (*neprilichno*) for him to defend his client vigorously. *Distsiplinarnoe proizvodstvo*, p. 88.

college members. In Smolensk, for example, each member of the college was reported to have given an average of eighteen speeches on legal topics in 1927.[204] One enterprising statistician, obviously intent on proving the civic consciousness of the Bar to the political authorities, calculated that in the Gul College members spent 6 percent of their time on public lectures.[205] In addition to giving lectures Soviet defenders during NEP also held discussions with housing and labor collectives and even staged mock trials to illustrate points of law and procedure.[206]

But this activity was engaged in without strict external supervision, at least until the end of NEP. Most advocates, therefore, restricted themselves in lectures to a straightforward description of the Soviet legal system without the requisite political commentary. In some cases advocates even used the public forum to draw unflattering comparisons between the Soviet and tsarist legal systems. One advocate was brought before a college disciplinary tribunal for commenting that he did not attack the bourgeois legal order during lectures, and did not plan to, given the meager income he was receiving under the Soviet system.[207] This undisciplined approach to legal propaganda came under attack by supervisory institutions as NEP drew to a close, and in many areas the state tightened up legal propaganda work. In Kaluga in 1927, for example, the regional court assumed direct responsibility for planning and vetting defenders' public lectures.[208]

The role of the advocate in the legal system was gradually being recast during NEP, apparently in the absence of an officially sponsored campaign directed from the center. The actions

[204] M. Stroev, "Obshchestvenno-pravovoia rabota sovetskoi zashchity," *Ezhenedel'nik sovetskoi iustitsii*, no. 4 (1927), p. 103.

[205] A. Korotkov, "Sovetskii advokat kak obshchestvennik," *Revoliutsionnaia zakonnost'*, no. 11-12 (1926), p. 47.

[206] The staging of moot court proceedings was a tradition among Russian advocates dating back to the Great Reform period.

[207] *Distsiplinarnoe proizvodstvo*, p. 71. The advocate was issued a reprimand (*vygovor*) by the tribunal.

[208] *Piat' let raboty kaluzhskoi*, p. 24.

and writings of legal officials sought to shift the loyalties of the defender away from the client and towards the state. This was illustrated by the increasingly frequent references to the Bar as a public (*obshchestvennyi*), and not a private, institution.[209] According to many government officials, the advocate's first duty was to defend state and social interests, which required the advocate to take a position independent of that of his client. An assistant procurator of the RSFSR Supreme Court spelled out a possible formulation of a defense speech if the advocate believed his client to be guilty:

> Citizen Judges, if you believe the accused you will acquit him. But since I am fully convinced that you will not believe him, I will touch on only those circumstances that in my opinion appear to mitigate his guilt.[210]

In the view of this official it was always possible to find mitigating circumstances in the client's favor.[211] Other writers, however, called on advocates to join the prosecutor in condemning the defendant if they were convinced of the client's guilt.[212] It was even suggested by one legal official that defenders themselves should be prosecuted if they accepted a criminal case knowing that the client was guilty.[213]

As NEP progressed, the advocate as an "objective" actor in legal proceedings emerged as the Soviet alternative to traditional bourgeois legal practice in which the defender represented the "subjective" interests of the client. Although the new approach

[209] L. Fishman, "Ob advokatskoi etike," *Rabochii sud*, no. 8-10 (1924), pp. 33-45.

[210] M. Andreev, "Imeet li pravo zashchitnik otkazat'sia ot zashchity vo vremia sudebnogo zasedaniia," *Rabochii sud*, no. 1 (1926), pp. 35-37.

[211] Ibid., p. 38.

[212] S. Vaisman, "Zashchitnik v ugolovnom protsesse," *Rabochii sud*, no. 3-4-5 (1924), p. 135.

[213] Fishman, "Ob advokatskoi," p. 48. Not only was privileged communication between lawyer and client not recognized in the Soviet legal system but some even favored giving police the right to search advocates' files for material relevant to a case in progress. I. Slavin, "O zashchitnikakh i zashchite," *Ezhenedel'nik sovetskoi iustitsii*, no. 1 (1923), p. 2.

had as yet a limited impact on the behavior of advocates, a journal article from 1925 approvingly cited two cases in which defenders sided with the prosecution in calling for the conviction of their clients.[214] Thus was launched a method of legal "defense" whose fullest expression would be achieved a decade later.

THE BREATHING SPELL COMES TO AN END

Although the policy toward the Bar established at the beginning of NEP was subject to isolated criticism, to occasional adjustments, and to some local variations in the method of implementation, it continued for four years to set a relatively stable course for the profession's development. At the end of 1926, however, increasingly vocal criticism of the profession by prominent political and legal officials reopened the debate on the appropriate role of the advocate in a Soviet legal system. Once again those responsible for forming policy were asking publicly whether a professional representative of private legal interests was necessary in a socialist society.[215]

One of the driving forces behind the hardening of policy toward the Bar appears to have been Aaron Solts, chairman of the party Central Control Commission, an organization that was instrumental in the mid-1920s in stifling opposition within the party.[216] Solts was entrusted with the articulation of party policy on the legal system during NEP, and in 1924 he presented the official report on revolutionary legality at the Fourteenth Party Conference, the first time that legal policy had been considered as a separate item on the agenda of a major party gathering.[217] While Solts was initially concerned with the commanding heights of

[214] S. Reisman, "O zashchitnikakh," *Rabochii sud*, no. 25-26 (1926), p. 1,054.

[215] A debate on this question was held among national and local justice officials at the Leningrad regional court in October 1927. "Nuzhen li obvinitel' i zashchitnik v sovetskom sude?" *Rabochii sud*, no. 1 (1928), p. 75.

[216] E. H. Carr, *Socialism in One Country*, 3 vols. (New York, 1958-1964), 2: 215-216.

[217] Ibid., p. 439.

the legal system, such as punitive policy, by the end of 1926 he was turning his attention to the problem of legal assistance.

On January 1, 1927, the Central Control Commission reversed earlier party policy by issuing a directive that prohibited Communists in the colleges of defenders from engaging in private practice.[218] This directive was rescinded several months later after complaints by Communist defenders that a purely consultation-based practice was not financially viable. It served to indicate, however, the desired direction of policy on the profession.[219]

Dissatisfied with the predominant role of the private practitioner in the delivery of legal services to the Soviet population, Solts assumed the leadership of a campaign to shift the burden of urban legal practice from the colleges of defenders to the legal aid system operated by the trade unions. The campaign appears to have been approved at the Fifteenth Party Conference held in October 1926 and launched several weeks later at the Seventh Congress of Trade Unions.[220] Within the space of a few months the trade union legal aid centers became the dominant channels for delivering legal services to the proletariat in some areas. In Leningrad the number of legal aid centers expanded from sixty-eight in October 1926 to one hundred in January 1927.[221] By the middle of 1927 the supporters of the syndicalist approach to legal assistance had succeeded in expelling consultation bureaus operated by the colleges of defenders from court buildings in Moscow. In their place union legal aid centers were established.[222]

The legal aid centers were, in general, staffed by persons

---

[218] "Zapreshchenie chastnoi praktiki kommunistov-chlenov kollegii zashchitnikov," *Ezhenedel'nik sovetskoi iustitsii*, no. 1 (1927), p. 18.

[219] "Rabota kommunistov v kollegiiakh zashchitnikov," *Ezhenedel'nik sovetskoi iustitsii*, no. 21 (1927), p. 646.

[220] L. Davidovich, "Profsoiuznaia iuridicheskaia pomoshch' i kollegiia zashchitnikov," *Rabochii sud*, no. 9 (1927), p. 787.

[221] Ia. Davidovich, "Iuridicheskaia pomoshch' leningradskikh profsoiuzov triudiashchimsia," *Rabochii sud*, no. 3 (1927), p. 227.

[222] M. Bukhov, "Novye formy pravovoi raboty profsoiuzov," *Rabochii sud*, no. 1 (1927), p. 16.

whose approach to the practice of law differed radically from that of the mainstream of the Bar. The legal advisors in the aid centers, drawn primarily from trade union officials and factory jurisconsults, refused to represent "hostile" elements in society or to take criminal cases, even from workers, if the evidence seemed to point to the defendant's guilt. When legal advisors did appear in court, they were pledged "to express first of all the opinions and interests of the union."[223]

The trade unions were unable over the long run, however, to sustain this foray into the field of legal aid. The attempt to fundamentally alter the organization and character of legal services seems to have been defeated by the intolerable financial burden that it placed on the trade unions and, more importantly, by the increasing disillusionment of the political leadership with a syndicalist approach to legal practice.[224] By the end of 1927, although certain local officials continued to press for the syndicalist alternative, it was the collectivization of the Bar, and not trade union legal assistance, that appeared to offer the most attractive way forward to those intent on reforming private legal practice.

[223] Davidovich, "Profsoiuznaia," p. 789.

[224] Since no charge was made for 85 percent of legal services rendered through the aid centers, their operation was dependent on a substantial subsidy from union funds. S. Chlenov, "Kollegii zashchitnikov i iuriskonsul'ty profsoiuzov," *Ezhenedel'nik sovetskoi iustitsii*, no. 4 (1927), p. 88. It appears that only the larger unions in Moscow were able to sustain this burden.

Chapter Four

THE BAR UNDER SIEGE, 1928-1932

Zakony uprostit', uprostit', i eshche raz uprostit.'

—*Soviet justice official, 1929*[1]

The pressure for a major reorientation of party policy on all fronts began to build through the mid-1920s as the original goals of the New Economic Policy—economic recovery and social stability—were realized. For the ideologically flexible partisans of Stalin as well as the party's unbending left wing, which, as Leonard Schapiro notes, "had never been reconciled to NEP,"[2] the tactical retreat introduced by Lenin in 1921 was viewed increasingly as an impediment to the construction of a socialist order. Impatient with the modest rate of economic growth and with the limitations of political control, the party leadership abandoned the politics of gradualism. In the early months of 1928 the New Economic Policy began to give way to a drive for the rapid industrialization, collectivization, and proletarianization of Soviet society.

The fundamental reforms of the social and economic order introduced during this second revolution had a profound effect on law and legal institutions. The legal system reverted in considerable measure to the nihilism of the civil war period, during which political commands were carried out among the population without the mediation of legal proceedings. This was especially true in the countryside, where collectivization was introduced

---

[1] "To simplify, simplify, and simplify again the laws." "Revoliutsionno-pravovye perspektivy," *Revoliutisiia prava*, no. 2 (1929), p. 9.

[2] L. Schapiro, *The Communist Party of the Soviet Union*, rev. ed. (New York, 1971), p. 383.

by armed party detachments and troops of the internal security organs operating outside the law.[3]

The increased reliance on administrative, rather than legal, methods to implement social change and maintain public order brought a corresponding revision of legal theory. The concept of the withering of state and law, which had been downplayed in the legal literature of the NEP period, was now a topic for serious study and debate. Some theorists argued that the traditional structure of law and legal institutions would soon be eliminated in the USSR. The pervasiveness of this approach in academic circles led to the running down of legal education as law acquired the reputation of a dying discipline.[4]

But the practical and theoretical assault on the legal system resulted in the reform, and not the complete abolition, of law and legal institutions. Whereas under NEP law had acted as the protector of the existing order, it was now called on to facilitate a revolution from above. In the words of party and government officials writing at the time this required the "politicization" of the legal system—that is, the return to a purely instrumental role for law.[5] If terror was the sword of the second revolution, then law was to be its chisel, faithfully carving out the precise contours of the new order.

The politicization of the legal system introduced during and, in some cases, in anticipation of the industrialization and collectivization drives had three primary elements. The first was the creation of a more flexible body of legal norms. Gone was the concern for legitimacy that had contributed to the stability of laws during NEP. The revolution from above demanded a more malleable legal system that would be responsive to rapidly

[3] See M. Fainsod, *Smolensk under Soviet Rule* (Cambridge, Mass., 1968), pp. 238-264.

[4] R. Sharlet, "Pashukanis and the Withering Away of Law in the USSR," *Cultural Revolution in Russia, 1928-1931*, ed. S. Fitzpatrick (Bloomington, Ind., 1978), pp. 181-186.

[5] The term *politicization* is used with reference to criminal procedure by M. Strogovich, "K reforme ugolovno-protsessual'nogo kodeksa," *Sovetskoe gosudarstvo*, no. 9-10 (1932), p. 164.

shifting political demands. The various codes of law and procedure introduced during NEP were either revised or lost much of their authority, as executive organs issued frequent substatutory (*podzakonnye*) acts[6] to direct the behavior of local legal institutions and personnel. This was most evident in the field of criminal procedure, where the provisions of the code were undermined by circulars of the Justice Commissariat.[7]

The reform of the legal system also involved a speedier handling of legal proceedings, particularly in criminal cases. This was accomplished through the simplification of the criminal process, which enabled judges to decide the majority of cases summarily, without the benefit of representatives for the prosecution or defense.

Finally, the politicization of the legal system encouraged the application of the harshest possible penalties for social deviance, especially on the part of *kulaks* or those whose actions could be construed as directed against the state. The uncompromising crusade against class enemies launched by the party in the late 1920s alerted judges to the need for the issuance of exemplary, and not simply punitive, sentences against offenders. For most judicial personnel it was easier to err on the side of severity. Indeed, the zeal of local officials often exceeded the requirements of those directing the campaign from the center. Speaking at a conference of local justice officials in 1931, the justice commissar of the RSFSR, N. Krylenko, warned against the imposition of overused sanctions (*trafaretnye sanktsii*) by judges. He gave as an example a case from Western Siberia of one Kuznetsov, who was charged under article 58—antistate agitation—for the theft of a harmonica. The harmonica, it seems, had been

---

[6] See Chapter 3, note 32.

[7] On the developments in the field of criminal procedure in this period, see pp. 168-179. In criminal law, as Peter Solomon points out, the second revolution led to proposals to eliminate altogether the special part of the criminal code. Although the special part was never abolished, some judges began to ignore it and to be guided instead only by the general principles of Soviet criminal law and their own revolutionary legal consciousness. P. Solomon, *Soviet Criminologists and Criminal Policy* (London, 1978), p. 23.

stolen from the village correspondent (*sel'kor*), a representative of Soviet power.[8]

The placing of the legal system on more "political rails" reopened the debate on the appropriate role for the advocate in Soviet society. It was a debate that took place in an atmosphere of cultural revolution, where, according to Sheila Fitzpatrick, "the social and generational tensions of NEP came to a climax in an onslaught . . . on privilege and established authority."[9] The advocates found themselves under siege, both as lawyers and as representatives of the old intelligentsia. While there was a consensus in political and legal circles that the profession could not continue to function in its existing form, serious disagreements were voiced over the extent and character of reform needed in the Bar. Some prominent officials even proposed the complete liquidation of the institution of advocates. Among this group was Aaron Solts, who participated in, and presumably helped to organize, a public debate on the future of the Bar in the Theater of the Revolution in Moscow in April 1928.[10]

Known as the conscience of the party, in part for his resistance to the Stalinist terror against the political elite in the mid-1930s, Solts refused to bend revolutionary principles to fit the realities of a backward population and a poorly trained bureaucracy. According to Solts, the advocates and the adversary process itself were remnants of the old order that had no place in a

---

[8] *Organy iustitsii na novom etape*, 5-oe soveshchanie rukovodiashchikh rabotnikov iustitsii RSFSR, iiun' 1931g. (Moscow, 1931), pp. 12-13. This example was one of a number given by Krylenko from practice in the regional courts. He noted that "if I were to take . . . cases from the people's courts, you would see even greater curiosities." See ibid., and "Otchet Narkomiusta," *Rabochii sud*, no. 1 (1929), pp. 23-27. The number of criminal convictions increased by over 40 percent from the beginning of 1928 to the end of 1929. See M. Kozhevnikov, *Istoriia sovetskogo suda 1917-1956* (Moscow, 1957), p. 201.

[9] S. Fitzpatrick, "Cultural Revolution as Class War," in *Cultural Revolution in Russia, 1928-1931*, ed. S. Fitzpatrick (Bloomington, Ind., 1978), p. 11.

[10] "Nuzhna li zashchita v sovetskom sude (disput, sostoiavshiisia v Moskve v Teatre Revoliutsii)," *Rabochii sud*, no. 11 (1928), pp. 851-855. On the life of Solts, see "K 90-letiiu so dnia rozhdeniia A.A. Sol'tsa," *Sotsialisticheskaia zakonnost'*, no. 4 (1962), p. 76.

socialist society. The introduction of a socialist system in Russia eliminated the fundamental antagonism between the individual and the state and thereby removed the logical underpinnings from the adversary process. The proletarian court, he argued, was itself able to defend the interests of the population. Instead of a contest between the two hostile sides of prosecution and defense, Solts envisioned court proceedings in which an officially appointed rapporteur would make an objective presentation of the evidence before the bench.[11] This system, which resembled the criminal process employed in Russia before 1864, would have brought to an end the institutions of defenders and prosecutors.

At the opposite pole in the debate stood Peter Stuchka. The former justice commissar of the RSFSR, who was demoted in 1927 to chairman of the RSFSR Supreme Court, viewed the adversary process as a "cultural achievement" that should not be discarded. Although Stuchka also engaged in the ritual criticism of the shortcomings of his former profession, he was conspicuous by his unwillingness to join the calls for a major reform of the Bar. Stuchka was supported in his moderate position by several other high-ranking judges, including A. Vinokurov, the chairman of the USSR Supreme Court.[12]

A defense of the status quo was also made by the advocates themselves. At a debate held in October 1927 in the criminal

[11] "Reforma sovetskogo ugolovnogo protsessa," *Revolutsiia prava*, no. 2 (1928), pp. 72-74.

[12] "Reforma sovetskogo ugolovnogo protsessa, doklad N. Krylenko," *Revoliutsiia prava*, no. 1 (1928), pp. 120-121. "Uproshchenie sudebnogo protsessa i rol' zashchitnika v sude (Mneniia rabotnikov suda, prokuratury, i profsoiuzov)," *Rabochii sud*, no. 3 (1928), pp. 253-255; V. Kuritsyn, "Stanovlenie sovetskoi advokatury," *Sovetskoe gosudarstvo i pravo*, no. 7 (1971), p. 117. A good analysis of the differences between Krylenko and Stuchka can be found in M. Strogovich, "K reforme," p. 163.

As a result of my reading of Stuchka's contribution to policy debates in the late 1920s, I cannot agree with Peter Juviler, who places Stuchka in the camp of radical jurists along with Krylenko and Pashukanis. Stuchka appears to have attempted whenever possible to slow down the movement towards legal nihilism. P. Juviler, *Revolutionary Law and Order* (New York, 1976), p. 43.

department of the Leningrad regional court an advocate from a rural district near Leningrad questioned whether Soviet judges functioning in so-called workers' courts really enjoyed the confidence of the masses. She argued that the system required the continued participation of advocates to maintain the support of the population and to assist the overworked judges in the hearing of complex cases. Another Leningrad advocate put the profession's position even more forcefully. "If you eliminate the adversary process, you might as well dispense with court proceedings altogether and leave the determination of guilt to the investigator."[13]

The vast majority of legal officials were in sympathy with Solts' critique of the profession, though unwilling for practical reasons to embrace his proposal to abolish the institution. For this group it was essential to retain at least the concept of court defense, even if the role of the advocate in legal proceedings was reduced to a minimum. The consensus among political and legal authorities that the adversary process, and hence the Bar, could not yet be eliminated appears to have stemmed from a fear that such a move would compromise the authority of the legal system among the masses. During a debate on the reform of criminal procedure held in the Communist Academy in early 1928, a participant commented, ". . . tell a peasant he has no right to defense—that is not permissible."[14] The statement could also have been applied to the worker. In answers to questionnaires distributed by the Leningrad journal *Rabochii sud* [The Workers' Court], the chairmen of the Metal Workers' Union, the Building Workers' Union, the Textile Workers' Union, and the Union of

[13] "Nuzhen li obvinitel' i zashchitnik v sovetskom sude?" *Rabochii sud*, no. 1 (1928), pp. 76, 82. In an attempt to deflect criticism from the profession the presidium of the Leningrad College of Defenders cited approvingly the remarks of Bukharin and Kalinin that the old intelligentsia was constantly coming over to the side of the proletariat. "Nuzhen li zashchitnik v sovetskom sude," *Rabochii sud*, no. 3 (1928), p. 247.

[14] "Reforma sovetskogo ugolovnogo protsessa," *Rabochii sud*, no. 2 (1928), p. 87.

Agricultural and Timber Workers regarded the preservation of the Bar as necessary for the protection of workers' rights.[15]

A policy of reform of the profession was therefore adopted. Because of the divergent views represented in institutions charged with formation and implementation of policy on the Bar and because of the frequent changes in the general political climate, the reform of the profession underwent shifts in intensity and direction in the four years from 1928 to 1932. The major elements in the reform included the collectivization of legal practice, the purging of suspect elements in the profession, and the weakening of the advocate's position in legal proceedings, each of which will be examined in detail in the following pages. According to one jurist, this "sovietization" of the profession was designed to produce defenders who would:

a) give a Soviet interpretation to our laws, never forgetting the limits of legality in a revolution;
b) understand in Soviet fashion the essence of legal cases;
c) have as their goal not the service of the client but the strengthening of the Soviet social system.[16]

COLLECTIVIZATION

In the waning months of NEP, with private practice still the dominant method of providing legal services, two alternative systems competed for clients and for the favor of the political leadership. The first was based on trade union legal aid centers,[17] the second on local collectives of advocates operating under the supervision of the regional college. Inspired by the beginnings of the collectivization movement in agriculture, the republican justice commissariats, which stood to lose control over legal assistance if trade union legal aid displaced the Bar, began to encourage the creation of collectives in the colleges of defenders

---

[15] "Uproshchenie sudebnogo protsessa," pp. 257-259.

[16] V. Undrevich, "Sovetskii sud i zashchita," *Revoliutsiia prava*, no. 5 (1928), p. 271.

[17] As described in Chapter 3.

at the end of 1927. Although experimental at first, the advocates' collectives soon emerged as the preferred replacement for private legal practice, whose continued existence was viewed as incompatible with the construction of a socialist economy.

With the direction of organizational policy on the Bar decided, much uncertainty remained over the methods and tempo of collectivization. Unlike collectivization in agriculture, the collectivization of the advocates went forward without clear guidelines or institutional control from the center. Party organs appear to have provided only the most infrequent and general directives, thus leaving the republican justice commissariats with considerable flexibility in the organization of advocates' collectives. In some republics, in turn, a large measure of responsibility devolved onto the regional courts, which were in the front line of the collectivization efforts in the Bar.

In the absence of all-union coordination the existence of differing attitudes toward the advocates and the varied temperaments among local justice officials resulted in not one, but several, collectivization campaigns in the profession. Republican, and in some cases regional, variations were evident in the pace of collectivization, in the methods employed in the formation of collectives, and in the character of the collectives themselves. As in the civil war period, attempts to transform the bases of the advocates' practice resulted in the breakdown of a relatively homogenous Bar into a profession with significant local distinctions.

The drive to collectivize the advocates was perhaps most cautious in the RSFSR, where the process began in January 1928 with the formation of an exemplary collective in the Leningrad College of Defenders. Known as the Labor Collective (*trudkollektiv*), it initially contained 55 of the college's 841 advocates. Its members operated three local legal consultation bureaus. Over the remainder of 1928 thirteen smaller collectives were formed in Leningrad, bringing the total number of advocates working in collectives in the city to 176 by the end of the year.[18]

---

[18] M. Ravich, "Ideia kollektivizatsii kollegii zashchitnikov," *Rabochii sud*, no.

In August 1928, apparently satisfied with the Leningrad experiment, the Justice Commissariat of the RSFSR directed regional courts in several other areas of the republic to begin to organize exemplary collectives in colleges of defenders.[19]

At first the collectives provided no incentives for entrance to advocates with even the most modest private practice, and therefore the members of these early collectives were drawn almost exclusively from among the most impoverished advocates in the profession.[20] In an attempt to force the pace of collectivization the presidia of some colleges of defenders in the republic—most likely acting on the instructions of impatient regional courts— brought before the rank and file proposals for the mass transfer of the membership into collectives. These moves were vigorously resisted by the profession. In Moscow, presidium proposals to collectivize the entire college were defeated overwhelmingly by a vote of the city's advocates.[21] In the Russian republic, at least, no administrative measures were taken as yet by party or government supervisory organs to overcome the resistance of the advocates to collectivization.

Justice officials in the RSFSR did begin, however, to offer some economic rewards for entering collectives. On June 4, 1929, the Justice Commissariat issued a ruling that placed advocates working in collectives in the same official category as workers and employees (*sluzhashchie*). This resulted in an immediate and substantial reduction in housing costs for collectivized advocates and promised to bring other benefits, such as lower taxes and trade union membership.[22] Given the high op-

---

24 (1928), pp. 1,749-1,755; "Otchet leningradskogo oblastnogo suda," *Rabochii sud*, no. 3-4 (1929), p. 253; E. Begun, "Na putiakh k novoi sovetskoi zashchite," *Sovetskaia iustitsiia*, no. 31 (1929), p. 722.

[19] E. Dubkov, Demokraticheskie osnovy organizatsii sovetskoi advokatury (*Kandidat* dissertation, Moscow, 1964), p. 51.

[20] The average income in the Leningrad collectives in 1928 reached only thirty to thirty-five rubles a month—approximately the wage of a semiskilled worker. "Otchet leningradskogo oblastnogo suda," p. 253.

[21] A. Malone, Jr., "The Soviet Bar," *Cornell Law Quarterly*, no. 2 (1961), p. 267.

[22] "O stavkakh kvartplaty dlia ChKZ, vstupaiushchikh v konsul'tatsionnye kol-

erating costs for the private practitioner and his widely fluc-
tuating income, these incentives made entrance into the collective increasingly attractive.

But the exodus from private practice did not begin in earnest
until the late summer of 1929, when a major purge of the profession was ordered by the People's Commissariat of Workers' and
Peasants' Inspection on instructions from the party Central Committee.[23] This was followed several months later by an all-out
offensive to collectivize the Bar. On January 11, 1930, after
hearing a report on the state of the advocates' collectives by the
vice-chairman of the republican Supreme Court, Nakhimson,
the Board of the RSFSR Justice Commissariat instructed all
regional courts that "had not taken the necessary steps in col-
lectivizing the Bar to do so at that time" and to submit reports
on their activities to the Supreme Court no later than March.[24]
Over the ensuing weeks a number of administrative measures
were taken (including the withdrawal of the right of private
practitioners to appear in court) that resulted, at least on paper,
in the complete collectivization of the Bar.[25]

Coming after two years of public campaigns against the prerevolutionary intelligentsia and specific attacks on private legal
practitioners, the collectivization offensive launched at the beginning of 1930 broke the resistance of the advocates. In the
midst of the offensive a general meeting of the Moscow College
of Defenders was held that symbolized the state's victory in the
collectivization of the profession. According to official accounts,

---

lektivy," Tsirkuliar no. 82 NKIu, June 5, 1929, *Sovetskaia iustitsiia*, no. 23 (1929),
p. 543.

[23] "O proverke i chistke sostava kollegii zashchitnikov po RSFSR," Tsirkuliar
no. 108 NKIu, September 8, 1929, *Ezhenedel'nik sovetskoi iustitsii*, no. 37 (1929),
p. 378.

[24] "Rabota konsul'tatsionnykh kollektivov chlenov kollegii zashchitnikov" (Iz pro-
tokola no. 514/1, zasedanie kollegii NKIu ot 11 ian. 1930g), *Sovetskaia iustitsiia*,
no. 4 (1930), pp. 26-27.

[25] "Ob ustranenii nepravil'nostei, dopuskaemykh pri organizatsii kollektivov
ChKZ," Tsirkuliar no. 67 NKIu 1931g, in *Sbornik tsirkuliarov i raz'iasnenii Narodnogo Komissariata iustitsii RSFSR deistvuiushchikh na 1 maia 1934g.* (Moscow,
1934), p. 21.

the 672 advocates present welcomed the transfer to a collective form of work and committed themselves "to follow unswervingly the line dictated by the party and soviet power."[26]

The banning of private practice in the RSFSR in early 1930 marked the last wave of the collectivization drive nationwide. But in many republics collectivization was completed much earlier. In Belorussia no sooner had collectives been put forward as the appropriate organizational form for the advocates than republican officials announced the elimination of private practice. By August 4, 1928, all advocates in Belorussia were organized into regionwide collectives, apparently by administrative fiat.[27] In Uzbekistan the republican Justice Commissariat issued instructions to the regional courts in December 1928 to organize all advocates into collectives,[28] and in Azerbaidzhan advocates entered collectives in May 1929 on the basis of a plan adopted by the republican colleges of defenders.[29]

Intensive efforts to collectivize the Bar also began early in the Ukraine. On January 7, 1928, a conference of leading judges, procurators, and advocates was called by the court organization section of the republican Justice Commissariat to discuss the reorganization of the Bar. Shortly after the conference the court organization section began drafting a law on advocates' collectives, and over the first months of 1928 republican authorities ordered the collectivization of selected colleges of defenders.[30] Among these were the colleges in Kharkov and in Zaporozhe, where collectivization was preceded by what one journalist termed the "reconstruction" of the profession's personnel by the republican Justice Commissariat.[31]

[26] "Moskovskaia kollegiia zashchitnikov privetstvuet kollegiiu NKIu," *Sovetskaia iustitsiia*, no. 4 (1930), p. 27.

[27] Dubkov, "Demokraticheskie osnovy organizatsii sovetskoi advokatury," p. 52.

[28] G. Sarkisiants, *Advokatura sovetskogo Uzbekistana* (Tashkent, 1972), p. 27.

[29] A. Abdullaev, "Iz istorii advokatury azerbaidzhanskoi SSR (1927-1930gg.), in *Trudy II* (NII pravovoi zashchity: Baku, 1970), pp. 21-22.

[30] "Reorganizatsiia advokatury," *Vestnik sovetskoi iustitsii*, no. 4 (1928), p. 117.

[31] "V zaporozhskoi kollegii zashchitnikov," *Vestnik sovetskoi iustitsii*, no. 7 (1928), p. 218.

Spontaneous attempts to collectivize other colleges were made by regional justice officials, though these were halted by the Justice Commissariat of the republic. In the Ukraine, as elsewhere, the impulse from below for radical change in legal affairs was long held in check by the central authorities. In a directive of October 1, 1928, the Ukrainian Justice Commissariat warned local officials that, according to party instructions, the collectivization of the Bar was still at an experimental stage and therefore the organization of collectives could not proceed without the prior approval of the Commissariat.[32] The final push to collectivize the remaining Ukrainian colleges of defenders began in the summer of 1929 and culminated in the outlawing of private legal practice on October 1, 1929.[33]

Although the authorities could claim to have completed the collectivization of the Bar throughout the country by the spring of 1930, a weakening of the collective bases of legal practice set in almost at once. The retreat from collectivization, which continued through much of the 1930s, led to the reappearance of open private practice on a limited scale, to the division of regional collectives into smaller organizations, and to increased tolerance of a more traditional relationship between clients and advocates working through collectives. This retreat, which has been passed over in silence or openly falsified by Soviet historians writing on the Bar,[34] began with a decree issued by the

[32] "Vremennoe dopolnitel'noe polozhenie o iuridicheskikh konsul'tatsiiakh k kotorym prikrepleni chleny kollegii zashchitnikov likvidirovshie svoi chastnye kabinety," *Vestnik sovetskoi iustitsii*, no. 21 (1928), p. 643.

[33] "Pro poperdni pidsumki kolektivizatsii kolegii oborontsiv," *Vestnik sovetskoi iustitsii* (in Ukrainian), no. 15-16 (1929), p. 480. After publishing for six years in Russian, the Ukrainian legal journal *Vestnik sovetskoi iustitsii* began to publish in Ukrainian in 1929.

[34] In general, the period from the end of NEP to the adoption of the 1939 Statute on the Bar is an awkward one for Soviet historians. Not wanting to admit the inconsistencies in policy towards the advocates and the failure of the collectivization effort, most writers feign the existence of an unbroken line of development by implying that collectivization was a successful bridging policy between the private practice of NEP and the formation of carefully supervised legal consultation bureaus in 1939. In his *Kandidat* dissertation the current deputy head of the Bar Section

RSFSR Justice Commissariat on March 21, 1930. Coming six days after the party ordered a temporary halt to the collectivization offensive in agriculture, the decree restored to citizens the right to seek legal assistance from a specific lawyer, a right that had been withdrawn in mid-Janaury.[35] It appears that the imposition of this restriction had considerably undermined the confidence of the masses in their ability to receive effective legal assistance from the Bar. Republican justice officials later admitted that in many areas the public simply refused to turn to the collectives when it discovered that advocates would be assigned to citizens by the management of the collective.[36] This undoubtedly led to increased demand for underground advocates, who remained a constant threat to a state-controlled system of legal aid.

Over the ensuing months the republican justice officials ordered the breakup of regionwide collectives of defenders that had been formed in many parts of the country. These collectives had united all the members of a college into a single "group practice," thus enabling the college presidium to control from the center the distribution of cadres over the region, the operation of the collective's legal consultation bureaus, and the level of fees charged and income received by advocates. A single regional collective was often found in areas dominated by leftist officials, who wished to maximize control over the advocates' practice and to ensure a minimal income differential within the profession.

The dismantling of regional collectives began in September 1930 after the issuance of a decree of the RSFSR Justice Com-

---

of the USSR Ministry of Justice, I. Sukharev, devoted only one page of a twenty-page historical introduction to the Bar in the period from 1924 to 1939. I. Sukharev, "Organizatsiia i deiatel'nost' advokatury SSSR" (*Kandidat* dissertation, Moscow, 1973), pp. 29-30. In an interview with Mr. Sukharev in Moscow in March 1980 I was unable to elicit more information from him on the formative years of the Bar.

[35] "Ob izmenenii p. 4 p.p. 'd' postanovleniia kollegii Narkomiusta po voprosu o rabote kollektivov chlenov kollegii zashchitnikov ot 11/I 1930g," *Sovetskaia iustitsiia*, no. 11 (1930), p. 26.

[36] "Ob ustranenii nepravil'nostei," p. 22.

missariat directing local officials to organize all collectives into self-governing bodies functioning on the district (*raion*) level.[37] In most areas this reform considerably reduced the ability of college presidia—and thereby local party and government supervisory organs—to regulate the internal affairs of the profession. Responsibility for the operation of the collectives passed to their governing bureaus, elected by the rank and file. These bureaus, although under the general supervision of the college presidia, enjoyed considerable autonomy, in large part because party cadres had entered only a very few collectives.[38]

Not all local authorities, however, complied with the "raionization" of advocates' collectives or the transfer of power from the regional Bar headquarters—the college presidia—to the governing organs of the collectives. In Leningrad advocates complained that "even the detailed affairs of the collectives are decided by the college presidium over the entirety of our vast region. In practice the chairmen of collectives are appointed by the presidium. The collective bureaus are therefore the presidium's reliable agents." In addition, some local courts refused to disband regionwide collectives. In other areas, however, the courts tolerated the existence of neighborhood collectives of less than five advocates.[39]

The diversity found in the size and degree of independence of the collectives was also evident in their methods of remuneration. There were, for example, at least three different systems adopted by the collectives for distributing income to advocates.[40] The payment system favored by left-wing justice

[37] E. Mashtaler, "Kak rabotaet kollegiia zashchitnikov ivanovskoi promyshlennoi oblasti," *Sovetskaia iustitsiia*, no. 14 (1932), p. 29.

[38] On the lack of progress in party penetration of the Bar in this period, see pp. 163-164.

[39] "Ob organizatsii kollegii zashchitnikov," *Za sotsialisticheskuiu zakonnost'*, no. 12 (1934), p. 37; Mashtaler, "Kak rabotaet kollegiia," p. 29; M. Koblents and M. Antselovich, "Bol'she vnimanie rabote ChKZ," *Sovetskaia iustitsiia*, no. 28 (1931), pp. 22-25. In the Rostov region, for example, nine collectives had only two advocates each (Koblents and Antselovich, "Bol'she vnimanie," pp. 22-25).

[40] In some cases all three systems were to be found in collectives in the same

officials and employed in many larger collectives divided income equally among all members of the collective. This distribution of advocates' income, referred to by its opponents as leveling (*uravnilovka*), came under severe criticism in the legal press beginning in 1931. Not only did *uravnilovka* allegedly reduce the productivity of advocates, who were accustomed to practicing on a piecework system, it also ran counter to the current political campaign to introduce greater differentials into industrial wages. By the end of 1931 many collectives began to abandon the equal pay system.[41]

Other collectives employed a scaled salary system that divided pooled receipts among the advocates on the basis of qualifications and professional experience. There were usually three to five salary levels, with the differential between highest and lowest approximately five to one. This system, however, was also criticized for stifling productivity by providing no direct material incentives to the more efficient members of the collective.[42]

Although some collectives continued to use alternative methods of payment through the 1930s, the preferred system was by piecework. Payment based on services rendered was essentially a continuation of the system used under NEP, and indeed before the Revolution, except that the fees were paid into the advocate's account in the collective and then disbursed to the advocate after deductions were made for the operating expenses of the collective and the regional college.[43] The piecework system clearly hindered the development of a collective practice. While obligated to receive clients in the collective's consultation bureau, to follow the collective's guidelines on fees, and to use

city. See Dubkov, "Demokraticheskie osnovy organizatsii sovetskoi advokatury," p. 170. The various payment systems are explained in M. Kozhevnikov, "Ocherki o nashei zashchite (O sisteme oplaty truda ChKZ," *Sovetskaia iustitsiia*, no. 13 (1937), p. 16.

[41] M. Shalamov, *Istoriia sovetskoi advokatury* (Moscow, 1939), p. 51.

[42] "Kak rabotaet cheliabinskoi kollektiv ChKZ," *Sovetskaia iustitsiia*, no. 4 (1930), p. 29; "Ob ustranenii nepravil'nostei," p. 21.

[43] "Sistema oplaty truda ChKZ," *Sovetskaia iustitsiia*, no. 19 (1935), p. 16; "Oplata truda zashchitnikov," *Sovetskaia iustitsiia*, no. 22 (1934), p. 7.

the collective's cashier for the collection of fees, advocates were permitted to develop their own clientele and to receive the income from that practice. This was in fact more individualistic than Western law firms, where the workload is usually coordinated from the center and payment is made on the basis of salaries or profit sharing. Most collectives were therefore not group practices at all but rather loosely structured cooperatives that serviced and supervised individual practitioners.

In many cases the collectives were no more than legal fictions created to satisfy the supervisory organs. This was particularly true in rural areas, where advocates had been placed in district (*raion*) collectives on paper during the height of the collectivization drive without any attempt to alter their method of practice. The private, home-based practice also continued unchanged in most smaller towns, though efforts were made in the larger cities to compel advocates to practice through the collectives' legal consultation bureaus. [44]

In June 1931 the Justice Commissariat of the RSFSR signaled a further retreat from collectivization by partially rehabilitating the private practitioner. This retreat was apparently prompted by the broader rehabilitation of bourgeois specialists declared by Stalin on June 23, 1931. [45] In a circular entitled "On the Elimination of Errors Committed in the Organization of the Advocates' Collective" the Commissariat noted that, while it regarded the collectives as the most appropriate organizational form for legal practice, "advocates may not be compelled to enter a collective." Every advocate, it continued, had the right to practice privately outside the collectives. [46]

This circular, the Commissariat claimed, was merely the reiteration of long-standing policy on the collectivization of the profession. If errors were committed, they occurred "in spite of the frequent directives of the People's Commissariat of Justice

[44] Abdullaev, "Iz istorii," p. 23.

[45] It was now necessary, Stalin argued, to "treat those specialists . . . of the old school who have definitely turned to the side of the working class with maximum care," I. Stalin, *Sochineniia*, 13: 77, cited in S. Fitzpatrick, *Education and Social Mobility in the Soviet Union, 1921-1934* (Cambridge, 1979), pp. 213-214.

[46] "Ob ustranenii nepravil'nostei," p. 21.

that entrance into the advocates' collectives should proceed only on a voluntary basis and that advocates not wishing to join the collectives reserved the right of private practice."[47] As in the campaign to collectivize agriculture, responsibility for the use of compulsory methods in the organization of collectives was laid at the feet of local authorities—in this case the regional courts. But the campaign to collectivize the Bar forcibly was in fact ordered and supervised by the Justice Commissariat. Although it certainly was not aware of all the actions of local authorities, it set down the general policy line and supported courts in their application of it. Its *post factum* denial of responsibility for the methods employed in the collectivization of the profession must be viewed as a disingenuous attempt to deflect from the central authorities criticism of the excesses associated with collectivization and to portray those same authorities as committed to the redress of popular grievances.

A mass exodus from the advocates' collectives did not of course occur in the wake of this announcement. Most advocates, undoubtedly fearful that departing a collectivized institution would place their careers in jeopardy, continued to practice through the collectives. It appears, though, that an increasing number of persons used the collectives as a front for private practice, and some advocates even began to engage openly in private practice during this period. A Western scholar who traveled to the Soviet Union in 1932 was told that about twenty Moscow advocates (slightly over 3 percent of the city's profession) did not belong to collectives.[48] In the North Caucasus a published report of the local college of defenders noted that twenty-one (3.5 percent) of the region's advocates were private practitioners.[49] Judging from reports on private legal practice in the mid-1930s, it seems that private practitioners became increasingly common from 1932 onwards.[50]

The state of the Bar at the end of the second revolution made

[47] Ibid.

[48] J. Davis, *The New Russia* (New York, 1933), p. 154.

[49] Koblents and Antselovich, "Bol'she vnimanie," pp. 23-24.

[50] "Po dokladu o rabote kollegii zashchitnikov ot 13 dek. 1933g," *Sovetskaia iustitsiia*, no. 7 (1934), p. 23.

clear the superficial nature of the collectivization of the profession. In some areas, to be sure, there existed collectives that carefully regulated the practice of advocates and eliminated the direct economic relationship between lawyer and client. But in most regions the temporarily suppressed tradition of private practice was rapidly reemerging to erode the bases of collective practice. In his annual report for 1932 the chairman of a college of defenders in Uzbekistan noted that the practice of advocates was "collective in form but private in content."[51] For a growing number of policy makers in Moscow it was becoming apparent that the Soviet state had not yet found the appropriate organizational form for legal practice.

CHANGES IN PERSONNEL AND POLITICAL CONTROL

The collectivization of the Bar appears to have been accompanied by a massive reduction in the size of the profession. The Moscow Bar, for example, was reduced from over twelve hundred members in 1929 to slightly over six hundred members in 1932.[52] Much of the decline in membership resulted from periodic purges, both national and local in character, carried out in the colleges of defenders by party and government supervisory organs. Although extensive local purges affected some colleges in 1928, the first purge to include most, if not all, of the country's advocates was ordered by the RSFSR Justice Commissariat in March 1929, shortly after the Sixth Congress of Justice Workers had adopted a new, and harsher, line on the advocates. This review of the composition of the college of defenders was conducted by the regional courts with the participation of the Procuracy, Rabkrin, party, soviet, and trade union organizations, and the leadership of the colleges of defenders. The task of the purge commissions was to expel from the Bar all "anti-Soviet, undisciplined, or self-seeking elements" and any advocates ex-

[51] M. Mumin, "Sozdanie i razvitie advokatury v Uzbekistane" (*Kandidat* dissertation, Tashkent, 1975), pp. 76-77.

[52] Davis, *The New Russia*, p. 154.

hibiting "an unwillingness or inability to correctly fulfill the tasks of the defender in the Soviet court."[53]

After four months of work, however, the purge commissions had not produced the desired results, at least in the eyes of the central political authorities. In early September 1929 Rabkrin of the Russian republic announced a new purge of the Bar to supersede the one already in progress. Attacking the Justice Commissariat for not ridding the profession of individuals unwilling to follow the class line and for at times removing from the colleges young and conscientious Soviet jurists, Rabkrin extended the existing purge of the government apparatus to the Bar. This purge was carried out in public sessions with the participation of party and trade union organizations as well as working-class clients served by the advocates.[54]

The purge of the Bar continued until the end of 1930.[55] Information on the number of advocates purged is far from complete, though extensive statistics do exist for Central Asia, where scholars in recent years have been more forthcoming in their treatment of Soviet legal history. In Samarkand the number of advocates fell from 43 in 1928 to 19 at the end of 1929. Tashkent, on the other hand, fared considerably better, losing only 15 of its 85 members over this period.[56] In the RSFSR the college in Saratov lost 40 of its 70 members during this purge.[57]

[53] "O peresmotre sostava kollegii zashchitnikov," Tsirkuliar no. 37 NKIu, *Ezhenedel'nik sovetskoi iustitsii*, no. 14 (1929), p. 327.

[54] "O proverke i chistke sostava," p. 378. Accompanying this circular was a directive from the Central Committee of Rabkrin that spelled out the methods to be employed in the purge. For the context of the class conflict between the intelligentsia and the proletariat in this period, see S. Fitzpatrick, "Cultural Revolution as Class War," in *Cultural Revolution in Russia, 1928-1931*, ed. S. Fitzpatrick (Bloomington, Ind., 1978), pp. 8-40.

[55] V. Undrevich, "Organy iustitsii v 1929-30gg," in *Ezhegodnik sovetskogo stroitel'stva i prava* (Moscow, 1931), p. 329. It should be noted that in this period the purges implied expulsion from the profession and not "liquidation."

[56] Mumin, "Sozdanie i razvitie," pp. 66-69. Mumin's dissertation further develops the work of his academic supervisor at Tashkent University, G. Sarkisiants, whose book also provides a relatively candid picture of the purges in the Uzbek Bar. Sarkisiants, *Advokatura sovetskogo Uzbekistana*, pp. 23-27.

[57] V. Liubkin, "Shest' mesiatsev raboty kollektiva zashchitnikov v Saratove," *Sovetskaia iustitsiia*, no. 6 (1930), p. 28.

From 1930 to 1933 there were indications of additional purges, though they seem to have been local in character. No mention was made of all-union or even republic-wide purges of the profession, with the exception of a review of personnel in the Uzbek Bar ordered by the Central Committee of the Uzbek Communist party.[58] If any central direction to the purge of the profession existed after 1930 it came through party signals and not through an official campaign organized by government institutions.

One of the primary purposes of the purges was to soften up a profession in the midst of organizational and procedural reforms. Just as purges, and the threat of purges, in the early years of NEP paved the way for the party's seizure of the governing organs of the Bar, so the wholesale purge of the second revolution broke down the resistance of advocates to forced collectivization and to a less extensive and vigorous role in legal proceedings. Recall the example of the Zaporozhe College, where the formation of advocates' collectives followed immediately after the "reconstruction" of the college's membership.

The purges were also a means for the state to alter the composition of a profession that was still regarded by most legal officials as replete with "agents of the private capitalist sector," to use the language of the head of the Communist fraction of the Moscow College of Defenders.[59] Indeed the purges enabled the state to pursue a reduction in the size of the Bar, which had grown rapidly in urban areas in the latter years of NEP, to remove advocates who maintained a commitment to the values of the old order, and to introduce new and reliable cadres into the profession from among *vydvizhentsy* and recent graduates from Soviet law faculties.[60]

The upheavals in the profession's personnel, however, did not bring a fundamental shift in the social composition of the col-

[58] Mumin, "Sozdanie i razvitie," p. 87.

[59] Platonov, "K kollektivizatsii moskovskoi kollegii zashchitnikov," *Sovetskaia iustitsiia*, no. 2 (1930), p. 19.

[60] "O rabote vydvizhentsev v kollektivakh zashchitnikov," *Sovetskaia iustitsiia*, no. 2 (1930), p. 29.

leges. In those areas for which information is available prerevolutionary jurists remained the dominant group in the profession. In the North Caucasus almost half of the 590 defenders in the regional college in 1931 had worked in the tsarist legal system, with that group divided almost evenly between former advocates and former court workers, many of whom had occupied high positions in the judiciary. Although the number of Soviet-trained defenders was increasing in the college—113 had graduated from Soviet institutions of higher learning—it appears that most of these were peasants by social origin. Only 5 members of the college had proletarian backgrounds, and these were not *vydvizhentsy*.[61]

In Moscow, as well, prerevolutionary jurists continued to dominate the profession. In 1932, 53 percent of Moscow advocates had received a higher legal education before the Revolution, compared to only 14 percent who had been trained in Soviet institutions. The remaining advocates appear to have been *vydvizhentsy* "recommended" to the college by local party and trade union organs.[62]

The influx of some new elements into the Bar from Soviet law institutions and the trade unions brought no appreciable rise in party membership in the profession. In Moscow, where party representation in the Bar had always been high relative to other areas, Communists still accounted for only 8 percent of the city's advocates in 1932.[63] In Uzbekistan, party members made up less than 7 percent of local advocates,[64] and in the North Caucasus regional college less than 2 percent of the 590 advocates were Communists.[65] These figures include, of course, the many party members who were in the profession solely to carry out political assignments on the colleges' governing bodies.

The continued low level of party membership in the Bar was all the more remarkable because of the party's drive during the

[61] Koblents and Antselovich, "Bol'she vnimanie," p. 22.
[62] Davis, *The New Russia*, p. 155.
[63] Ibid.
[64] Mumin, "Sozdanie i razvitie," p. 90.
[65] Koblents and Antselovich, "Bol'she vnimanie," p. 23.

second revolution to penetrate professional groups. In other branches of the legal community, for example, party membership reached the saturation point in this period. The proportion of Communists among people's court judges rose from 83 percent in 1927 to 92 percent in 1931. Over 95 percent of regional court judges were party members by 1931.[66]

In those groups that had not been subjected to extensive party penetration during NEP the second revolution brought a massive infusion of Communist cadres. In 1930 alone, 3,500 engineers and technicians became party members.[67] Even in the Academy of Sciences, one of the institutions most resistant to political domination, party membership increased from 2 officials in 1928 to 350 in 1933.[68] The exemption of the advocates from this campaign illustrated the lack of importance attached to a profession that did not make a direct contribution to the great leap forward in the economy. It also reflected, no doubt, the continuing unwillingness of the party to expose large numbers of Communists to work that placed them in an adversarial relationship with the state.

Due to the continuing dearth of party cadres and the strength of prerevolutionary elements in the Bar, the assertion of rigid political control over the advocates was especially difficult in this period. When advocates' collectives were created as a means of linking the regional colleges and the mass of the profession, responsibilty for much of the governance of the Bar devolved onto the collectives, which were outside of party control. Although the collectives were subject to the supervision of the college presidium, they had their own organs of self-government—a general meeting, a governing bureau, and an auditing commission—that decided most questions relating to the oper-

[66] Kozhevnikov, *Istoriia sovetskogo suda*, pp. 264-265.

[67] K. E. Bailes, *Technology and Society under Lenin and Stalin: Origins of the Soviet Technical Intelligentsia, 1917-1941* (Princeton, N.J., 1978), p. 138.

[68] L. Graham, *The Soviet Academy of Sciences and the Communist Party, 1927-1932* (Princeton, N.J., 1967), p. 148. The increase in the party component of the Academy was due largely to the influx of Communist graduate students and support staff.

ation of the collectives. Not only did the governing bureaus oversee the legal practice of the members of the collective, they also had the authority to accept new members into the profession, subject to confirmation by the college presidium. Furthermore, direct responsibility for the training of young advocates and for legal propaganda work passed from the college presidium to the collective's governing bureau.[69] This significantly reduced the ability of party and government organs to shape the political and social composition of the profession.

Paradoxically, then, the collectivization of the Bar resulted in the weakening of the structure of political supervision over the profession. By placing the collectives between the rank and file of the profession and the existing regional colleges, the authorities had obviously hoped to establish effective control over the advocates at the local level. But the lack of party penetration of the collectives, taken together with the virtual absence of government supervision at the district level, gave the advocates in many areas greater organizational autonomy than they had enjoyed under NEP.

The reluctance of advocates to fully exploit the relative autonomy of the collectives was undoubtedly explained by the general political climate of the period. A major element of the second revolution was the campaign to root out bourgeois specialists who refused to respond to the new demands of industrialization and collectivization. Staged trials of bourgeois technical specialists, such as the Shakhty Case of 1928, alerted the entire prerevolutionary intelligentsia to the dangers of the slightest deviation from expected behavior.[70] Thus, even without a well-developed system of institutional control at the local level, the state was able to ensure its domination of the rank and file

---

[69] "Polozhenie o kollektivakh chlenov kollegii zashchitnikov," *Sovetskaia iustitsiia*, no. 6-7 (1932), pp. 57-59. It was an indication of the uncertainties of official policy towards the advocates that this authoritative legislation on collectives in the RSFSR did not appear until two years after the profession had been declared collectivized.

[70] See the excellent discussion of the Shakhty Trial and its effect on the technical intelligentsia in Bailes, *Technology and Society*, pp. 69-140.

of the Bar by instilling fear and despair over the direction of political developments. After more than a decade of Soviet rule the remaining resistance in the Bar was not hostile to Soviet power writ large but to further encroachment on the autonomy of the profession.

Over the period from 1928 to 1932 some governmental supervision of the profession was carried out by the republican justice commissariats and their regional subordinates, the courts. At this time the soviets ceased to play a significant role in the oversight of the Bar. But despite the concentration of supervisory responsibility within the so-called organs of justice, the methods and intensity of government control varied considerably from one college to the next. As during NEP, the central political leadership made no provisions for the coordination of supervisory policy on the Bar at the all-union level. With a USSR Justice Commissariat yet to be established, it was left to the republican commissariats to fashion their own approaches to the advocates.

In most republics it seems the commissariats engaged in only the most general and infrequent supervision of the profession, issuing directives when prompted by the demands of a larger campaign, such as the collectivization of the countryside.[71] It was only in the Ukraine where the Justice Commissariat adopted a markedly interventionist posture towards the Bar. The Ukrainian justice officials were less interested, however, in supervising the colleges than in financing the republic's underfunded state legal institutions at the advocates' expense. Over the early 1930s the Ukrainian Justice Commissariat extorted 1,800,000 rubles from the general funds of various colleges of defenders in the republic. According to official sources, this money was used to pay the salaries of Procuracy and Justice Commissariat staffs.[72]

Advocates in other areas were also subject to extraordinary

[71] Of the hundreds of circulars published by the RSFSR Justice Commissariat over the period from 1930 to 1933, only six related to the Bar. For the most important of these, see *Sbornik tsirkuliarov* (1934), pp. 19-34.

[72] "Ob organizatsii kollegii zashchitnikov," *Za sotsialisticheskuiu zakonnost'*, no. 12 (1934), pp. 46-47.

state demands on their collegial funds. At an oblast conference of advocates in 1933 three colleges "volunteered" to finance the construction of two tanks for the Soviet Army. Appropriately, the tanks were named the N. Krylenko and the A. Vyshinsky.[73]

One of the most flagrant violations of the colleges' limited autonomy occurred in the midst of the collectivization drive, when, responding to republican directives to improve the system of legal aid in the countryside, many regional courts banished large numbers of advocates to rural areas.[74] But this forced exile of advocates into the villages for long periods succeeded only in uniting the entire profession against the courts. The policy was later reversed by order of the republican justice commissariats.[75]

Although there was a continual erosion of the court's respect for the limited autonomy of the profession—with policies increasingly imposed on, and not suggested to, the college presidia—the relationship between the colleges and the regional courts varied widely, depending on the amount of guidance from the republican commissariat, the political attitudes of the judges, and the attention given to the colleges' affairs by the court. This last factor was particularly important. While the Soviet political and legal system was grounded on the theory of the careful monitoring of the behavior of intermediary organizations such as the Bar, supervisory institutions often found it impossible to allocate sufficient resources to fulfill the many oversight tasks assigned to them. In their monitoring of the Bar the courts were hampered by an overloaded docket and could not afford to assign individual judges or other court staff to oversee the advocates. Besides carrying out normal judicial functions the regional courts were responsible for the direct management of lower court organs, the investigative apparatus, the notaries, and the colleges of defenders. Thus, their supervision was largely restricted to

---

[73] "Organy iustitsii—krepite oboronu SSSR," *Sovetskaia iustitsiia*, no. 9 (1933), p. 7.

[74] "O meropriatiia po organizatsii iuridicheskoi pomoshchi naseleniiu," *Sovetskaia iustitsiia*, no. 14 (1929), pp. 326-327.

[75] "Ob ustranenii nepravil'nostei," pp. 21-22.

discussions with college leaders at periodic plenary meetings of the court. Although harsh in their dealings with advocates, the courts were often ineffective in influencing the behavior of the profession.[76]

The advocates were therefore able, even in the conditions of the second revolution, to maintain a measure of continuity in their professional lives. With the bureaucracy of control over the Bar still in its formative stages, the state was unable to ensure a sustained and systematic application of policy directives toward the advocates. This "authority leakage" contributed greatly to the decollectivization of the Bar over the mid-1930s.

SIMPLIFICATION OF CRIMINAL PROCEDURE

During the second revolution, the most vigorous policy debate relating to the Bar concerned the nature and extent of the advocate's participation in criminal proceedings.[77] This debate, which began in earnest in mid-1927 and passed through several

[76] In 1931 the RSFSR Justice Commissariat complained that the regional courts exercised only a *pro forma* supervision of the colleges of defenders. Their activities were normally limited to the hearing of periodic reports by the representatives of the profession and to the issuing of general guidelines. "O iuridicheskoi pomoshchi naseleniiu," Postanovlenie kollegii NKIu, 9 dek. 1931g, in *Sbornik tsirkuliarov* (1934), p. 33.

[77] The advocates' civil practice, which went into decline with the demise of NEP, was all but ignored in this period by legal journalists. In fact, very little is known concerning the participation of advocates in either criminal or civil cases after 1929. Not only was the legal press less forthright in its description of the legal system from 1930 onwards but the rich variety of sources publishing information on legal affairs under NEP did not survive the second revolution. After 1927 the yearly reports of the colleges of defenders were no longer published. Perhaps the greatest loss for the researcher on legal affairs in the interwar period was the disappearance by 1931 of legal journals such as *Rabochii sud*, published by the Leningrad regional court, *Proletarskii sud*, published by the Moscow regional court, *Vestnik sovetskoi iustitsii*, published by the Ukrainian Justice Commissariat, and the minor national legal journals, such as *Pravo i zhizn'* and *Sovetskoe pravo*. The concentration of editorial responsibility at the center paved the way for the introduction of a monolithic approach to legal affairs in the wake of the second revolution. On the legal press in the interwar period, see P. Solomon, "Legal Journals and Soviet Social History" (1983).

inconclusive stages before being redefined in 1933, engaged the most distinguished and influential members of the Soviet legal community. Characterized by conflicts on the personal, institutional, and ideological levels, the debate led to a marked decline in the role of the defender in legal proceedings.

Discussion of the advocate's rights in the criminal process took place in the context of a movement to simplify criminal procedure. The movement was launched in June 1927 with the publication of a draft Code of Criminal Procedure prepared by the RSFSR Justice Commissariat. This draft was based on the theses of the then Deputy Justice Commissar and Procurator of the RSFSR Krylenko, who appears to have been the dominant figure in the Commissariat, overshadowing the new Justice Commissar N. Ianson, a party activist from Estonia with no legal background. Krylenko became the draft's most visible proponent in the long, and eventually unsuccessful, bid to introduce it into law.[78]

Perhaps the most disputed feature of the draft was its size. The draft code contained only thirty-two articles, in comparison with four hundred in the existing code. According to Krylenko, the draft represented a move away from the capitalist fetish with rigid norms towards a socialist court system capable of responding to the changing demands of the proletarian dictatorship.[79] But the character of the courts' response to changing political developments was not left to local initiative under the proposals of the Justice Commissariat. Court behavior was to be shaped from the center by frequent directives on criminal procedure issued by the Commissariat.[80]

As the opponents of the draft were quick to point out, this two-tiered system of procedural norms gave the Justice Commissariat, and its effective head, Krylenko, extraordinary powers over the determination of procedural policy. Whereas changes

[78] Strogovich, "K reforme," p. 162. On the nihilist movement in other areas of law, see Sharlet, "Pashukanis and the Withering Away of Law," pp. 169-188.

[79] "Reforma sovetskogo ugolovnogo protsessa, doklad N. Krylenko," *Revoliutsia prava*, no. 1 (1928), pp. 105, 119.

[80] Ibid., p. 119.

in criminal procedure had previously required legislative confirmation by the All-Russian Central Executive Committee, under the proposed system the Justice Commissariat would be able to alter court procedure without discussing the reforms with higher government organs. While accepting the need for the simplification of criminal procedure, many legal officials opposed this bold attempt by Krylenko to appropriate for his institution exclusive control over criminal procedure.[81]

Krylenko had long been an imposing figure in revolutionary law and politics. Trained in law and history at St. Petersburg University, he joined the Bolshevik party in 1904 and shared the fate of many prominent revolutionaries in the last decade of tsarist rule: agitation in Russia, arrest, and exile. Mobilized into the Russian Army in 1916, Krylenko was given important assignments by the party in the armed forces in the wake of the February and October revolutions. At the end of 1917 he was named high commander of the nascent Soviet military. After the signing of the Brest-Litovsk Treaty with the Germans in March 1918 Krylenko began his career in the justice system, organizing show trials in the revolutionary tribunals on the instructions of the Sovnarkom. One observer remembers a particularly complex trial where Krylenko spoke for the prosecution for three hours without a note and without missing a detail. Having made his name during the Civil War as a talented and ruthless state prosecutor in political cases, he joined with Lenin at the beginning of the 1920s to campaign for the revival of a centralized Procuracy. During NEP, Krylenko served as the first procurator of the RSFSR and as deputy justice commissar of the RSFSR. He was appointed RSFSR justice commissar in 1931.[82]

---

[81] Ibid., pp. 112-121.

[82] Krylenko, the uncompromising justice official, was an experienced alpinist, a writer of travelogues, and an expert marksman. Like many of the old Bolsheviks, he was also a revolutionary ascetic. Krylenko was reported by a biographer to have forsaken his state car in the 1920s for a bike that he rode through the streets of Moscow dressed in cap, velvet field jacket, and riding breeches. See E. Boboritskii and S. Bogunov, "Tribun revoliutsii," *Sotsialisticheskaia zakonnost'*, no. 5 (1962), pp. 31-35; A. Vaksberg, "Politik, tribun, uchenyi, iurist (k 90-letiiu so dnia rozhdeniia N.V. Krylenko)," *Sovetskoe gosudarstvo i pravo*, no. 5 (1975), pp. 114-121;

Resistance to Krylenko's proposals for reform of the justice system were motivated in part by personal and institutional rivalry. But moderate elements in the Soviet legal community also disagreed strongly with Krylenko's attitude toward law and justice and were clearly worried by the procedural changes that would be introduced by the Justice Commissariat if the old codes were abandoned. Of particular concern were Krylenko's plans for a bifurcated judiciary. Krylenko advocated a return to the dual system of extraordinary and regular courts that had been the hallmark of Soviet justice during the Revolution and Civil War. In Krylenko's proposals the existing regional courts would function as extraordinary tribunals, hearing cases involving bourgeois elements or crimes against the state. These courts would operate under essentially inquisitional procedure, which excluded both prosecution and defense. The people's courts, in turn, would hear ordinary cases using trial procedure that retained certain elements of the adversarial system.[83]

But the adversarial elements in the commissariat draft were in fact reduced to a minimum. Whereas under NEP the presence of an advocate was obligatory in certain instances in the people's court, the draft code eliminated these provisions and permitted the advocate to appear in trial proceedings only at the discretion of the court. Furthermore, once admitted to the court, the advocate's ability to defend was severely undermined by the draft code, which gave judges the option of dispensing with the advocate's speech.[84]

The most vigorous opposition to the Commissariat draft and to Krylenko's maximalist approach to the simplification of criminal procedure coalesced around the legal section of the Com-

---

"Biografiia tov. Krylenko," *Sovetskaia iustitsiia*, no. 13 (1931), pp. 2-4; *Bol'shaia sovetskaia entsiklopediia*, vol. 13 (Moscow, 1973), pp. 1,502-1,503; M. Simonian, *Zhizn' dlia revoliutsii* (Moscow, 1963).

[83] "Reforma sovetskogo ugolovnogo protsessa, doklad," pp. 103, 109-110; Strogovich, "K reforme," pp. 162-163.

[84] G. Meren, "Zamechaniia k reforme UPK," *Rabochii sud*, no. 3 (1928), pp. 227-233; "Plenum okrsuda Leningrada," *Rabochii sud*, no. 13 (1928), pp. 106-107.

munist Academy, which was headed by E. Pashukanis. The jurists in the Communist Academy accepted the need for the further politicization of legal procedure but favored a fuller statement of procedural norms in the code itself and the retention of more traditional elements of criminal procedure. They held, for example, that the right to defense implied the right to a professional defender who participated actively in court proceedings. The court, in their view, was still not capable of managing without professional prosecution and defense.[85] In a rebuttal to the theses of Krylenko, the Academy jurist Estrin warned that it was time to stand up to the justice commissar lest the adversary system be abandoned altogether.[86]

It is ironic, then, that in subsequent Soviet accounts of the movement to simplify criminal procedure Pashukanis should be portrayed as a nihilist. This label appears to have been attached to him by Vyshinsky and his supporters who, during the move towards greater stability of laws that followed the second revolution, sought to discredit Pashukanis by associating him with the legal nihilism of Krylenko.[87] This is unfortunately a label that Pashukanis still wears in the Soviet Union and even in the West.[88] Although the theoretical implications of Pashukanis's "commodity exchange" view of law gave his opponents ammunition for portraying him as a nihilist, in the debate on criminal procedure in this period he showed himself to be a moderate

---

[85] "Reforma sovetskogo ugolovnogo protsessa, doklad," pp. 112-115.

[86] Ibid., p. 113. The strongest attack on Krylenko came from the jurist M. Klimov, who accused the justice commissar of being motivated only by institutional interests. "Reforma sovetskogo ugolovnogo protsessa," *Revoliutsiia prava*, no. 2 (1928), pp. 68-69.

[87] See, for example, Vyshinsky's comments on the "double-dealer" Pashukanis in A. Vyshinsky, *K polozheniiu na fronte pravovoi teorii* (Moscow, 1937), pp. 4-5.

[88] Juviler, *Revolutionary Law and Order*, pp. 41-44. The main student of Pashukanis in the West, Robert Sharlet, does not to my mind distinguish carefully enough between Pashukanis' general theory of law and his approach to legal policy problems during the second revolution. See R. Sharlet, "Stalinism and Soviet Legal Culture," in *Stalinism: Essays in Historical Interpretation*, ed. R. Tucker (New York, 1977), pp. 155-179.

who believed that Soviet society was not yet ripe for the elimination of the legal form.

As a result of resistance to the original Commissariat draft within the legal community, a number of amendments were introduced to the draft code. This represented a significant defeat for Krylenko. The number of fixed articles in the code was to be raised, thereby restricting somewhat the ability of the Justice Commissariat to shape procedure through administrative directives. In addition, the procedural position of the professional defender was strengthened by making the participation of an advocate obligatory when a prosecutor was present. Furthermore, proposals to employ two distinct forms of criminal procedure for the people's courts and the regional courts were eliminated.[89] This revised draft was then discussed, with apparently inconclusive results, at the Sixth Congress of Procuracy, Court, and Investigative Workers in February 1929.[90]

In late 1929, after two years of debate on criminal procedure, the amended draft was submitted for legislative review to the Council of People's Commissars of the RSFSR. The Sovnarkom made a number of important changes that redressed the flagrant procedural imbalance between prosecution and defense still present in the draft. First, it eliminated the article that gave the prosecution the sole right to decide which witnesses the court could call. Second, the provisions on court defense were also revised to extend the participatory rights of the advocates. Whereas in the Commissariat draft "the defense was to be admitted as a rule at the discretion of the court," the Sovnarkom version allowed the court to exclude the advocate only when the accused was caught red-handed or when the case was not especially complex. And finally, the Sovnarkom also insisted that the participation of a professional defender be obligatory when the defendant was physically or mentally incapable of conducting his own defense (e.g., in the case of minors) and when social

[89] Strogovich, "K reforme," pp. 164-168.
[90] Ibid., and A. Estrin, "VI s'ezd prokurorskikh, sudebnykh i sledovatel'nykh rabotnikov RSFSR," *Revoliutsiia prava*, no. 3 (1929), pp. 87-97.

organizations, such as a defendant's trade union, called for the presence of a defender.[91]

With these revisions, the draft Code of Criminal Procedure was submitted to VTsIK for legislative enactment. But VTsIK failed to adopt the legislation, apparently because of continuing conflicts among the republic's political leadership over the degree of simplification required in criminal proceedings. A number of provisions in the draft were introduced, however, as amendments to the existing Code of Criminal Procedure by a decree of October 20, 1929, issued jointly by the Sovnarkom and VTsIK.[92]

The stalemate on criminal procedure policy in the RSFSR continued over the ensuing years. In mid-1931, after almost two years in which criminal procedure did not appear on the political agenda, the republican Sovnarkom directed the Justice Commissariat and the Communist Academy to rework the draft code. The precise details of the third draft, which emerged from the Justice Commissariat in August 1931, are not known. But contemporary accounts of the document portray it as even more "political" than earlier drafts in providing maximum flexibility to the judge in the determination of court procedure. While rejecting the formal division between extraordinary and normal criminal procedure proposed by Krylenko, the new draft did set out a differentiated system of procedure. There would not be two distinct procedures in law but "a unified procedural order that would be so flexible and elastic that it would enable the court to vary its approach to different criminal cases." This would mean "a single procedure with two approaches determined by class differentiation."[93]

Although the third draft contained 134 articles, it appears to have simplified criminal procedure to an even greater extent than the previous version. In essence, under the new draft the wide discretion accorded to the regional court in earlier for-

[91] V. Undrevich, "O proekte UPK RSFSR," *Sovetskoe gosudarstvo i revoliutsiia prava*, no. 1 (1930), pp. 103-104.

[92] Strogovich, "K reforme," p. 164.

[93] Ibid, pp. 164-168

mulations was extended to the people's court. The courts were empowered to dispense with the questioning of witnesses and with the debate between the sides (*prenie storon*). The admission of the advocate to the court was left in most cases to the discretion of the judge, though provision was made for the obligatory participation of a defender in a limited number of cases.[94]

Like its forerunners, the third draft was never introduced into law. In fact, it appears that the draft was not even considered by the legislative organs of the RSFSR. After the draft was returned to the Justice Commissariat for further revision to bring it into line with the new approach to legal policy adopted at the Seventeenth Party Conference, public debate on criminal procedure ceased and did not begin again until 1933, at which time the legal nihilism of the second revolution was being abandoned by the political leadership.[95] After five years of discussion and three draft statutes officials in the Russian Republic were unable to agree on a new Code of Criminal Procedure.

The lack of central direction in the movement to simplify criminal procedure was evident in the adoption of new codes of criminal procedure in two non-Russian republics where the resistance to legal nihilism was less intense. The Uzbek Code of Criminal Procedure, introduced in 1929, and the Turkmen Code of Criminal Procedure, introduced in 1932, adhered closely to the theses on criminal procedure laid out by Krylenko in 1927.[96] In Uzbekistan, for example, the new code gave judges complete discretionary power over the admission of advocates to the criminal process. It also permitted advocates to refuse to accept a case if there appeared to be no grounds for a defense. This "freedom of conscience" clause for the advocates had been favored for some time by left-wing jurists.[97]

The absence of an all-union approach to criminal procedure was apparently due to the relegation of the issue to a low level of priority in party policy making. The central party organs in

---

[94] Ibid., p. 166.

[95] Ibid., p. 168.

[96] M. Strogovich, *Kurs sovetskogo ugolovnogo protsessa* (Moscow, 1958), p. 67.

[97] Mumin, "Sozdanie i razvitie," pp. 77-78.

this period seem to have interested themselves only in the general contours of legal policy. Without clear party signals on criminal procedure, decision making fell by default to government institutions—in this case to government institutions at the republican level, since legal affairs were not yet under the jurisdiction of an all-union commissariat.

The failure of most republics to introduce simplified codes of criminal procedure did not mean, however, that the procedural norms in place at the end of NEP continued to govern the advocates' position in the criminal process. Although Krylenko did not gain formal legislative approval in most jurisdictions for his approach to criminal procedure, he was able, at least in the RSFSR, to thoroughly undermine the existing Code of Criminal Procedure. He did this by issuing through the RSFSR Justice Commissariat scores of directives to the courts on procedural questions.[98]

This body of Commissariat directives, which in effect replaced the code, greatly simplified criminal procedure by widening the discretionary power of the judges. But perhaps more importantly, the constant barrage of instructions from the Commissariat, frequently overlapping with earlier directives, created such confusion at the lower level that judges often ignored written guidelines, relying instead on their own revolutionary legal consciousness to determine court procedure. Because of the hostility of judges towards the advocates, fewer constraints on judicial behavior resulted in a significant weakening of the advocate's role as criminal defender.

The hostility of the judges towards the Bar, which reached an unprecedented level of intensity in this period, appears to have had two primary sources. The first was class hatred. Whereas the advocates were drawn primarily from the prerevolutionary intelligentsia, judges came overwhelmingly from the laboring classes. Furthermore, during the second revolution, the bench

---

[98] Strogovich, "K reforme" p. 161. For examples of "simplifying" directives, see M. Undrevich, "Organy iustitsii v 1929-30g," *Ezhegodnik sovetskogo stroitel'stva i prava* (1931), pp. 329-333; and "O zashchite v sude," Postanovlenie kollegii NKIu, *Ezhenedel'nik sovetskoi iustitsii*, no. 26 (1928), p. 749.

was filled increasingly with worker-*vydvizhentsy* who had no legal training. On July 1, 1928, former workers comprised 34 percent of people's court judges in the RSFSR. Four years later the proportion of former workers was over 53 percent. A similar proletarianization of the courts took place at the regional level.[99]

The advocates, therefore, became ever more incongruous figures in the Soviet courtroom. Writing of his visits to Soviet courts in this period, the Western jurist J. Zelitch noted:

> The advocate . . . not infrequently sounds a complete disharmony by his attire, appearance, and manner of speech. He is often a person of a different sphere, politically as well as psychologically.[100]

For most judges the advocates represented the decaying bourgeois world that the Soviet state was dedicated to eliminating.

The class hatred of the judges towards the advocates led to the social, as well as professional, isolation of the Bar. In one region judges forbade court personnel from shaking hands with the advocates or offering them cigarettes.[101] This isolation was no doubt exacerbated by the rising antisemitism in Soviet society accompanying the *vydvizhenstvo* movement, which placed ill-prepared, though politically reliable, workers in responsible positions. In an exposé of the Bar issued in 1931 by the publishing house of the RSFSR Justice Commissariat, one finds for the first time in print antisemitic references to Jewish advocates.[102]

Another factor contributing to the hostile attitude of judges towards the advocates was the income differential between the two branches of the legal community—a differential that was

[99] Kozhevnikov, *Istoriia sovetskogo suda*, pp. 264-265; A. Vyshinsky, "Rol' kollegii zashchitnikov v bor'be za revoliutsionnuiu zakonnost'," *Sovetskoe stroitel'stvo*, no. 5-6 (1933), p. 8.

[100] J. Zelitch, *Soviet Administration of Criminal Law* (Philadelphia, 1931), p. 361.

[101] "Provesti ogosudarstvlenie instituta sovetskoi zashchity," *Sovetskaia iustitsiia*, no. 1 (1931), p. 25.

[102] V. Valerin, *Volch'ia staia—Zapiski chlena kollegii zashchitnikov* (Moscow, 1931), pp. 21-22.

heightened in some cases by the advocates' acceptance of *mikst*, or under-the-table payment from clients. In 1939 a judge was reported to have complained: "We work hard to earn eight hundred rubles a month and you defenders do nothing and receive a thousand."[103] Of course, some of the hostility between the judges and advocates was also due to the conflicts between these two groups in court. Many advocates continued to use defense tactics learned under tsarist rule, which in the view of the judges served only to obstruct the proceedings. It was claimed by court workers in Moscow that 70 to 80 percent of red tape in court proceedings was due to the advocates.[104] Furthermore, advocates still employed an "apolitical" approach in cases concerning such sensitive issues as the collectivization of the peasantry and speculation in scarce goods.[105]

Given the poor relations between the judges and criminal defenders and the heavy load of criminal cases assumed by the court (the number of convictions in the RSFSR rose from 1.1 million in 1928 to almost 1.6 million in 1931),[106] judges used their discretionary power to reduce to a minimum the participation of advocates in criminal proceedings. It appears that in this period advocates were admitted to people's courts as defenders only when a state prosecutor was present—that is, in about 5 percent of the cases. Advocates were excluded altogether from both first instance and appellate cases heard in higher-level courts.[107]

In most criminal cases the procedure employed in this period was little different from the inquisitional process used by Russian judges before the Judicial Reform of 1864. The judges rendered

[103] "Sud'i i zashchitniki," *Sovetskaia iustitsiia*, no. 12 (1939), p. 36.

[104] A. Vroblevskii, "Otvet sovetskogo zashchitnika nekotorym avtoram, mniashchim sebia uchiteliami," *Sotsialisticheskaia zakonnost'* no. 10 (1937), p. 92, citing an unspecified issue of *Vechernaia Moskva* of 1928.

[105] A. Vyshinsky, *Revoliutsionnaia zakonnost' i zadachi sovetskoi zaschity* (Moscow, 1934), p. 35; E. Mashtaler, "Kak rabotaet kollegiia zashchitnikov," p. 29.

[106] Juviler, *Revolutionary Law and Order*, p. 50.

[107] "Reforma sovetskogo ugolovnogo protsessa," *Revoliutsiia prava*, no. 2 (1928), p. 80.

decisions based on a cursory reading of the indictment, without benefit of either witnesses or defense and prosecution. And the indictment was itself suspect because reforms introduced during the second revolution enabled the case to proceed to the court directly from the police inquest (*doznanie*), thereby circumventing the intervening stages of the preliminary investigation (*predvaritel'noe sledstvie*) and the preliminary court hearing (*predanie sudu*).[108] Once again, as in the latter stages of the civil war, legal defense was all but suspended.[109]

[108] Strogovich, *Kurs sovetskogo ugolovnogo protsessa*, p. 66.

[109] The weakening of legal defense in Soviet courts was, of course, overshadowed by the widespread use of extrajudicial repression in the second revolution. In many millions of cases Soviet justice was applied on the spot in the exile or shooting of "kulaks" and other "antistate elements." In other instances punitive measures taken by the security police were hurriedly confirmed by the three-man special sessions of the OGPU—better known as the *troiki*. It is in this context that the erosion of the advocate's ability to defend Soviet citizens in regular legal proceedings must be understood.

Chapter Five

THE BAR AND THE TRIUMPH OF STALINISM, 1933-1939

You must know that there are two ways of
governing—by law and by force. The first is
proper to men; the second to beasts. But
because many times the first is insufficient,
recourse must be had to the second. A prince
must possess the nature of both beast and
man.

—*Machiavelli, as quoted by Vyshinsky in the
Case of the Trotskyite-Zinoviev Terrorist
Center, 1936*[1]

THE END OF LEGAL NIHILISM

The year 1932 witnessed the beginning of a gradual reorientation
of Soviet legal policy. Once the major social and economic transformations of the second revolution had been achieved, the role
of law began to shift from a facilitator of social change to a
protector of the status quo. In the language of Soviet historiog-
raphy this represented a movement away from legal nihilism and
toward the stability of law.[2]

---

[1] *Report of Court Proceedings in the Case of the Trotskyite-Zinoviev Terrorist Centre*
(Moscow, 1936), p. 138. In his prosecuting speech Vyshinsky accused Kamenev,
who had several years earlier contributed a preface to a translation of Machiavelli,
of sharing Machiavelli's approach to politics. It was Vyshinsky himself, however,
who appeared to be most influenced by Machiavelli's arguments for combining law
and terror.

[2] The Stalin Constitution of 1936 is commonly viewed by Western scholars as
initiating the stability of law movement. H. Berman, *Justice in the USSR: An Interpretation of Soviet Law*, rev. ed. (Cambridge, Mass., 1963), p. 63. R. Sharlet notes
that "there were earlier signs, but the publication of the draft constitution in June
1936 clearly foreshadowed the impending major changes in legal policy." "Stalinism
and Soviet Legal Culture," in *Stalinism: Essays in Historical Interpretation*, ed.

While the RSFSR Justice Commissar Krylenko and others remained wedded to the nihilist approach to law in the early 1930s, the RSFSR Procurator A. Vyshinsky, apparently enjoying the patronage of powerful forces within the party leadership, was rediscovering the potential for law under state socialism. In late June 1932, immediately following the issuance of a joint decree of the USSR Council of People's Commissars and the USSR Central Executive Committee (TsIK) "On Revolutionary Legality,"[3] Vyshinsky outlined his new approach to the legal system in a *Pravda* article and in a report to an open party meeting in the RSFSR Justice Commissariat.[4] Although the challenge to legal nihilism had little impact initially, by the end of 1933 the ideas of Vyshinsky were beginning to dominate the debate over the way forward in legal policy.

In the writings of most traditional Marxist legal theorists, foremost among them Pashukanis, the legal form was inextricably linked with capitalism.[5] But Vyshinsky stood Marxist theory on

---

R. Tucker (New York, 1977), p. 168. P. Juviler dates the shift in legal policy from 1934/1935. *Revolutionary Law and Order* (New York, 1976), pp. 58-59. But the movement toward stability of law began in fact at the end of the second revolution, in 1932 or 1933. Therefore, the Stalin Constitution should properly be regarded as the culmination of the movement's rather protracted first phase. A revision of the conventional wisdom on this point is long overdue.

[3] O revoliutsionnoi zakonnosti, *Sobranie zakonov i rasporiazhenii Raboche-Krestianskogo Pravitel'stva SSSR* (1932), no. 50, art. 298. This decree (*postanovlenie*), coming several months after the Seventeenth Party Conference, appears to have initiated the retreat from legal nihilism.

[4] See Polianskii, *Ocherk razvitiia sovetskoi nauki ugolovnogo protsessa* (Moscow, 1960), p. 48. This book, written by the prerevolutionary jurist Polianskii, is remarkable for its academic rigor and its willingness to discuss the politics of criminal procedure in the early years of Soviet rule.

The shift in policy on legal affairs was but one part of a broader movement to introduce a stable, monolithic brand of state socialism. Less than a month separated the beginnings of the campaign for socialist realism in the literary community from Vyshinsky's initial challenge to the legal nihilists. See A. Kemp-Welch, "The Origins and Formative Years of the Writers' Union of the USSR, 1932-1936" (Ph.D. dissertation, London School of Economics and Political Science, University of London, 1976), p. 31.

[5] See E. Pashukanis, *Law and Marxism: A General Theory* (London, 1978), and

its head by arguing that it was in fact under socialism that law reached its fullest expression. Instead of suspending traditional legal norms, he insisted that state policy should be directed towards the creation of a coherent body of distinctly socialist laws that enjoyed the respect of justice workers and the population at large.[6] This reversal of conventional thinking represented an extension to legal theory of Stalin's pronouncements of April 1929, when, in the final throes of his battle with Bukharin, the general secretary called for the strengthening, not the withering away, of the Soviet state. If the intensification of the class struggle envisioned by Stalin warranted a more powerful state, then surely law, integrally linked with the state in the minds of all Marxists, should be strengthened accordingly. For this application of the logic of Stalinism to the legal order, Vyshinsky, the ex-Menshevik, was propelled to a position of prominence in Soviet legal affairs.[7]

The new emphasis on socialist legality did not signify, however, a reduction in state repression. Indeed, in the view of Vyshinsky, state repression was "cultured activity" (*kul'turnaia deiatel'nost'*). Writing in 1934, he asserted that "at this stage revolutionary violence appears a manifestation of the highest act of human will that is directed towards the building of a new, higher socioeconomic structure." At stake was not the use of terror but who would control it and how.[8]

It was, paradoxically, the weakness of Vyshinsky's personal background that may have recommended him to the Stalinist political leadership as a spokesman on legal affairs in the wake of the second revolution. Compared to the then dominant per-

R. Sharlet, "Pashukanis and the Commodity Exchange Theory of Law, 1924-1930: A Study of Soviet Marxist Legal Thought" (Ph.D. dissertation, Indiana University, 1968).

[6] A. Vyshinsky, "Revoliutsionnaia zakonnost' i nashi zadachi," *Pravda*, June 28, 1932, p. 2.

[7] L. Schapiro, *The Communist Party of the Soviet Union*, rev. ed. (New York, 1971), pp. 471-473.

[8] A. Vyshinsky, *Revoliutsionnaia zakonnost' i zadachi sovetskoi zashchity* (Moscow, 1934), p. 27.

sonalities in the legal system, the old Bolshevik Krylenko and the brilliant theorist Pashukanis, Vyshinsky was an upstart. A Menshevik for fourteen years before the Revolution, Vyshinsky only joined the Bolshevik party in 1920. During the 1920s, he occupied positions in the educational and legal communities, often simultaneously. He was a lecturer, department chairman, and rector at Moscow State University before becoming a member of the Board of the Commissariat of Education in 1928. In the legal system he was assigned by the party to the presidium of the Moscow Bar for a brief stint in 1922 (he had practiced part-time as an advocate-in-training in Moscow from 1915 to 1917). He later worked as a prosecutor and as a judge, presiding in the Shakhty Trial in 1928. By the time of his appointment as procurator of the RSFSR in 1931 he had considerable experience in legal affairs. He did not have, however, the personal following or the attachment to a specific approach to law of his professional seniors, Krylenko or Pashukanis. He was well positioned, therefore, to lead a movement that would replace the heterodoxy of law of the second revolution with a Stalinist orthodoxy.[9]

The movement away from legal nihilism engineered by Vyshinsky appears to have been inspired in large measure by the desire of the political leadership to reassert firm, centralized control over the legal system. The increasing concentration of political power at the apex of Soviet society during the second revolution contrasted sharply with the devolution of decision-making responsibility in the court system. In order to rein in judicial power and thereby eliminate the spontaneity and localism associated with the erosion of legal norms, the state began to demand of judicial personnel strict adherence to centrally imposed guidelines.

The reconstruction of a stable edifice of legal norms began in

---

[9] *Bol'shaia sovetskaia entsiklopedia*, vol. 9 (Moscow, 1951), p. 540; R. Sharlet and P. Beirne, "In Search of Vyshinsky: The Paradox of Law and Terror," *International Journal of the Sociology of Law* 12 (1984): 153-177; V. Tol'ts, "A. Vyshinskii—Zhertva, akter, i rezhisser spektaklia sovetskogo prava (k 100-letiiu so dnia rozhdeniia)," in *Materialy issledovatel'skogo otdela*, Radio Svoboda, December 12, 1983.

1934 with the assembling of various legislative drafting commissions. [10] Although policy disagreements and the disruptive effects of the Great Purges prevented legislation from being introduced in this period on all areas of substantive and procedural law, a number of important measures were adopted, including the most celebrated product of law reform, the Stalin Constitution. By the end of the 1930s a new and more stable, if not wholly systematized, set of legal norms was in place. [11]

These legal norms were intended to replace revolutionary legal consciousness as the primary source of judicial decision making. No longer would the state tolerate the diversity in judicial behavior that had characterized the second revolution. This new policy was communicated to the judges through the public pronouncements of prominent legal officials, such as Vyshinsky, and through written directives, such as Supreme Court guiding explanations, which became more frequent and authoritative in this period. In a decree of the plenum of the USSR Supreme Court issued on June 7, 1934, lower court judges were directed to strictly observe all norms of criminal procedure, including even those that affected the "culture" of court proceedings, such as the composing of the court transcript. [12]

The reimposition of rigid discipline on the judiciary, many of whose members continued to favor a nihilistic approach to law, was also accomplished in this period through the centralization of the court system itself. Initially this meant the development of more active appellate oversight, with the higher-level courts hearing ever larger number of cases on appeal and by way of extraordinary protest (*v poriadke nadzora*). [13] This general su-

[10] A. Vinokurov, "K voprosu o novom polozhenii o sudoustroistve Soiuza SSR i soiuznykh respublik," *Za sotsialisticheskuiu zakonnost'*, no. 1 (1935), p. 35.

[11] Those laws affecting the Bar most directly were Polozhenie o sudoustroistve, *Vedomosti Verkhovnogo Soveta SSSR* (1938), no. 11, and Polozhenie ob advokature SSSR, *Sovetskaia iustitsiia*, no. 15-16 (1939), pp. 41-43.

[12] "O neobkhodimosti sobliudeniia sudami ugolovno-protsessual'nykh norm," Postanovlenie no. 47 plenuma Verkhovnogo Suda SSSR (7 iiunia 1934g), *Sbornik tsirkuliarov Verkhovnogo Suda* (Moscow, 1935), no. 88.

[13] In Soviet criminal procedure, cassation appeals are initiated by the defense or prosecution immediately after the decision (*prigovor*) is handed down. Once a de-

pervision soon degenerated, however, into the direct assumption of people's court cases by the Supreme Court of the USSR, which emasculated court institutions at the republican and regional levels. The increasing centralization of judicial decision making can be seen in the expansion of the membership of the USSR Supreme Court from eight judges in 1929, to forty-five judges in 1938, and to sixty-nine judges in 1946.[14]

The strengthening of the supervisory role of the USSR Supreme Court was accompanied by the formation and development of the Procuracy on the all-union level. Previously the Procuracy, which was responsible for criminal investigation and prosecution as well as the general supervision of legality, had existed at the republican level attached to the republican justice commissariats. The establishment of the USSR Procuracy in June 1933 was yet another step in the drive to centralize control over the legal system. But it was also a means of eroding the institutional prominence of the justice commissariats. Thus, in terms of the developing struggle between Vyshinsky and Krylenko for pre-eminence in legal affairs, this reform represented a clear victory for Vyshinsky, who became deputy procurator of the USSR.[15] Not only was the institutional base of Krylenko in the RSFSR Justice Commissariat weakened by the hiving off of the Procuracy but with the appointment of Vyshinsky as procurator-general of the USSR in March 1935 the new head of the Procuracy became only the second major legal official with all-union credentials. The other was Iagoda, the head of the People's Commissariat of

---

cision has gone into effect, the case may only be reopened by way of extraordinary protest (*v poriadke nadzora*) by higher-level Procuracy or court officials. Such protests are often prompted by the requests of advocates. Unlike cassation proceedings, hearings based on extraordinary protests are not restricted as to the questions that can be considered by the court.

[14] T. Dobrovol'skaia, *Verkhovnyi Sud SSSR* (Moscow, 1964), p. 56; *Vsia Moskva* (Moscow, 1929), p. 139.

[15] Whereas before the formation of the USSR Procuracy Vyshinsky, as RSFSR procurator, was administratively subordinate to Krylenko, in his new post Vyshinsky answered to the Procurator-General I. Akulov, who had been brought in from his party post in the Donbass to head the Procuracy. *Sovetskaia prokuratura-istoriia i sovremennost'* (Moscow, 1977), p. 109.

Internal Affairs (NKVD). Krylenko did not achieve all-union status until 1936, when he was appointed head of the newly created USSR Justice Commissariat.

In addition to the centralization of control over legal affairs the new course of Vyshinsky called for a renewed emphasis on the legal system as "a school to educate and reeducate unreliable elements among the working classes." It also sought to restore the credibility of legal proceedings among the population.[16] The arbitrariness of Soviet justice in this period, reminiscent of the civil war years, belied the claims of the state to faithfully represent the interests of the laboring masses. For all the talk of repression of class enemies, over 90 percent of criminal defendants in Soviet courts during the second revolution came from among the workers and peasants.[17]

While maintaining firm political control over the courts, it was therefore in the interests of the political leadership to create a stable system of laws in which justice at least appeared to be done. This sensitivity to the image of the Soviet legal system among the masses set Vyshinsky apart from Krylenko and other leftist elements in the legal community and helps to explain the seeming paradox noted by Western scholars between terror and the increasing respect for the legal form in the era of the Great Purges.[18] As the ideas of Vyshinsky displaced legal nihilism, the Soviet Union in the 1930s moved towards a new formalism in law in which legal norms became an important guarantor of the legitimacy and operation of the social and economic system.

A major part of the effort to restore legitimacy to the legal system involved a campaign to enhance the formal procedural rights of citizens in legal proceedings. This led, in turn, to the revitalization of the Bar. Criticizing the poor state of legal defense in the country, Vyshinsky asserted that the Bar was not an

[16] Vyshinsky, "Revoliutsionnaia zakonnost' i nashi zadachi," p. 2.

[17] V. Undrevich, "O proekte UPK RSFSR," *Sovetskoe gosudarstvo i revoliutsiia prava*, no. 1 (1930), p. 107.

[18] As R. Sharlet notes in the opening line of his essay "Stalinism and Soviet Legal Culture," "one of the paradoxes of Soviet history is that a major movement to revive legality occurred at the very height of the Great Purges of the Thirties" (p. 155).

outmoded institution; on the contrary, it was essential to the functioning of a socialist legal system. This signaled, however, not a return to the model of NEP but the full integration of the advocates "as soldiers in the socialist army who help the court to quickly and accurately decide the tasks of Soviet justice, in keeping with the interests of the masses and socialist construction."[19]

Vyshinsky's interest in a revitalized Bar appears to date from the beginning of 1933, when he made his first public pronouncement on the future of the profession before a general meeting of advocates in the Chernozem region.[20] His proposals to restore the Bar to a more respected place in the Soviet legal system were developed further in the opening article of *Sovetskoe stroitel'stvo* [Soviet Construction] of May/June 1933 and in December 1933 in a speech before the Moscow College of Defenders, a forum to which he would return several times over the ensuing years. In his article and in the Moscow speech, which was published with revisions as *Revolutionary Legality and the Tasks of Soviet Legal Defense*, Vyshinsky laid the foundations for a new policy on the Bar by offering apparent compromises on organizational questions of concern to the advocates in exchange for their commitment to a Soviet style of legal practice.[21]

Acknowledging the failure of the forced collectivization of the profession, Vyshinsky proposed the adoption of a strictly voluntary method of organizing advocates' collectives. Although he reminded Moscow advocates that it was necessary to reject proposals circulating within the profession for a wholesale return to private practice, he did admit that the transfer to voluntary collectivization would result in an expansion of the ranks of

---

[19] A. Vyshinsky, "Rol' kollegii zashchitnikov v bor'be za revoliutsionnuiu zakonnost' (po dokladu, sdelannomu na desiatiletii kollegii zashchitnikov)," *Sovetskoe stroitel'stvo*, no. 5-6 (1933), p. 12.

[20] "Tretaia oblastnaia konferentsiia kollegii zashchitnikov TsChO," *Sovetskaia iustitsiia*, no. 10 (1933), p. 15.

[21] Vyshinsky, "Rol' kollegii zashchitnikov," pp. 1-12; Vyshinsky, *Revoliutsionnaia zakonnost'*, pp. 28-42.

private practitioners "over a certain period." Only following "significant preparatory work and careful selection of cadres" would the collectivization of the profession begin anew, this time with the collectives able to "illustrate their practical advantages over the private practitioners."[22]

This conciliatory posture on collectivization was accompanied by an effort to enhance the position of the advocates as members of the legal community. Vyshinsky strongly criticized judges and prosecutors for underestimating the role of advocates in legal proceedings—an attitude that he seemed to attribute to the continuing appeal of legal nihilism among justice workers. He reminded court officials in Moscow that their "novel" approach to legal defense in fact reflected practice in Russian courts before the era of the Great Reforms.[23]

Vyshinsky's patronage of the Bar appears to have been welcomed by the profession. After a blistering public condemnation by Vyshinsky of the condescending attitudes of judges and prosecutors toward the advocates, the Leningrad college ordered that copies of the speech be distributed to all the city's advocates.[24] But his intervention was not without costs. The improvement of the profession's position in the legal system was made contingent on the advocates' ridding their practice of vestiges from the bourgeois past. One such vestige was "the tendency for the advocate to view his work in the Soviet court more from the point of view of the interests of the client than of the interests of the proletarian state as a whole."[25]

The correct approach to legal defense, according to Vyshinsky, was to be found in the show trials of bourgeois specialists, such as the Shakhty Trial and the Industrial Party Trial, where the defenders were able to adhere to "the principles of socialist construction . . . without harm to the professional responsibility

[22] Vyshinsky, *Revoliutsionnaia zakonnost'*, pp. 40-41.

[23] Ibid., p. 30.

[24] "Polozhit' predel prenebrezhitel'nomu otnosheniiu k zashchitnikam v protsesse," *Sovetskaia iustitsiia*, no. 21 (1934), p. 13.

[25] Vyshinsky, *Revoliutsionnaia zakonnost'*, p. 32.

of the defender."[26] In these cases the advocate accepted without question the arguments of the prosecutor establishing the guilt of the accused. In fact, I. Braude, the defender for Kuprianov in the Industrial Party Trial, began his defense summation by congratulating the prosecutor on his historical accusatorial speech. By way of justifying his own failure to put questions to the various defendants during the trial, Braude commented that "there was nothing to ask about." His only disagreement with the prosecutor related to the severity of the punishment: physical liquidation of his client, Braude argued, was unnecessary.[27] In this style of defense the advocate did not challenge the bases of the prosecution or even seek to mitigate his client's guilt. Instead, he pleaded for mercy.

While Vyshinsky's overtures to the advocates were made in a conciliatory tone, the clear threat of sanctions lay behind them if conformity to state expectations was not forthcoming. Toward the end of his speech to advocates in Moscow he warned: "To carry out the work of a defender or consultant is not easy. Your words, like an Australian boomerang, may return to strike you. It's all right if they strike only you—you will answer for it: but if they strike others, it's our common concern. Then what?"[28]

The personal intervention of Vyshinsky to revive the debate on the Bar appears to have been linked to his campaign to strengthen the Procuracy and in particular its division of state prosecutors. During the second revolution, the role of state pros-

[26] Ibid., p. 34.

[27] *Protsess Prompartii* (Moscow, 1931), pp. 488-495. In spite of his behavior as a cooperative defense counsel in the show trials of the 1930s, the Moscow advocate I. Braude enjoys a reputation as a courageous and talented jurist among Soviet and émigré advocates. The numerous émigré jurists with whom I have spoken consider his participation in the carefully scripted purge trials to have been forced and unavoidable. For a fascinating portrait of Braude at work in the 1930s petitioning the authorities for clemency for victims of the purges, see the recently published memoirs of Faina Baazava, *Prokazhennye* (Jerusalem, 1980), pp. 111-130. I am grateful to Peter Solomon for bringing this source to my attention.

[28] Vyshinsky, *Revoliutsionnaia zakonnost'*, p. 37. Vyshinsky also reminded the advocates that to criticize too severely the representatives of the state was to raise "objectively" the banner of counterrevolution. Ibid., p. 35.

ecutors declined significantly as adversarial trials were replaced by inquisitional proceedings conducted by judges without benefit of the sides. As noted earlier, prosecutors participated in only about 5 percent of all criminal trials in this period.[29] The movement away from legal nihilism brought a restoration of the adversarial bases of trial proceedings and therefore the reintroduction of state prosecutors and professional defenders into the courtroom. With the fate of state prosecution bound inextricably with that of legal defense in the minds of Soviet jurists, the drive to restore state prosecutors to prominence required a strengthening of at least the formal participation rights of the advocates in the criminal process.[30]

Vyshinsky was also conscious of the role played by advocates as transmitters of "signals from below"—signals that could assist the Procuracy in carrying out its supervisory function over the legal system. In applying on behalf of a client for the rehearing of a case by way of extraordinary protest, the advocates were able to communicate directly to higher-level procurators. This provided those in charge of the general supervision of legality with an additional source of information on local political and legal officials. For example, in October 1934 Vyshinsky issued an exemplary decree on the criminal acts of two militia workers that had been covered up by local officials. The investigation of the case was prompted by a letter to the procurator-general from a Moscow advocate.[31]

Vyshinsky's interest in the Bar and his proposals for its reform seem to have derived, then, from the broader struggle for power and policy in which he was engaged. While consolidating his own institutional base in the Procuracy, he sought to reduce the influence of his two major rivals, the RSFSR Justice Commissariat headed by Krylenko and the NKVD headed by Iagoda,

[29] "Reforma sovetskogo ugolovnogo protsessa," *Revoliutsiia prava*, no. 2 (1928), p. 80.

[30] Vyshinsky, "Rol' kollegii zashchitnikov," p. 1.

[31] "Za bezdushnoi biurokratizm k otvetu," Prikaz po Prokurature SSSR, no. 296 ot 8 okt. 1934g., *Sovetskaia iustitsiia*, no. 28 (1934), p. 7. The order (*prikaz*) was signed by Vyshinsky as Deputy Procurator of the USSR.

and later Ezhov. By putting himself forward as the patron of the advocates, Vyshinsky claimed for the Procuracy the authority to shape policy in an area previously subject to the supervisory jurisdiction of the Justice Commissariat. By stressing the educative and legitimating role of legal proceedings, he hoped to convince the political leadership of the advantages of open, exemplary justice over the secretive, summary proceedings of the NKVD, whose officials, Vyshinsky complained, often treated procurators with the same contempt that procurators reserved for the advocates.[32] Why hold a counterrevolutionary trial behind closed doors, he argued, when show trials such as the Shakhty and Industrial party cases heightened the vigilance of the masses and their support for the regime? Law was therefore not a façade for the terror of the NKVD but an alternative to it—an alternative that provided greater legitimacy and a more effective check on spontaneity in the use of repression at the local level. It was the commitment of Vyshinsky to "the development of the open, public, and adversarial character" (*razvertyvanie glasnosti, publichnosti, sostiazatel'nosti*) of Soviet justice that led him to campaign to revive the Bar.[33]

Although the intervention of Vyshinsky did not result in an immediate reform of the profession, it did place the issue on the political agenda. As a result, the Bar began to receive greater attention from its supervisory institutions and from the press. In mid-1933 the presidium of the Supreme Court of the RSFSR issued a detailed instruction on the work of the colleges of defenders. After noting the important role to be played by the profession in the strengthening of socialist legality, the court called for the imposition of stricter control over the advocates. This was to be accomplished in part by transferring the responsibility for supervising the Bar from the courts as institutions to individual judges. The Supreme Court also provided specific recommendations for improvements in the profession, including

[32] A. Vyshinsky, "Nashi zadachi," *Za sotsialisticheskuiu zakonnost'*, no. 5 (1935), p. 12.

[33] Ibid., p. 15.

an increased reliance on material incentives to raise productivity, the elimination of improper attitudes of court workers towards the advocates, and more extensive participation of advocates in defense activities.[34]

The encouragement given to advocates to involve themselves more fully in legal proceedings was, of course, highly qualified. While criticizing the advocates' failure to file appeals, their reluctance to meet clients under detention, and their generally weak defense of the accused, the court also complained that the advocates prolonged the proceedings unnecessarily, were willing to use any method to get the case dismissed, and disputed "obvious facts" of the indictment.[35] The authorities did appear, however, to sanction some increase in the quality as well as the quantity of advocates' participation in legal proceedings. In the spring of 1934 the RSFSR Supreme Court restored to membership in the Bar four advocates who had been expelled by a lower court for an overly vigorous defense of the accused. The lower court had ordered the expulsions when, after persistent attempts to reclassify the charge from a counterrevolutionary offense to a less serious crime had failed, the advocates appealed to the republican Supreme Court for a reversal of the verdict. The reinstatement of the advocates was reported prominently in the most widely read legal journal *Sovetskaia iustitsiia* [Soviet Justice] and was cited approvingly by the Armenian justice commissar during discussions at the First All-Union Conference of Court and Procuratorial Workers.[36]

The debate on the Bar initiated by Vyshinsky led to the drafting of new legislation on the profession at the end of 1934. A drafting commission headed by the secretary of the Central Executive Committee of the USSR, Enukidze, produced draft de-

[34] "Po dokladu o rabote kollegii zashchitnikov," Postanovlenie prezidiuma Verkhovnogo Suda RSFSR ot 13 dek. 1933g., *Sovetskaia iustitsiia*, no. 7 (1934), pp. 23-24.

[35] Ibid.

[36] "V prezidiume Verkhovnogo Suda RSFSR," *Sovetskaia iustitsiia*, no. 14 (1934), p. 20; "Pervoe vsesoiuznoe soveshchanie sudebno-prokurorskikh rabotnikov," *Za sotsialisticheskuiu zakonnost'*, no. 6 (1934), p. 39.

crees on the colleges of defenders and on court organization that were discussed in the January 1935 issue of the journal of the USSR Procuracy *Za sotsialisticheskuiu zakonnost'* [For Socialist Legality]. The contents of the draft on the colleges of defenders were in stark contrast to the official policy towards the advocates during the second revolution. While upholding the collectives as the preferred structure for legal practice, the legislation proposed by the Enukidze Commission permitted individual private practice. And, although the fees of private practitioners were to be based "as a rule" on a fee schedule, private arrangements with clients were also to be allowed.[37]

At the same time the draft attempted to tighten control over the profession by establishing colleges at the district level and by clarifying the supervisory responsibility of government bodies toward the advocates. At the republican level general supervision of the Bar was to be shifted from the justice commissariats to the supreme courts, thereby confirming a transfer of responsibility that had occurred in practice over a year earlier. Within the republican supreme courts the draft decree envisioned the formation of special departments for the supervision of legal defense (*osobye sektory po delam zashchity*).[38]

The draft was never submitted for legislative enactment, however. In fact, it appears to have been hastily withdrawn from consideration in February 1935, along with the draft on court organization. The demise of the draft legislation was almost certainly linked to the disgrace of the chairman of the drafting commission, Enukidze, who was removed from TsIK in early March 1935 and expelled from the party three months later.[39] His projects and allies at TsIK were naturally condemned by association. At a meeting of the leading cadres (*aktiv*) of the Moscow Party Organization on June 10, 1935, N. Khrushchev

---

[37] Vinokurov, "K voprosu o novom polozhenii," pp. 35-38.

[38] Ibid., p. 37

[39] Enukidze was expelled at the Central Committee plenum of June 5 to 7, 1935. See *Za sotsialisticheskuiu zakonnost'*, no. 7 (1935), p. 4, and Schapiro, *The Communist Party of the Soviet Union*, pp. 408-409.

assailed Enukidze for his "rotten liberalism" and his refusal to purge his own secretariat in spite of repeated warnings.[40]

The fall of Enukidze occurred in the midst of a wave of repression unleashed in December 1934 by the assassination of the Leningrad party chief, Kirov. The extraordinary measures introduced after Kirov's death were apparently designed to crush the opposition of party moderates to Stalin. As an ardent follower of Stalin, Vyshinsky was a major beneficiary of this campaign and, in particular, of the Enukidze shake-up. Enukidze's removal from TsIK was accompanied by the elevation of Vyshinsky to the post of procurator-general of the USSR. The previous procurator-general, Akulov, replaced Enukidze as secretary of TsIK.[41]

The attack on moderate elements in government and party institutions brought a hardening of official attitudes towards the advocates. The renewed emphasis on vigilance and the rooting out of internal enemies altered the tone of relations between the state and the profession and led to demands for a purge of hostile elements from the colleges. According to a legal commentator writing in the spring of 1935, it was pointless to discuss raising

[40] "Doklad tov. Khrushcheva na sobranii moskovskogo partiinogo aktiva," *Pravda*, June 16, 1936, p. 3.

[41] See *Za sotsialisticheskuiu zakonnost'*, no. 3 (1935). In his book on the Stalinist period Roy Medvedev asserts that Akulov was replaced because of his unwillingness to sanction the increased role for the NKVD. According to Medvedev, Iagoda and Vyshinsky conspired with the support of Stalin to remove Akulov. R. Medvedev, *Let History Judge: The Origins and Consequences of Stalinism*, ed. David Joravsky and Georges Haupt (New York, 1971), p. 217; Schapiro, *The Communist Party of the Soviet Union*, pp. 408-409.

See also the recent work of J. Arch Getty, *Origins of the Great Purges: The Soviet Communist Party Reconsidered, 1933-1938* (Cambridge, 1985), which challenges traditional scholarship on the triumph of Stalinism by uncoupling the Kirov assassination and the party expulsions (*chistki*) of 1933 to 1936 from the Great Purges. While Getty's research in the journals and archives of the period illustrates well the depth of policy disagreements and center-periphery conflict in the Communist party of the 1930s, it does not warrant his conclusions, which stress voluntarism everywhere except in the person of Stalin.

the authority of the Bar until unhealthy forces had been removed from the profession.[42]

Given the paucity of membership statistics on the Bar in this period it is not possible to reach firm conclusions about the effects of this crackdown on the profession. Although a nation-wide purge of advocates was launched, it was applied with vary-ing degrees of intensity throughout the country. In Uzbekistan, where a thorough purge of the colleges had been carried out over the winter of 1933-1934, the advocates were little af-fected.[43] In Moscow, on the other hand, an émigré study pub-lished in the early 1950s reported that four hundred advocates, most of whom had backgrounds as prerevolutionary lawyers, were expelled from the city's college in 1935.[44]

Whatever the scale of the purge, the Bar entered the era of the Great Purges a leaner and more carefully scrutinized insti-tution. After more than three years of preparation the Bar was now poised for a period of intense development, during which the state would seek to resolve once and for all problems of personnel, organization, and legal practice.

THE BAR IN THE YEARS OF THE GREAT PURGES, 1936-1938

Cadre Reform

Despite the public commitment of legal officials to restore the Bar to a prominent position in the legal system, the membership of the profession, which had been depleted during the second revolution, was not expanded over the period from 1933 to 1936.

[42] "Rabotu kollegii zashchitnikov—na vysshuiu stupen'," *Sovetskaia iustitsiia*, no. 11 (1935), p. 23.

[43] G. Sarkisiants, *Advokatura sovetskogo Uzbekistana* (Tashkent, 1972), p. 61. For a description of the purge nationwide, see M. Kozhevnikov, "Ocherki o za-shchite—kadry," *Sovetskaia iustitsiia*, no. 8 (1937), p. 36.

[44] A. Malone Jr., "The Soviet Bar," *Cornell Law Quarterly* (1961), p. 260. If the information is accurate, this purge would have reduced the membership of the college by one half.

In fact, it appears to have declined further. This left the Bar in the mid-1930s with a greatly reduced membership when compared to the latter years of NEP. As a result of natural attrition, purges, voluntary retirement from a declining profession, and the inability, or perhaps reluctance,[45] of the college to replenish its ranks, the Moscow Bar declined in size from slightly over 1,000 members in 1929 to approximately 500 in 1935.[46] The decline in Leningrad was on a similar scale, with approximately 350 members in the local college in 1936 compared to over 600 seven years earlier.[47] In Uzbekistan 120 advocates served the republic in 1936, whereas 163 had done so in 1928.[48]

The reduction in the size of the profession did not bring a significant realignment of the social groups comprising the Bar, though there was some displacement of prerevolutionary lawyers by graduates of Soviet legal institutions. Legal education, which had gone into decline during the second revolution, was finally revived in the spring of 1935 with the formation of the All-Union Legal Academy to train leading justice workers and with the development of subordinate legal institutes and schools, with programs lasting from three months to two years, to educate other legal personnel.[49] But the Bar occupied only a peripheral

[45] Like professional associations in capitalist states, the Soviet Bar has been reluctant to increase competition within the profession by expanding its membership. From the late 1950s to the present the number of practicing advocates in the city of Moscow has not increased, in spite of a significant rise in the city's population. E. Huskey, "The Limits to Institutional Autonomy in the Soviet Union: The Case of the *Advokatura*," *Soviet Studies*, no. 2 (1982), p. 214.

[46] P. Topalov, "K voprosu o reorganizatsii kollegii zashchitnikov," *Proletarskii sud*, no. 8 (1928), p. 8. In order to reach the figure 500 I estimated that in addition to the 360 advocates registered as working in collectives (*Vsia Moskva* [Moscow, 1936], pp. 65-67), 140 advocates were working as private practitioners.

[47] A. Liberman, "Kritika snizu i . . . antikritika sverkhu," *Sovetskaia iustitsiia*, no. 1 (1938), p. 42; "Otchet leningradskogo oblastnogo suda," *Rabochii sud*, no. 3-4 (1929), p. 253.

[48] M. Mumin, "Sozdanie i razvitie advokatury v Uzbekistane" (*Kandidat* dissertation, Tashkent, 1975), pp. 66, 90.

[49] O meropriiatiiakh po razvertyvaniiu i uluchsheniiu pravovogo obrazovaniia, *Sobranie uzakonenii* (1935), no. 13, art. 96, pp. 166-169. This decree contains much detail on the diverse legal programs offered and on the planned enrollments in the country's legal institutions.

place in the scheme to rejuvenate legal training. It seems that the major legal faculties prepared students exclusively for the Procuracy, the courts, and other state institutions. Students preparing for work in the state sector had almost no exposure to questions of legal defense. Those desiring to enter the Bar were usually educated in separate, inferior institutions, whose curriculum was less thorough.[50]

This lack of commitment to the training of a new generation of Soviet advocates meant that advocates from the old regime continued to make up a large and vocal minority of the profession. Indeed, in Moscow as late as 1937 more than half of the city's advocates had worked in the tsarist legal system.[51] The only exception to this pattern appears to have been in certain areas of the Ukraine, where the ranks of prerevolutionary lawyers in the Bar were devastated by purges during the second revolution. In Kiev the proportion of prerevolutionary lawyers among the city's advocates had been reduced to well under 20 percent by 1936.[52]

The continued prominence of bourgeois specialists in most colleges, which distinguished the Bar not only from other branches of the legal profession but also from most other professional groups, prompted the state to launch a determined drive in 1936 to alter the social complexion of the colleges of defenders. This was to be achieved primarily through the addition of large numbers of young Soviet cadres into the profession, though it was not clear where the cadres were to come from. In Moscow a goal of 500 new members was set for the local college of defenders, which promised to expand the college's membership by more than 60 percent. Figures from the first year of this campaign, 1936 to 1937, show that 145 new members were

[50] J. Hazard, *Law Student Life in Moscow* (Zug, 1978), letters 34, 49, 60; course notes (court organization), pp. 39 and 143. The collected letters and course notes of John Hazard's days in Moscow in the 1930s are an invaluable source on the Soviet legal system during this period.

[51] "Na sobranii moskovskikh advokatov," *Sovetskaia iustitsiia*, no. 22 (1937), pp. 42-43.

[52] M. Kozhevnikov, "Zashchita na Ukraine," *Sovetskaia iustitsiia*, no. 16 (1937), p. 25.

accepted into the Moscow college, including 90 individuals recently graduated from Soviet law faculties. But many of the remaining Soviet cadres were drawn from the ranks of former court and procuratorial workers who were forced out of state institutions for reasons of incompetence or political unreliability. Only moderate progress appears to have been made in bringing *vydvizhentsy* with proletarian backgrounds into the profession. In Moscow former workers accounted for less than 8 percent of the city's advocates in 1937.[53]

Although the membership goals set for the colleges of defenders do not appear to have been met in this period, the profession did undergo a significant expansion. By the middle of 1938 the Soviet Bar included more than six thousand members, which approached the size of the profession in the latter years of NEP. Advocates with a prerevolutionary university education now accounted for less than 30 percent of the profession.[54]

The expansion of the profession was accompanied by periodic purges. Over the years 1936 and 1937 the removal of advocates appears to have occurred gradually and on a small scale. Most expulsions came as a result of disciplinary proceedings carried out by the colleges themselves on the basis of complaints by party and government organs. Disciplinary cases in Moscow, for example, were sometimes heard during all-night sessions of the college presidium, thus indicating its reliance on instructions from the ever vigilant repressive organs.[55] Although the exact number of expulsions by disciplinary means is not known, the USSR Justice Commissariat did report in late 1937 that it had

[53] "Na sobranii moskovskikh advokatov," pp. 42-43. Dina Kaminskaya notes that in the late 1930s "most of the newer members [of the Bar] were former investigators of the NKVD or judges who had been dismissed from the bench and by order of the party were fixed up with jobs in advocacy." See Kaminskaya, *Final Judgment: My Life as a Soviet Defense Attorney* (New York, 1982), p. 28, and personal interview with D. Kaminskaya and K. Simis, Arlington, Virginia, December 1980.

[54] Spektorov, "Reshitel'no uluchshit' rabotu sovetskoi advokatury," *Sovetskaia iustitsiia*, no. 16 (1928), p. 24.

[55] "Na sobranii moskovskikh advokatov," p. 43.

just reviewed eighty-one applications from advocates seeking reinstatement to the profession.[56]

The methods and intensity of the purges changed in early 1938 after the arrest of Krylenko and the resulting shake-up in the USSR Justice Commissariat.[57] At meetings of the new *aktiv* of the USSR Justice Commissariat between March 14 and 16, 1938, the colleges of advocates were condemned as commercial enterprises whose membership was made up primarily of "former people" (*byvshie liudi*). The colleges of defenders, which it was alleged had been protected by liberal elements in the organs of justice, were now subjected to an investigation by party, trade union, and other organs.[58] Information on the purges spawned by this investigation is incomplete, but it was reported by the émigré Procurator Semenov that 165 advocates were arrested in a single night in Moscow. The émigrée A. Mal'ginova, who lost a brother in the purge of March 1938, estimated that 150 advocates in the city disappeared that day. Although it might have been expected that the repression would fall most heavily on prerevolutionary elements in the profession, this evidently was not the case. Mal'ginova, a practicing advocate in Moscow in this period, saw no link between social and occupational background and the purge, while Semenov claimed that in the Moscow college most of those purged entered the Bar during the Soviet period.[59] The purges did not, therefore, seem to contribute to a realignment of social forces in the profession.

[56] "O poriadke rassmotreniia distsiplinarnykh del chlenov kollegii zashchitnikov," *Sovetskaia iustitsiia*, no. 23 (1937), p. 55. Thirty of the requests were granted.

[57] Krylenko's place as USSR justice commissar was taken by N. Rychkov, a little-known justice official who posed no threat to the dominance of the Procurator-General Vyshinsky or the NKVD head Ezhov in legal affairs. On Krylenko's fate after his arrest, see A. Solzhenitsyn, *The Gulag Archipelago*, 3 vols. (New York, 1973-1974), 1: 395.

[58] Spektorov, "Reshitel'no uluchshit'," p. 25.

[59] Personal interview with A. Mal'ginova, Brighton, Massachusetts, January 9, 1984. Malone, "The Soviet Bar," p. 269, citing N. Semenov, "Advokatura v SSSR" (Munich, 1954), p. 17. The unpublished manuscript by Semenov was written while the author was an associate with the Institute for the Study of the USSR in Munich. I have tried for several years, without success, to locate this manuscript.

Party and Government Control over the Advocates

While a measure of success was achieved in introducing Soviet-trained personnel into the Bar over the period from 1936 to 1938, the cadre reform did not bring a significant increase in party penetration of the profession. Virtually all the new entrants to the colleges came from nonparty backgrounds. The proportion of party members in the Bar in this period appears to have been less than 10 percent nationwide. In the two largest colleges in the country, those in Moscow and Leningrad, party members accounted for only 7 and 9 percent, respectively, of the cities' advocates in 1937.[60] But party penetration was even weaker than these figures indicate, since a high proportion of Communist advocates continued to be affiliated with the colleges only for part-time political work. In Moscow, one-half of the party members of the college were not engaged in the practice of law.[61]

Traditionally the primary function of Communist advocates had been to ensure party domination of the governing organ of the college, the presidium. As described earlier, party control of the presidium had been achieved with some difficulty during NEP.[62] But in the late 1930s advocates in several areas began to successfully challenge the single slate of presidium candidates put forward by the party. On a number of occasions reelections had to be called by the supervisory institutions after the advocates had installed "undesirable" elements on the presidium.[63] In other cases the supervisory institutions removed unwanted individuals from the presidium by administrative means, as in the Ukraine in 1937, when the Kharkov Regional Party Com-

---

[60] "Na sobranii moskovskikh advokatov," pp. 42-43; Liberman, "Kritika snizu," p. 42.

[61] "Na sobranii moskovskikh advokaktov," pp. 42-43.

[62] See Chapter 3.

[63] Kozhevnikov, "Zashchita na Ukraine," p. 25; T. Kruglov, "Novyi etap v deiatel'nosti sovetskoi advokatury," *Sovetskaia iustitsiia*, no. 15-16 (1939), p. 38.

mittee ordered the expulsion of the chairman of the local college presidium.[64]

The erosion of party control over the colleges of defenders was facilitated by serious divisions among party and government officials over the appropriate personnel and policies to guide the Bar. These divisions reflected the struggle for power between the Procurator-General Vyshinsky and the newly appointed USSR Justice Commissar Krylenko, whose commissariat was given direct responsibility for the supervision of the Bar upon its formation in 1936. As the forces hostile to Krylenko made their final assault on the justice commissar, the advocates were faced with a breakdown in supervisory authority, which they appeared to exploit by challenging party control of the leadership selection process.

The conflict for control of the legal system and the contradictory signals that it produced for the Bar were illustrated during a four-day general meeting of Moscow advocates held from September 11 to 14, 1937. The appearance of Krylenko at the opening session of the meeting was followed by a *Pravda* article the next day rebuking the chairman of the Moscow College Alexandrov for his reference to the justice commissar as "our honored guest."[65] In its coverage of Krylenko's speech to the advocates on the final day of the proceedings *Pravda* criticized the justice commissar directly for his failure to integrate the Bar into the Soviet legal system.[66]

Amid the uncertainties of official policy toward the Bar the USSR Justice Commissariat in mid-October 1937 adopted a "Decree on Elections to the Presidium and Revision Commission of the College of Defenders" that provided a fillip to the efforts of the rank and file to play a larger role in the selection of the profession's leaders. Evidently inspired by the campaign to ex-

---

[64] "O rezul'tatakh revizii kharkovskoi i kievskoi kollegii zashchitnikov," *Sovetskaia iustitsiia*, no. 13 (1937), p. 54.

[65] "Na sobranii moskovskikh advokatov," *Pravda*, September 12, 1937, p. 6.

[66] A. Dunaevskii, "Na sobranii advokatov," *Pravda*, September 15, 1937, p. 6.

tend formal voting rights in party and soviet elections,[67] the new decree called, in effect, for the dismantling of the system of voting that had enabled the party to seize and maintain control of the colleges' governing organs. Henceforth, all voting was to be done by secret ballot, including the selection of a presidium chairman by the members of that body. More importantly, the rank and file of the colleges was given the right to nominate candidates and to discuss the merits of the candidates on an individual basis and not by list (*po spisku*) as had previously been the custom. In fact, the composing of slates of candidates in advance was forbidden by the decree.[68]

If the introduction of the decree was designed to test the political reliability of the profession, the results were not long in coming. At the end of 1937 a carefully organized meeting of Leningrad advocates was held to elect a new presidium for the college and to subject the city's advocates to criticism for what was termed their professional incompetence and political inactivity. But the election did not go as planned by the organizers. Several official candidates failed to receive a majority in the first round of voting, and it appears that the rank and file was prevented from installing several of its own choices on the presidium only by a change in the voting procedure between rounds that shortened the list of candidates. When this step was challenged by some advocates, the college was subjected to the "persuasion" of prominent observers at the meeting, among whom were the first secretaries of the regional and district party committees, the head of the legal defense section of the USSR Justice Commissariat, and the chairman of the Moscow College of Defenders.

[67] The new election rules in the Bar appeared to be patterned on the changes in party voting procedures that were introduced on March 21, 1937. Schapiro, *The Communist Party of the Soviet Union*, pp. 419-420. The effects of the rule-changes on party elections are discussed by Getty, *Origins of the Great Purges*, pp. 153-163. He argues that the dramatic democratization of voting procedure was an attempt by the center "to unleash criticism of the middle-level *apparat* by the rank-and-file activists" (p. 155).

[68] "Instruktsiia o vyborakh v prezidium i revizionnuiu komissiiu kollegii zashchitnikov i biuro kollektivov," *Sovetskaia iustitsiia*, no. 23 (1937), p. 53.

Thus, the advocates elected a presidium smaller than that desired by the organizers but with the requisite political complexion.[69]

Neither the experience in Leningrad nor the arrest of Krylenko in February 1938 resulted in a formal revision of voting procedure in the colleges. At least until the beginning of 1939 advocates in some areas continued to use the liberal election system to limit external control of the profession. At a general meeting of the Moscow College of Defenders in January 1939 the rank and file refused to accept the discipline that the party had imposed on other institutions in Soviet society. This prompted a legal commentator to complain that the college had learned nothing from the criticism to which it had been exposed by *Pravda* in September 1937. Instead of an orderly process of nominating and balloting, the election of members to the presidium occurred amid "inadmissible shouts and screams." Although the results of the vote were not published, it was revealed that the secretary of the college party committee failed to be elected to the presidium. In fact, when his name was mentioned at the meeting, it was greeted by shouts of "Who is that?" (*Kto eto takoi?*).[70]

The apparently successful resistance of the advocates to complete party domination raises a number of questions that cannot be answered without access to closed Soviet archives. It is not known to what extent divisions among party and government officials over the Bar contributed to the development of parallel divisions in the colleges of defenders; or whether the reform of the voting system was prompted by an excessive confidence in the party's standing in the profession or by a cynical desire to flush out the opposition. Nor is there any indication of the differences in behavior between prerevolutionary lawyers and young Soviet-trained advocates in professional disputes. All that is certain is the state's decision in the wake of the January 1939

[69] Liberman, "Kritika snizu," p. 42.

[70] "Obshchee sobranie moskovskoi gorodskoi kollegii zashchitnikov," *Sotsialisticheskaia zakonnost'*, no. 2 (1939), p. 67.

meeting of Moscow advocates to suspend the liberal voting system and embark on a massive infusion of party cadres into the Bar.[71]

While the party's internal control of the profession was in disarray over the period from 1936 to 1938, the permanent structural foundations were being laid for external supervision by government institutions. After more than a decade in which the supervision of the advocates was shared by various local and republican legal institutions, responsibility for supervisory policy was centralized in 1936 in the newly created Justice Commissariat of the USSR. In order to facilitate supervision of the profession the Department of Legal Defense (*otdel sudebnoi zashchity*) was created in the USSR Justice Commissariat on November 20, 1936. Subordinate departments of legal defense were subsequently established within the republican justice commissariats.[72]

Heading the all-union Department of Legal Defense was the moderate jurist M. Kozhevnikov, who initiated an ambitious campaign during the first few months of his tenure to institutionalize supervisory policy on the Bar by substituting bureaucratized control for control based on terror. Under the old and rather haphazard system of supervision, Kozhevnikov argued, control over the profession had been achieved largely through the use of periodic purges of the colleges of defenders. He proposed replacing this episodic and disruptive style of control with a method of supervision that relied primarily on a constant monitoring and influencing of advocates' behavior. This implied, of course, the establishment of a firm set of guidelines for professional behavior that had been lacking in the past.[73]

[71] See Kruglov, "Novyi etap v deiatel'nosti," pp. 39-40. I attempted to raise some of these difficult questions with M. Strogovich in an interview in Moscow in March 1980. Unfortunately, Strogovich, who was a leading reformist in the post-Stalin period, was unwilling to discuss his role in the legal system under Stalin.

[72] M. Kozhevnikov, "Slova i delo," *Sotsialisticheskaia zakonnost'*, no. 8 (1937), p. 118.

[73] M. Kozhevnikov, "Ocherki o nashei zashchite—rukovodstvo zashchitoi," *Sovetskaia iustitsiia*, no. 17 (1937), p. 15.

The development of a system of centralized control over the advocates began at the end of 1936 with an assessment of the state of the profession. Basic information on cadres, college activities (such as disciplinary proceedings), and legal practice—none of which had been collected systematically since the end of NEP—was compiled by the all-union Department of Legal Defense on the basis of responses by college leaders to a national questionnaire. An analysis of written materials received from the profession was followed by the summoning of chairmen from fifty-one local colleges to Moscow to provide reports on the colleges' affairs. With this initial background Kozhevnikov instituted a program of on-the-spot inspections of local colleges carried out by inspectors from the Department of Legal Defense. By the middle of 1937 colleges in seven republics had been inspected.[74]

Although Kozhevnikov succeeded in developing a viable structure of supervision over the Bar and in producing a number of written guidelines for the profession, the effectiveness of governmental supervisory policy was severely limited by the low priority given to legal defense by the leadership of the Justice Commissariat. Over nine months after the creation of the all-union Department of Legal Defense, Kozhevnikov complained that it had not yet been given its basic staff.[75] The republican departments of legal defense, for their part, appear to have contributed little to the supervision of the profession. The only reference to the republican departments in the legal journals of the period came in mid-1938, when the Ukrainian Justice Commissariat, after transferring the head of the Department of Legal Defense to other work, sought to close the department altogether. It was retained only after the intervention of the USSR Justice Commissariat.[76]

More importantly, however, the efforts of Kozhevnikov to construct a system of external supervision over the advocates were

[74] Ibid.; Kozhevnikov, "Ocherki o zashchite—kadry," p. 36; Kozhevnikov, "Slova i delo," pp. 119-120.

[75] Kozhevnikov, "Slova i delo," p. 118.

[76] Spektorov, "Reshitel'no uluchshit'," pp. 24-25.

compromised by the campaign against Krylenko. Although Kozh-evnikov's approach to the Bar differed significantly from that of Krylenko, who in 1936 was still insisting on a prominent role for trade unions in legal aid, his work in the Department of Legal Defense was condemned by institutional association with the justice commissar.[77]

The first direct blow against Kozhevnikov and his department came in the spring of 1937 in an article published in the Proc-uracy's journal *Sotsialisticheskaia zakonnost'* [Socialist Legality]. Not only did the author criticize the activities of the Department of Legal Defense but in a note appended to the article the journal editors requested that Krylenko personally investigate the "in-comprehensible methods" employed by his commissariat in the supervision of the Bar.[78] Responding to this attack from the Procuracy in a lengthy article published in *Sotsialisticheskaia zakonnost'* in the summer of 1937, Kozhevnikov admitted that minor mistakes had been committed but argued that the De-partment of Legal Defense had made considerable progress given its small staff and the absence of a coherent supervisory policy toward the advocates before 1936. This did not satisfy his critics. In an unusually long postscript to the response of Kozhevnikov the editors of the journal rejected his explanations and again called on Krylenko to ensure that the Department of Legal De-fense adopt an appropriate supervisory policy toward the advocates.[79]

Caught in the broader campaign against Krylenko, Kozhev-nikov lost his post during the massive purge of the Justice Com-missariat of the USSR that followed Krylenko's arrest in February 1938. But whereas earlier Kozhevnikov had been criticized for his harshness towards the Bar, he was now accused of a lack of vigilance towards the profession, an indication that it was indeed

---

[77] N. Krylenko, "Zadachi sovetskoi zashchity," *Sovetskaia iustitsiia*, no. 27 (1936), p. 3.

[78] N. N., "Slova i delo," *Sotsialisticheskaia zakonnost'*, no. 4 (1937), pp. 82-84. In 1935 the title of the Procuracy journal *Za sotsialisticheskuiu zakonnost'* was changed to *Sotsialisticheskaia zakonnost'*.

[79] Kozhevnikov, "Slova i delo," pp. 118-120.

considerations of power and not policy that motivated his crit-ics.[80] With Kozhevnikov removed from the Justice Commissariat, government supervision over the advocates appears to have re-verted, at least temporarily, to the pre-1936 pattern. The regular, bureaucratic monitoring and influencing of the profession's ac-tivities was replaced by a system of supervision that relied on large-scale purges and administrative measures to ensure the advocates' compliance with state policy.

Organizational Questions

A major impediment to the establishment of an institutionalized form of supervision over the Bar continued to be the very struc-ture of the profession. A completed chain of supervisory com-mand over the advocates would have required either the elim-ination of the private practitioner and the bureaucratic subordination of local collectives to the college presidia or the establishment of direct party and government oversight of the profession at the district (*raion*) level and below. Neither was introduced in this period. Although the advocates were organized for associational purposes into regional colleges whose presidia were supervised directly by party and governmental organs, their daily professional activities continued to be performed through individual, private practices or through small, local collectives, which were largely self-governing. The Moscow presidium was accused in a *Pravda* article in 1937 of exercising no supervision whatever over the collectives in the city.[81]

In spite of the ideological and practical problems posed for the state by the continued existence of private legal practitioners and the many cliquish collectives (*zamknutye kollektivy*), no fundamental revision of the profession's structure was proposed during the Great Purges. Indeed, when a new draft law on the Bar emerged in the middle of 1937, during a short lull in the terror, it accepted private legal practice as a legitimate alter-

---

[80] "Bol'nye voprosy advokatury," *Sovetskaia iustitsiia*, no. 14 (1938), pp. 16-17.
[81] "Na sobranii moskovskikh advokatov" (*Sovetskaia iustitsiia*), p. 42.

native to the "basic" form of legal practice, the collective. According to the draft, private practice was to be governed by a supplementary "Directive on Defenders Practicing Individually."[82]

The first legislative reform of the profession to be advanced since the Enukidze Commission draft of early 1935, the draft law on the Bar of 1937 bore the unmistakable imprint of prerevolutionary jurists. Composed by Kozhevnikov in conjunction with several leading members of the Moscow College of Defenders, the draft provided not only for the protection of private practice but also for a partial return to the language and customs of the old profession of sworn advocates. The term defender was to be replaced by the more internationally recognizable term advocate, and the colleges of defenders were to be renamed councils of advocates (*sovety advokatury*), in keeping with the prerevolutionary tradition (*sovet prisiazhnykh poverennykh*).[83] In another provision that satisfied the traditionalists in the profession, full-time legal consultants (*jurisconsults*) working in enterprises and government institutions were to be excluded from membership in the Bar.[84]

While granting a number of concessions to the advocates, the draft did promise further restrictions on the autonomy of legal

[82] M. Kozhevnikov, "Proekt novogo polozheniia ob advokature," *Sovetskaia iustitsiia*, no. 15 (1937), p. 15. A potentially important reform of the Bar was contained in the December 8, 1936, law creating the USSR Justice Commissariat. The legislation called for the formation of state Bar organizations in outlying areas not served by the colleges of defenders. However, this legislative provision, which was in keeping with Krylenko's preference for alternatives to the traditional organization of the Bar, was never implemented. "Polozhenie o NKIu SSSR," Postanovlenie TsIK i SNK SSSR, 8 dek. 1936g., *Sovetskaia iustitsiia*, no. 1 (1937), p. 4.

[83] Ibid. The draft also included a provision for an institution of advocates-in-training (*pomoshchniki advokatov*), who would serve for two years in an apprentice program. The question of dropping the term defender in favor of advocate was first raised publicly at the beginning of 1937 by an anonymous author who noted the advantages of employing a term that was recognizable in the West. See "Sovetskaia advokatura," *Sovetskaia iustitsiia*, no. 1 (1937), p. 8.

[84] "Sovetskaia advokatura," p. 8. This was designed to exclude from the Bar the large number of college members whose income was based on contracts with one or more institutional employers.

collectives by redefining, or more accurately, distorting, the concept of voluntary collectives. According to Kozhevnikov, the principle of voluntariness (*printsip dobrovol'nosti*) did not signify that collectives were to make their own personnel decisions independently. Rather it meant that "each advocate had the right to enter a collective voluntarily, to leave a collective voluntarily, and to voluntarily select individual or collective practices."[85] This redefinition was clearly designed to break up small, tight-knit collectives that excluded professionally incompetent or politically committed advocates.

Shortly after the major provisions of the draft law on the Bar were described in outline form by Kozhevnikov in the spring of 1937 the proposed legislation was subjected to fierce criticism, particularly by legal specialists writing in the journal of the Procuracy. Over the remainder of 1937 and the first weeks of 1938 the draft remained a topic of discussion in the specialist literature, with many authors complaining that the legislation had been drafted secretly and that it was unnecessarily harsh towards the Bar.[86] But with the shake-up in the Justice Commissariat in early 1938, the debate on the draft law ceased. There followed instead a series of articles that condemned Kozhevnikov and others in the Justice Commissariat for being wreckers who had "undermined the work of collectives and encouraged private practice." It was subsequently reported that a second draft law on the Bar was being composed, this time by a newly formed section of the USSR Justice Commissariat in conjunction with the All-Union Research Institute of Juridical Sciences (VNIIIuN).[87]

As in supervisory policy towards the advocates, the February 1938 purge of the USSR Justice Commissariat brought a fun-

---

[85] Kozhevnikov, "Proekt novogo polozheniia ob advokature," p. 15.

[86] S. Bronshtein, "Dostizheniia' otdela sudebnoi zashchity NKIu SSSR," *Sotsialisticheskaia zakonnost'*, no. 12 (1937), p. 99; A Liberman, "K proektu polozheniia ob advokature," *Sovetskaia iustitsiia*, no. 23 (1937), p. 33; T. Livshits, "Voprosy reorganizatsii advokatury na soveshchanii pri Narkomiustitsii Ukrainy," *Sotsialisticheskaia zakonnost'*, no. 7 (1937), p. 82.

[87] Spektorov, "Reshitel'no uluchshit'," pp. 24-25.

damental shift in the official line on the organization of the Bar. Not only was private practice to be eliminated but the collectives were to be subjected to administrative control by the regional colleges of defenders. A prominent writer on legal affairs noted that henceforth "the relationship between the bureaus of the legal collectives and the college presidia should be analogous to that between agriculture brigades and *kolkhozy*,"[88] that is, as between production units and management.

Legal Practice

The era of the Great Purges brought further pressure on the advocates to abandon traditional methods of legal defense and adopt instead a position of complete independence from the client. The model of this new type of Soviet legal defender was I. Braude, who presented arguments for the defense in two of the great show trials, the Case of the Anti-Soviet Trotskyite Center (January 1937) and the Case of the Anti-Soviet Bloc of Rights and Trotskyites (March 1938).[89] Braude, who joined the Soviet Bar under NEP, had practiced as a sworn advocate in Moscow and Petersburg before the Revolution. Drafted into the tsarist army in 1916, he was at the front at the time of the October Revolution when, according to official Soviet sources, he immediately allied himself with the Bolshevik cause. After the Revolution he worked for several years as a state criminal investigator in the Ukraine, eventually rising to the post of Ukrainian chief investigator before entering legal practice in the 1920s.[90]

In the opening lines of his defense of the accused Kniazev in the Case of the Anti-Soviet Trotskyite Center, Braude provided

[88] M. Rivkin, "Organizatsionnye voprosy sovetskoi advokatury," *Sovetskaia iustitsiia*, no. 14 (1938), p. 17.

[89] *Report of Court Proceedings in the Case of the Anti-Soviet Trotskyite Centre* (Moscow, 1937); *Report of Court Proceedings in the Case of the Anti-Soviet Bloc of Rights and Trotskyites* (Moscow, 1938).

[90] I. Braude, *Zapiski advokata* (Moscow, 1974), pp. 5-6.

a telling description of the desired role for the advocate in the Soviet courtroom:

> Comrade Judges, I will not conceal from you the exceptionally difficult, the unprecedently difficult position in which the defense finds itself in this case. First of all, Comrade Judges, the Counsel for the Defense is a son of his country. He, too, is a citizen of the Great Soviet Union, and the great indignation, anger, and horror which is now felt by the whole population of our country, old and young, the feeling which the Prosecutor so strikingly expressed in his speech, cannot but be shared by Counsel.
>
> But, Comrade Judges, according to Soviet law, according to Stalin's Constitution, which ensures every accused person the right to defense, irrespective of the gravity of his crime, we are obliged, it is our professional duty, to help those of the accused who have wished to avail themselves of this right, to exercise this right.
>
> In this case, Comrade Judges, there is no dispute about the facts. Comrade Procurator was quite right when he said that from all points of view, from the point of view of the documents available in the case, from the point of view of the examination of the witnesses who were summoned here, and the cross-examination of the accused, all this has deprived us of the possibility of disputing the evidence. All the facts have been proved, and in this sphere the defense does not intend to enter into any controversy with the Procurator. Nor can there be any controversy with the Procurator concerning the appraisal of the political and moral aspects of the case. Here, too, the case is so clear, the political appraisal made here by the Procurator is so clear, that the defense cannot but wholly and entirely associate itself with that part of his speech.
>
> While fully subscribing to the political and moral appraisal of the case given by the Procurator, what does the defense regard its task to be in this case? It is the task of the defense to seek what the Procurator spoke of at the end of his speech,

to seek those considerations which would justify a plea for clemency. Such is the task of Kniazev's defense counsel."[91]

This defense strategy, which was undoubtedly approved, if not developed directly, by the trial's chief prosecutor, Vyshinsky, reduced the advocate to a minor actor in the courtroom. Adhering to the political and evidentiary position of the prosecutor, the advocate was expected to restrict himself to arguments that mitigated his client's guilt. In this Stalinist model of legal defense the advocate was obliged to openly recognize the guilt of his client if it "was established by the circumstances of the case."[92]

How effective was this model in influencing the behavior of advocates in less publicized cases? The evidence suggests that the attempts to introduce a more acceptable style of legal defense were often met with confusion or resistance in the ranks of the advocates. Some advocates, anxious to illustrate their loyalty to the regime, exceeded their brief by seeking harsher penalties for their clients than was requested by the prosecutor.[93] Although this approach may have pleased many local judges and prosecutors, it was criticized severely by the central authorities. The overzealous conduct by advocates tarnished the legal image of Soviet socialism that the state sought to project to internal and international audiences. Writing in 1938, Vyshinsky complained that the advocates-turned-prosecutors created the impression that the rights of defendants were being transgressed.[94]

Probably more numerous in this period, however, were advocates who continued to employ, even if somewhat more cautiously, traditional methods of legal defense. In her professional autobiography, *Final Judgment*, the Soviet émigrée advocate

[91] *Case of the Anti-Soviet Trotskyite Centre*, p. 517.

[92] I. Shmarov, "Zashchitnik v sovetskom ugolovnom protsesse" (*Kandidat* dissertation, Moscow, 1955), p. 90.

[93] Ibid., p. 33; D. Golubovskii, "Uzlovye voprosy zashchity," *Sotsialisticheskaia zakonnost'*, no. 6 (1936), p. 50; N. Lagovier, "Zashchita v sovetskom sude," *Sovetskaia iustitsiia*, no. 4 (1937), p. 32; V. Raskol'nikov, "Sovetskii zashchitnik," *Sovetskaia iustitsiia*, no. 16 (1938), p. 27.

[94] Cited in Shmarov, "Zashchitnik," p. 33.

Dina Kaminskaya writes of prerevolutionary jurists such as L. Kats who in the late 1930s "retained an old conception of legal defense."[95] The persistence of the prerevolutionary traditions of oral advocacy undoubtedly accounts for the large number of disciplinary cases brought against advocates by judges and prosecutors in this period. In 1936 sixty-one disciplinary cases against advocates were initiated in Moscow on the basis of complaints from the courts and the Procuracy. At least one of these cases resulted in the expulsion of an advocate from the city's profession for engaging in anti-Soviet behavior in his legal practice.[96]

The unwillingness of many advocates to adopt the Stalinist approach to legal practice appears to have strengthened the hand of those political and legal authorities who opposed expanded participation for the advocates in legal proceedings. During the legal debates sparked by the drafting of the Stalin Constitution in 1936, many jurists favored enhancing the advocate's procedural position in criminal cases. Writing in the summer of 1936, Vyshinsky remarked that it was appropriate to consider extending the defendant's rights at the pretrial stage of the criminal process by admitting the advocate to the preliminary investigation.[97] This proposal was supported by many jurists in subsequent debates over a new Code of Criminal Procedure.[98]

[95] Kaminskaya, *Final Judgment*, pp. 26-28.

[96] "Na sobranii moskovskikh advokatov" (*Sovetskaia iustitsiia*), p. 42.

[97] A. Vyshinsky, "Stalinskaia konstitutsiia i zadachi organov iustitsii," *Sotsialisticheskaia zakonnost'*, no. 8 (1936), p. 18.

[98] M. Strogovich, "Voprosy ugolovnogo prava i novaia konstitutsiia," *Sotsialisticheskaia zakonnost'*, no. 7 (1936), p. 43; A. Vol'skii, "Obespechenie obvinaemomu prava na zashchitu i sovetskaia advokatura," *Sovetskaia iustitsiia*, no. 22 (1936), p. 5; M. Tarnova, "Zashchita v sovetskom sude," *Sovetskaia iustitsiia*, no. 26 (1936), p. 13; Raskol'nikov, "Znachenie sovetskoi zashchity," *Sovetskaia iustitsiia*, no. 31 (1936), p. 6.

Intensive discussion of a proposed Code of Criminal Procedure began in the All-Union Institute of Juridical Sciences in February 1939, with the academic legal community solidly behind expanded participation for the advocate in the pretrial stage. N. Polianskii, *Ocherk razvitiia sovetskoi nauki ugolovnogo protsessa* (Moscow, 1960), pp. 62-64. New legislation on criminal procedure was not introduced, however, until the post-Stalin period.

But despite open support in the legal community for an expansion of the advocate's participatory rights, no major revision of existing legislation was forthcoming. The Stalin Constitution did contain an article that guaranteed citizens a "right of defense" (article 111), but this guarantee remained open to varying interpretations. In fact, hard-line jurists insisted that the right to defense signified only that the accused had the right to speak in his own defense in open court—a seemingly ludicrous interpretation unless one recalls the tradition of inquisitional proceedings in pre-Reform Russia.[99]

If the extent of the advocate's participation in court proceedings remained little changed, so too did the conditions of legal practice. Although the legal journals continued to exhort judges to treat the advocates with greater respect, the press was replete with complaints about the attitudes of state legal personnel toward the Bar. The "shocking disrespect" that judges exhibited towards the advocates during public trials was reportedly even more pronounced in closed cassation hearings.[100] Prosecutors, too, shared the bench's intolerance towards the advocates. One prosecutor asked that an advocate be expelled from the profession for having smiled at a sensitive point in the trial.[101]

In general, the operation of the courts impeded, rather than facilitated, legal defense. In court-appointed cases judges often gave the defender only forty-eight hours to prepare for the trial.[102] Furthermore, advocates were still obliged to stand in the queue with ordinary citizens in order to submit and receive court documents.[103] The advocates were also denied separate chambers

---

[99] "Sodoklad M. A. Chel'tsova, Zashchita po proektu ugolovno-protsessual'nogo kodeksa," in *Trudy pervoi nauchnoi sessii vsesoiuznogo instituta iuridicheskikh nauk*, ed. I. Goliakov (Moscow, 1940), pp. 234-235.

[100] A. Liberman, "Zashchita v kassatsionnom sude," *Sovetskaia iustitsiia*, no. 17 (1937), p. 26.

[101] N. Lagovier, "Zashchita v sovetskom sude," *Sovetskaia iustitsiia*, no. 4 (1937), p. 32.

[102] Rivkin, "V zashchitu zashchitnikov," *Sovetskaia iustitsiia*, no. 2-3 (1938), p. 52.

[103] "Na sobranii moskovskikh advokatov" (*Sovetskaia iustitsiia*), p. 42. This was also true in the Procuracy, where advocates were sometimes forced to wait in line

in court buildings and gathered instead around an "advocates' table" in the corridors outside the courtroom. This was all the more demeaning since the advocate often waited hours for his case to be called.[104] Thus, in spite of the promises of Vyshinsky and others to elevate the Bar to a respected place in the legal community, the advocate through his daily practice was continually reminded of his inferior position in the Soviet legal system.

THE FINAL ASSAULT ON THE BAR

The Great Purges brought a noticeable hardening of policy towards the advocates, but it was not until the end of 1938 that the final offensive against the profession began. On December 22, 1938, nine months after the purges had replaced its leading cadres, the USSR Justice Commissariat issued a directive "On the Work of the Colleges of Defenders," which initiated a short, sharp campaign to complete the transformation of the Bar into a compliant Soviet institution.[105] The campaign culminated in August 1939 with the adoption of a new USSR Statute on the Bar. This was the first such law since 1922 and the model for all subsequent legislation on the profession.[106]

A major part of the reorientation of policy on the profession in 1939 was the abolition of legal collectives, whose autonomy was now regarded as "harmful" to the legal order.[107] Legal practice was to be conducted instead through local legal consultation bureaus (*iuridicheskie konsul'tatsii*), which were administratively subordinated to the presidium of the colleges of advocates, as the regional professional associations were to be known hence-

four or five hours to submit documents (ibid.). In some cases advocates found it difficult to gain access to court transcripts that were needed to compose appeals. See F. Kamenskii, "Distsiplinarnaia deiatel'nost' prezidiuma moskovskoi kollegii zashchitnikov," *Sovetskaia iustitsiia*, no. 4 (1938), p. 59.

[104] Kamenskii, "Distsiplinarnaia," p. 59.

[105] "Mery uluchsheniia raboty advokatury," *Sovetskaia iustitsiia*, no. 3 (1939), pp. 63-64.

[106] Polozhenie ob advokature SSSR, *Sovetskaia iustitsiia*, no. 15-16 (1939), pp. 41-43.

[107] Kruglov, "Novyi etap v deiatel'nosti'," p. 39.

forth. Under the 1939 Statute on the Bar the college presidium was empowered to select the site and membership of the bureaus as well as their managers (*zaveduiushchie*). The managers, who answered directly to the presidium and not to the members of the bureau, were responsible for overseeing the professional behavior of advocates. They also distributed the workload among the advocates and determined the level of payment when the provisions of the fee schedule were unclear.[108] It was, in effect, "one-man management" (*edinonachal'e*) applied to the basic production unit of the advocates. This new structure enabled the college presidium, and through it party and government supervisory organs, to establish effective oversight of the rank and file of the profession for the first time.

Private legal practice was all but eliminated by the new Statute on the Bar. Hundreds of private practitioners were forced to abandon their practice in 1939 and affiliate with legal consultation bureaus. A few exceptions were made, however, for those advocates who had rendered special service to the state. With dispensations granted by the USSR Justice Commissariat, a handful of advocates continued to practice privately for some years. One such advocate was I. Braude.[109]

The 1939 statute also resolved the long-standing dispute over the relationship between the Bar and the profession of jurisconsults. Advocates had been able since the introduction of NEP to hold joint appointments as members of the Bar and as staff jurisconsults in government institutions and enterprises. In Kiev it was reported in 1937 that 60 percent of Bar members were jurisconsults. They retained their professional affiliation with the

---

[108] Ibid. The introduction of the Statute on the Bar was followed immediately by the issuance of a fee schedule by the USSR Justice Commissariat. "Instruktsiia o poriadke oplaty iuridicheskoi pomoshchi, okazyvaemoi advokatami naseleniiu," *Sovetskaia iustitsiia*, no. 17-18 (1939), pp. 79-80. This eliminated, at least for a time, the diversity in payment systems that existed across the country.

[109] I. Sukharev, "Organizatsiia i deiatel'nost' advokatury SSSR" (*Kandidat* dissertation, Moscow, 1973), p. 32. The 1939 statute also permitted members of the rural intelligentsia, such as doctors and teachers, to engage in part-time private legal practice in remote regions. Ibid.

Bar in order to have a means of livelihood in case their consulting contracts were not renewed. The combining of full-time government legal service with membership in the Bar was prohibited, however, by the new statute, thus forcing large numbers of lawyers to choose between the state sector and the Bar. Advocates continued, of course, to provide legal services to government institutions and enterprises but no longer as in-house consultants.[110]

The final assault on the Bar brought cadre reform on a massive scale. After the extensive purges of late 1938 and early 1939 had cleansed the profession of "harmful elements," large numbers of *vydvishentsy* were directed into the Bar.[111] The profession expanded from approximately 6,000 members in 1938, to 8,000 members in 1939, and 10,500 members in 1941. This number would increase to over 13,000 by 1947.[112]

Although some of the growth can be explained by the desire of the state to extend legal services into the less populated areas of the country, which were very poorly served by the Bar, the basic motivation was to bring an irreversible shift in the political complexion of the profession.[113] Thus, in spite of the strict ed-

---

[110] M. Kozhevnikov, "Zashchita na Ukraine," p. 25. On the profession of jurisconsults, see Y. Luryi, "Jurisconsults in the Soviet Economy," in *Soviet Law after Stalin*, part 3, ed. D. Barry, F. Feldbrugge, G. Ginsburgs, and P. Maggs (Alphen aan den Rijn, 1979), p. 168; J. Giddings, "The Jurisconsult in the USSR," *Review of Socialist Law*, no. 1 (1975), p. 171; L. Shelley, *Lawyers in Soviet Work Life* (New Brunswick, N.J., 1984).

[111] Zubkov, "Moskovskie advokaty izuchaiut istoriiu VKP (b)," *Sovetskaia iustitsiia*, no. 17-18 (1939), p. 38; T. Neishtadt, *Sovetskii advokat* (Moscow, 1958), p. 10.

[112] Spektorov, "Reshitel'no uluchshit'," p. 25; D. Barry and H. Berman, "The Jurists," in *Interest Groups in Soviet Politics*, ed. H. Skilling and F. Griffiths (Princeton, N.J., 1971), p. 304; S. Kucherov, *The Organs of Soviet Administration of Justice* (Leiden, 1970), p. 459.

[113] It appears that only a small percentage of the advocates flooding into the profession over the decade from 1939 to 1949 were directed into rural areas. Complaints about the concentration of advocates in urban areas continued to be heard, and by the beginning of the 1960s over one hundred districts (*raiony*) in the RSFSR were still without advocates. A. Sukharev, "Nastoiashchie zadachi sovetskoi advokatury," *Sovetskoe gosudarstvo i pravo*, no. 14 (1964), p. 26.

ucational requirements for advocates laid out in the 1939 Statute on the Bar, political, not professional, qualifications were most evident among the new recruits to the Bar. In Uzbekistan less than 20 percent of individuals entering the profession from 1936 to 1939 had received a higher education.[114] The stress on the political reliability of new cadres, taken together with the purge of considerable numbers of prerevolutionary jurists, led to a rapid decline in the educational standards of the profession nationwide. The proportion of Soviet advocates with a higher education fell from 53.3 percent in 1938 to 37 percent in 1939.[115]

Party membership in the Bar, on the other hand, increased dramatically during this period. In the Moscow City College of Advocates membership as a whole expanded only marginally from 1937 to 1939 (apparently as a result of large-scale purges), but the number of party members rose from 58 to 160.[116] In Uzbekistan the influx of party cadres into the profession was even more marked. Whereas 5 of 151 advocates in the republic were party members in 1936, by 1941, 102 of 391 advocates were Communists.[117] This massive injection of Communists into the colleges of defenders altered two decades of cadre policy toward the Bar and began a process of party saturation that raised the proportion of Communists in the profession to almost 70 percent by the end of the 1950s.[118]

The push to sovietize the personnel of the Bar was accompanied by other measures that tightened political control. In

---

[114] Mumin, "Sozdanie i razvitie, pp. 90, 100-102.

[115] Spektorov, "Reshitel'no uluchshit'," p. 25; *Stenograficheskii otchet*, Verkhovnogo Soveta SSSR, 6-aia sessaia (4-i sozyv) (Moscow, 1957), p. 462.

[116] "Na sobranii moskovskikh advokatov" (*Sovetskaia iustitsiia*), p. 22; "Obshchee sobranie moskovskoi gorodskoi kollegii zashchitnikov," p. 67.

[117] Mumin, "Sozdanie i razvitie," pp. 90, 100-102. As Rigby points out, the years from 1939 to 1941 were distinguished not only by the large number of new recruits to the party but also by the white-collar bias in recruitment. White-collar workers accounted for approximately 70 percent of new members and candidates to the party in this period. T. H. Rigby, *Communist Party Membership in the USSR, 1917-1967* (Princeton, N.J., 1968), pp. 219-225.

[118] *Stenograficheskii otchet*, Verkhovnogo Soveta SSSR, p. 462.

some regions the functions of the college presidium were handed over temporarily to a smaller, more reliable organizational bureau (*orgburo*) that carried out the transformation of the profession. In other areas the supervisory organs called new elections to the college presidia. These elections, for which the democratic voting procedures introduced in 1937 were apparently not applied, installed on the college presidia more compliant and politically orthodox leaders.[119]

The new presidium members moved quickly to fully integrate the colleges into Soviet political life. Shortly after assuming power in early 1939 the new leadership of the Moscow City College organized a lecture series on political topics that was attended by three-quarters of Moscow advocates. To bring the Bar into line with other Soviet institutions, the Moscow presidium challenged the Leningrad College of Advocates to a socialist competition drive in the field of ideological work.[120]

Finally, regular supervision of the Bar by government institutions was restored in 1939. According to the new USSR Statute on the Bar, which superseded existing republican laws on the advocates, supervisory power over the profession was vested in the USSR Justice Commissariat, the republican justice commissariats, and the departments of justice (*upravleniia Narkomiusta soiuznykh respublik*) at the regional level.[121] Besides maintaining oversight of the Bar and acting as the final arbiter on questions of personnel and professional discipline, these institutions issued periodic directives that were binding on the regional colleges of advocates. Selected directives from the all-union Justice Commissariat published in 1942 provided guidelines to the profession on such questions as voting procedure for presidium elections, the maintenance of labor discipline in the legal consultation bureaus, and legal fees.[122] Instructions from

[119] N. Levin, "Zashchita v sovetskom ugolovnom protsesse (v formal'nom smysle)" (*Kandidat* dissertation, Leningrad, 1946), p. 138; Zubkov, "Moskovskie advokaty," p. 38.

[120] Zubkov, "Moskovskie advokaty," p. 38.

[121] Polozhenie ob advokature SSSR, art. 2.

[122] *Sovetskaia advokatura* (Moscow, 1942).

the republican and regional levels of the Justice Commissariat, had they been published, would undoubtedly have revealed an even more thorough intrusion of the state into a profession that, according to the 1939 Statute of the Bar, should have enjoyed self-government "on all questions relating to the organization and functioning of the colleges of advocates."[123]

The Legacy of the Bar's Transformation

The events of 1939 marked the end of the formative stage in the development of the Soviet Bar. Over the ensuing decades the position of the profession in the Soviet legal system has been much debated, and on two occasions new laws on the Bar have been introduced.[124] The period since 1939 has also witnessed a gradual improvement in the working conditions of advocates and a moderate extension of their formal rights in legal proceedings. But the contemporary profession of advocates continues to rest on the foundations that were laid in the first two decades of Soviet rule. The restrictions imposed in this period on the organizational independence of the profession and on the ability of individual advocates to represent their clients in a system of unbridled state power remain intact.[125]

To say that the Soviet Bar acquired its permanent shape in the years from 1917 to 1939 does not signify, however, that it

---

[123] Polozhenie ob advokature SSSR, art. 14.

[124] In the early 1960s republican laws on the advocates replaced the single, all-union statute of 1939. A translation and annotation of the 1961 RSFSR Statute on the Bar can be found in L. Friedman and Z. Zile, "Soviet Legal Profession: Recent Developments in Law and Practice," *Wisconsin Law Review* (January 1964), pp. 32-77.

Following the introduction of the Brezhnev Constitution in 1977, the legislative fundamentals on the advocates were set out anew in Zakon ob advokature SSSR, *Stenograficheskii otchet*, Verkhovnogo Soveta SSSR, 2-aia sessiia (10-i sozyv) (Moscow, 1979), pp. 384-391. Subsequently, more detailed republican statutes on the advocates were introduced. See Polozhenie ob advokature RSFSR, *Vedomosti Verkhovnogo Soveta RSFSR*, no. 48, 1980, item 11.

[125] See Kaminskaya, *Final Judgment*, and Huskey, "The Limits to Institutional Autonomy."

was transformed into a wholly orthodox Soviet institution. Despite attempts to transfer the loyalties of the advocates from the client to the state, traditional approaches to legal defense have continued to exert a considerable influence on the profession. Throughout Soviet history some advocates have been willing to represent the interests of their clients with vigor and professional acumen, in some cases even at great personal risk. After pursuing an uncompromising line of defense in the 1968 trial of the dissident A. Ginzburg, the Moscow advocate B. Zolotukhin was stripped of his party membership and expelled from the profession.[126]

The advocates have also been able to preserve a degree of institutional autonomy that is rare, if not unique, in the Soviet system. Although operating under the close scrutiny of party and government organs, the colleges of advocates have not been integrated into the formal bureaucratic hierarchy of the Soviet state. They remain, at least formally, part of a "self-governing profession." As nonstate organizations outside of the administrative chain of command, the colleges have been able to exercise considerable control over certain areas of professional policy and administration, such as those concerning disciplinary practice and financial expenditures. More importantly, the advocates have continued to resist, where possible, the party's imposition of leaders on the profession. On several occasions in recent years delegates to the conferences of the Moscow City College of Advocates, a majority of whom were Communists, voted down candidates for the college presidium proposed on the official slate.[127]

The refusal of the profession to submit completely to the process of *Gleichschaltung* owes much to the ability of the colleges of advocates to attract individuals with a commitment to *zakonnost'* [legality] rather than *partiinost'* [party spirit]. The Bar offers the independent-minded law graduate an alternative to the rigid hierarchies of state legal institutions. Moreover, once

---

[126] Kaminskaya, *Final Judgment*, pp. 257-308.

[127] Huskey, "The Limits to Institutional Autonomy," pp. 207-210.

in the Bar advocates are subjected to a professional socialization that places them in an adversarial relationship with state authorities. For some advocates, like Dina Kaminskaya, who began legal practice in the 1930s as a loyal Komsomol member, years of work in the Soviet legal system aroused a desire to defend not only clients but the Bar itself against state power.[128] However, the position of the advocates in the Soviet Union depends finally on the state. If the Bar has been granted a measure of immunity from the heavy hand of the bureaucratic apparatus it is because the existence of a formally self-governing profession of advocates is essential for the legitimation of the Soviet legal system at home and abroad. As long as the state remains concerned about the image of Soviet justice, it will continue to allow the Bar to occupy its anomalous place in the Soviet order.

[128] Kaminskaya, *Final Judgment*.

Chapter Six

CONCLUSION: THE BAR AND THE TRANSFORMATION OF SOVIET PROFESSIONS

One of the major questions raised by this study of the formative years of the Soviet Bar is why the transformation of the advocates was more protracted and more qualified than in other groups in Soviet society. Whereas the prerevolutionary traditions, institutions, and personnel of such diverse groups as the writers, the doctors, and the engineers had been thoroughly transformed by 1934,[1] the final triumph of the state over the advocates was achieved only in 1939. The most compelling explanation for this is the low priority attached to the advocates' function by the political leadership. In providing legal assistance to individuals and enterprises, the advocates were not engaged in the essential services of socialist construction. Lenin appealed to the doctors to attack the typhus epidemic that was ravaging the country during the Civil War.[2] The writers—those "engineers of human souls"—were exhorted to create a *"magnitostroi* of literature" during the second revolution.[3] But for the advocates the expectations were less grand. Struggling to find a way to involve the Bar in the campaign to collectivize the countryside, the RSFSR Justice Commissariat could only encourage the profession to

[1] See E. Brown, *The Proletarian Episode in Russian Literature, 1928-1932* (New York, 1971); A. Kemp-Welch, "The Origins and Formative Years of the Writers' Union of the USSR, 1932-1936" (Ph.D. dissertation, London School of Economics and Political Science, University of London, 1976); M. Field, *Doctor and Patient in Soviet Russia* (Cambridge, Mass., 1957); K. E. Bailes, *Technology and Society under Lenin and Stalin: Origins of the Soviet Technical Intelligentsia, 1917-1941* (Princeton, N.J., 1978); S. Fitzpatrick, *Education and Social Mobility in the Soviet Union, 1921-1934* (Cambridge, 1979).

[2] Field, *Doctor and Patient*, pp. 15-16.

[3] Brown, *The Proletarian Episode*, p. 190.

extend more legal aid to the peasantry.[4] The nature of the advocates' labor, therefore, made its mass mobilization in the interests of the state impractical. This lowered the standing of the profession in the eyes of the political and legal authorities and, ultimately, of Soviet society as a whole.

The Bar remained the occasional concern of the central political leadership during Lenin's lifetime, apparently because of the oppositionist temperament of the profession in the wake of the revolution and Lenin's own penchant for involvement in the day-to-day administration of legal affairs. But after Lenin's death policy towards the advocates was shaped by officials of lesser rank. Besides Solts, who intervened briefly in the debate on the future of the Bar in the late 1920s, only Vyshinsky among the second level of Soviet leaders displayed an active interest in the affairs of the profession. Stalin appears never to have mentioned the advocates in his public speeches and writings, and the profession went unnoticed in major party meetings.[5]

Thus, while the decision to solve the problem of diversity in the literary community by "organizational" means was taken by Stalin personally,[6] policy toward the advocates during the Stalinist period had to be derived from the general line of the party by legal officials in the government apparatus. The party's neglect of the profession gave full rein to disputes in government institutions at the center and periphery over policy toward the advocates. This hindered the adoption of a single, coherent approach to the transformation of the Bar and exempted the advocates from the kind of concerted, public campaign launched against the bourgeois specialists in the technical intelligentsia during the second revolution.[7] Without close party coordination

---

[4] O iuridicheskoi pomoshchi naseleniiu, Postanovlenie kollegii NKIu, 9 dek. 1931g., *Sbornik tsirkuliarov i raz'iasnenii Narodnogo Komissariata iustitsii RSFSR deistvuiushchikh na 1 maia 1934g.* (Moscow, 1934), p. 33.

[5] After the death of Lenin legal policy seems to have been discussed at only two major gatherings, the Fourteenth Party Conference in 1925 and the Joint Plenum of the Central Committee and Central Control Commission in January 1933.

[6] Brown, *The Proletarian Episode*, p. 200.

[7] Bailes, *Technology and Society*, pp. 69-140.

government institutions seemed incapable of carrying the transformation of the profession through to its conclusion.

The low priority accorded to the advocates by the political leadership was evident in the reluctance of the state to commit scarce human resources to the profession. Not only were Communist cadres in the Bar kept to a minimum, but even young, nonparty graduates from Soviet law institutes were discouraged from entering the colleges of defenders. The neglect of recruitment and training for the Bar deprived the state of one of its most effective means of elite transformation. The medical profession, for example, which had been unreservedly hostile to the Bolshevik takeover in 1917, was thoroughly transformed over the first decade of Soviet rule by the infusion of large numbers of Soviet-trained cadres. By 1928 the number of doctors in the country was three times the level of 1917.[8]

Furthermore, the political leadership was unwilling to offer significant financial incentives to achieve the transformation of the Bar. Attempts to attract the advocates into collectives at the end of the 1920s with promises of economic rewards were only half-hearted, and even at the end of the 1930s the eligibility of the advocates for trade union membership was still in dispute.[9] Thus, the creation of a relationship of economic dependency between the state and society, which was instrumental in the coopting of occupational groups in the Soviet Union, did not extend in full measure to the Bar. While the judges spent their lunch breaks in the state-subsidized dining hall, the defenders ate sandwiches at the advocates' table in the corridor.[10]

The refusal of the state to channel funds into the Bar retarded the absorption of the profession into the Soviet system. But perhaps more importantly, it helped to maintain the traditional economic relationship between lawyer and client. Although most

[8] Field, *Doctor and Patient*, pp. 45, 54.

[9] Kirzner, "O profsoiuznom chlenstve individual'no-praktuiushchikh advokatov," *Sovetskaia iustitsiia*, no. 23 (1937), p. 44; M. Mamontov, "Pravo na zashchitu," *Sotsialisticheskaia zakonnost'*, no. 11 (1938), p. 62.

[10] D. Golubovskii, "Zametki zashchitnika," *Sotsialisticheskaia zakonnost'*, no. 2 (1939), p. 69.

legal officials appeared to favor in principle the creation of a state Bar, they were not prepared to support the institution with state funds.[11] They reluctantly acquiesced, therefore, to the policies of the more moderate elements in the legal community, who proposed a self-financing profession. Unlike the doctors, who were transferred to employee status in the new regime, the advocates were permitted to collect fees from clients within limits set by the state. In retaining the economic link between advocate and client the state made more difficult the attainment of its self-proclaimed goal of transforming the advocates from representatives of clients to representatives of the interests of society.

The failure of the state to subject the Bar to direct administrative subordination was also due to the very function of the advocates as representatives of the individual in the legal system. To have eliminated altogether the corporate character of the profession would have undermined the legitimacy of the Soviet legal process and led to the resurgence of an underground Bar, many of whose members would have been drawn from the ranks of government legal personnel.[12] The impulse of state socialism toward maximum political and social control was therefore tempered in the case of the advocates by a desire to reestablish the appearance of the impartiality of law. If it wished to ensure the confidence of the masses in the legal order, the Soviet state was bound to reach some accommodation with the advocates, much as it did with the creative intelligentsia, whose labor, like that of the advocates, could not be directed solely by administrative fiat.

The accommodation was made easier in the case of the Bar by the tightly controlled environment in which the advocates

[11] A rare admission of the importance of financial considerations in shaping policy toward the Bar was made in "K voprosu o gosudarstvennoi zashchite," *Sovetskaia iustitsiia*, no. 49 (1929), p. 1,155.

[12] In a discussion at the Sixteenth Party Conference on the purge of the government apparatus, the rapporteur, Ia. Iakovlev, offered as an example of those to be removed from office people's court judges who were practicing as underground advocates. *Stenograficheskii otchet*, 16-aia konferentisiia VKP (b), aprel' 1929g. (Moscow, 1962), p. 463.

worked. Those in charge of the "commanding heights" of the legal system—government personnel responsible for legal investigations, judicial decision making, and the oversight of legality—acted as instruments of the state to severely limit the effectiveness of the advocate in the legal process. Moreover, the scope of the advocates' traditional functions was narrowed. In criminal cases the advocates were excluded altogether from pretrial proceedings, and at the trial itself they were no longer able to argue before a jury. In civil law the development of a state committed to the extension of benefits through administrative entitlements, and not formal legal rights, shifted dispute resolution in many civil cases from the legal process to the government bureaucracy, where the advocates generally were not welcome. If the transformation of the profession lacked a sense of urgency, it was because the advocates were reduced to legal actors of secondary importance in the aftermath of the Revolution.

Against the loss of influence and prestige in the Soviet legal order, however, the advocates could claim to have retained a corporate identity, limited institutional autonomy, certain traditional elements of legal practice, and an apparently secure future in the legal system of state socialism. This accommodation of the Soviet state to Russian lawyers represented a concession to a nation that refused to accept the complete congruence of individual and state interests. The revival of law and the Bar under NEP and in the wake of the second revolution was in part, then, a response to the failure of the policies of the legal nihilists among the population.[13]

But a developed legal order gave the Soviet political leadership more than legitimacy and stability. It also provided an effective means of centralized rule over society. During the Civil War and the second revolution, the simplification of law devolved decision-making responsibility onto local party and justice cadres.

---

[13] In *The Great Retreat* (New York, 1946) N. Timasheff argues that the 1930s witnessed not the victory of socialism but the "victory, though partial only, of the nation against the reckless dictatorship" (p. 359).

Although repression and social control were directed in these periods by signals from the center, uniformity in the application of the policy could not be ensured. With the triumph of Stalinism in the mid-1930s, law was called on to combat spontaneity and localism. Cadres were ordered to reject revolutionary legal consciousness in favor of a rigid adherence to written rules. By virtue of its ability to promote organization and discipline law became one of the essential components in the construction of a centralized Stalinist bureaucracy. The renewed emphasis on law in the 1930s did not represent, therefore, a "Great Retreat" to earlier traditions but a belated recognition by the political leadership of the power of law in the service of state socialism.

Glossary of Russian Terms

Cheka (Extraordinary Committee for the Struggle against Counterrevolution, Sabotage, and Speculation)

The Cheka grew out of the Military-Revolutionary Committee that led the revolutionary insurrection in October 1917. Originally established to investigate political offenses and bureaucratic corruption, the Cheka rapidly acquired wide powers over ordinary criminal investigations. In the fall of 1918 it was assigned the leading role in the Red Terror, the campaign to eliminate opposition to Bolshevik rule. In 1922 the Cheka was replaced by the GPU (renamed the OGPU in 1924). These institutions are the forerunners of the present-day KGB.

Colleges of Defenders (*kollegii zashchitnikov*)

From 1922 to 1939 Bar associations in the Soviet Union were known as colleges of defenders. Since 1939 they have been called colleges of advocates (*kollegii advokatov*).

NEP (New Economic Policy)

Announced by Lenin at the Tenth Party Congress in March 1921, the New Economic Policy was a tactical retreat from the extreme centralization and repression of the civil war period. It reintroduced some capitalist elements into the economy and brought a partial revival of the legal institutions and legal thought of the old regime. NEP was abandoned at the end of the 1920s.

NKVD (People's Commissariat of Internal Affairs)

From the October Revolution of 1917 until 1934 the NKVD included the regular police force (the militia) and the prison and labor camp administrations. In 1934 the functions of the OGPU (see Cheka above) were transferred to the NKVD, thus giving the NKVD a monopoly over law enforcement. This monopoly ended after World War II with the reestablishment of a separate institution for the secret police. The present-day Ministry of Internal Affairs is the successor to the NKVD of the 1917 to 1934 period.

People's Commissariat of Justice (*Narodnyi Kommissariat iustitsii*)

Created in the wake of the Bolshevik takeover in October 1917, the Justice Commissariat was the weakest of state legal institutions. Its responsibilities lay outside of law enforcement, in areas such as legislative drafting, criminology research, and the general supervision of the courts and the Bar. It is the forerunner of the present-day Ministry of Justice.

Procuracy (*prokuratura*)

The Procuracy is the state legal institution responsible for criminal prosecution, for the supervision of criminal investigations (and the conduct of some investigations), and for the general oversight of adherence to legal norms by individuals and institutions. Originally established in 1722 by Peter the Great to act as the eyes of the tsar in the country, the Procuracy was abolished immediately following the Bolshevik Revolution. It was revived in 1922 and functions to this day as the Communist party's watchdog over legal affairs. Operating initially as part of the People's Commissariat of Justice, the Procuracy was granted full institutional independence in 1936.

Rabkrin (People's Commissariat of Workers' and Peasants' Inspection)

The successor to the People's Commissariat of State Control, Rabkrin was charged with discovering abuse and inefficiency in Soviet government institutions. Created in 1920, its mandate was to recruit representatives from the laboring masses and to grant them limited power to inspect and discipline government bureaucracies. However, like its parallel in the Communist party apparatus, the Central Control Commission, Rabkrin soon became an institution of elite, not popular, control. It was abolished in 1934. Rabkrin is a forerunner of the present-day People's Control Committee.

RSFSR (Russian Soviet Federated Socialist Republic)

The original nucleus of the Soviet state, the RSFSR has been the largest republic in the Union of Soviet Socialist Republics (USSR) since the early 1920s. Although the population of the RSFSR is predominantly Russian, the republic includes many other ethnic groups.

Sovnarkom (Council of People's Commissars)

Headed by Lenin from its inception at the time of the October Revolution, the Sovnarkom was the supreme executive organ of the Soviet government. This cabinetlike body included among its members heads of the government bureaucracies who were known as people's commissars. The Sovnarkom is the forerunner of the present-day Council of Ministers.

VTsIK (All-Russian Central Executive Committee)

Established as the permanent arm of the All-Russian Congress of Soviets, which was an unwieldy body with infrequent meetings, VTsIK was in constitutional terms the preeminent executive and legislative institution in the Soviet Union. However, its executive power was eroded by the Sovnarkom and its legislative authority usurped by the Communist party. Although largely stripped of influence, VTsIK remained a forum for relatively open debate, by Soviet standards. With the formation of the USSR in 1922, TsIK USSR superseded VTsIK as the highest organ of state authority in the country. VTsIK and TsIK USSR are the forerunners of the present-day RSFSR and USSR supreme soviets.

VTsSPS (All-Union Central Council of Trade Unions)

VTsSPS is the highest organ of Soviet trade unions. During the interwar period, VTsSPS was repeatedly petitioned by members of the Bar who sought admission to the ranks of trade unions. Trade union membership carried with it numerous social and economic benefits.

Vydvizhentsy

Vydvizhentsy were workers and peasants promoted to responsible positions in the Soviet state and society, often with little education or professional training. They were beneficiaries of the large-scale removal of bourgeois specialists during the cultural revolution of 1928 to 1932. The rise of underqualified and politically malleable personnel facilitated the triumph of Stalinism in the 1930s.

Bibliography

I. Periodicals

Included here are newspapers and journals read thoroughly for material relating to the Bar. For periodicals whose titles changed the earlier name(s) appear in parentheses.

Izvestiia VTsIK, 1918
Nash vek (Vek, Rech', Svobodnaia rech'), 1917-1918
Pravda (Rabochii put'), 1917-1918
Pravo, 1917
Pravo i zhizn', 1922-1927
Problemy sotsialisticheskogo prava, 1937-1939
Proletarskaia revoliutsiia i pravo, 1918-1919, 1921
Proletarskii sud, 1922-1928
Rabochii sud, 1923-1930
Revoliutsionnaia zakonnost', 1926
Russkie vedomosti, 1917-1918
Sotsialisticheskaia zakonnost' (Za sotsialisticheskuiu zakonnost'), 1934-1940
Sovetskaia iustitsiia (Ezhenedel'nik sovetskoi iustitsii), 1922-1940
Sovetskoe gosudarstvo i pravo (Revoliutsiia prava; Sovetskoe gosudarstvo i revoliutsiia prava; Sovetskoe gosudarstvo), 1927-1940
Sovetskoe pravo, 1922-1929
Sovetskoe stroitel'stvo, 1933-1937
Vestnik sovetskoi iustitsii, 1923-1930
Vestnik statistiki, 1923-1928

II. Official Documents and Bar Reports

Arsen'ev, K. *Zametki o russkoi advokature (obzor deiatel'nosti s-peterburgskogo soveta prisiazhnykh poverennykh za 1866-74gg)*. St. Petersburg, 1875.

Distsiplinarnoe proizvodstvo za 1926g. Moscow, 1926.

Dva goda raboty pravitel'stva RSFSR. Materialy k otchetu pravitel'stva za 1924-1925 i 1925-1926gg. Moscow, 1927.

God raboty pravitel'stva RSFSR. Materialy k otchetu pravitel'stva za 1926-1927g. Moscow, 1928.

God raboty pravitel'stva RSFSR. Materialy k otchetu pravitel'stva za 1927-1928g. Moscow, 1929.

Instruktsiia po provedeniiu revizii v prezidiumakh i iuridicheskikh konsul'tatsiiakh. Ministerstvo iustitsii RSFSR, Otdel advokatury. Moscow, 1947.

Iuridicheskii kalendar'. Moscow, 1923-1930.

Materialy Narodnogo Komissariata iustitsii. Vypusk 1. Pervyi vserossiiskii s'ezd oblastnykh i gubernskikh komissarov iustitsii. Moscow, 1918.

———. Vypusk 3. Vtoroi vserossiiskii s'ezd oblastnykh i gubernskikh komissarov iustitsii. Moscow, 1918.

———. Vypusk 11-12. Tret'ii vserossiiskii s'ezd deiatelei sovetskoi iustitsii. Moscow, 1921.

Narodnyi Komissariat iustitsii. *Otchet IX vserossiiskomu s'ezdu sovetov*. Moscow, 1921.

Narodyi sud. *Materialy Narodnogo Komissariata iustitsii*. Moscow, 1918.

Nos. A., ed. *Sbornik materialov otnosiashchikhsia do sosloviia prisiazhnykh poverennykh okruga moskovskoi sudebnoi palaty s 23 aprelia 1866g. po 23 aprelia 1891g*. Moscow, 1891.

Ob'edinenie russkikh advokatov vo Frantsii. Paris, 1932.

Organy iustitsii na novom etape. 5-oe soveshchanie rukovodiashchikh rabotnikov iustitsii RSFSR, iiun' 1931g. Moscow, 1931.

Organy iustitsii na rubezhe vtoroi piatiletki. Materialy VIII rasshirennogo soveshcheniia rabotnikov iustitsii, mart 1933g. Moscow, 1933.

Otchet o deiatel'nosti prezidiuma leningradskoi gubernskoi kollegii zashchitnikov po ugolovnym i grazhdanskim delam pri leningradskom gubsude za chetyre polugodiia (s 15 marta 1923 po 1 aprelia 1925). Leningrad, 1925.

Otchet prezidiuma moskovskoi gubernskoi kollegii zashchitnikov za pervoe polugodie (s 8 okt. 1922 po 1 aprelia 1923). Moscow, 1923.

Otchet prezidiuma moskovskoi gubernskoi kollegii zashchitnikov za 2-oe polugodie (s l aprelia po 1 okt. 1923). Moscow, 1924.

Otchet prezidiuma moskovskoi gubernskoi kollegii zashchitnikov za 3-i otchetnyi period (1 okt. 1923 po 1 aprelia 1924). Moscow, 1924.

Otchet prezidiuma novonikolaevskoi gubernskoi kollegii zashchitnikov za vremia s 1 dek. 1924 po 1 noiabria 1925. Novonikolaevsk, 1925.

Otchet prezidiuma novosibirskoi kollegii zashchitnikov za 1926g. Novosibirsk, 1927.

Otchet prezidiuma omskoi gubernskoi kollegii zashchitnikov za 1925 god. Omsk, 1926.

Piat' let raboty kaluzhskoi gubernskoi kollegii zashchitnikov (1922-1927). Kaluga, 1927.

Protsess Prompartii. Moscow, 1931.

Report of Court Proceedings in the Case of the Anti-Soviet Bloc of Rights and Trotskyites. Moscow, 1938.

Report of Court Proceedings in the Case of the Anti-Soviet Trotskyite Centre. Moscow, 1937.

Report of Court Proceedings in the Case of the Trotskyite-Zinoviev Terrorist Centre. Moscow, 1936.

Sbornik otchetov i rukovodiashchikh postanovlenii prezidiuma kostromskoi gubernskoi kollegii zashchitnikov s 1 avg. 1922 po 1 iiunia 1924. Kostroma, 1924.

Sbornik prikazov i instruktsii Ministerstva iustitsii SSSR 1936-1948. Moscow, 1948.

Sbornik tsirkuliarov i raz'iasnenii Narodnogo Komissariata ius-

titsii RSFSR deistvuiushchikh na 1 maia 1934g. Moscow, 1934.

Sbornik tsirkuliarov Narodnogo Komissariata iustitsii RSFSR za 1922-1925. Moscow, 1926.

Sovetskaia advokatura. Narodnyi Komissariat iustitsii SSSR. Tambov, n.d.

Sudebnye ustavy 20-go noiabria 1864g. za 50 let. Petrograd, 1914.

Trudy pervoi nauchnoi sessii vsesoiuznogo instituta iuridicheskikh nauk. Moscow, 1940.

Uchastie advokata po ugolovnomu delu v sude pervoi instantsii. Narodnyi Komissariat iustitsii RSFSR, Otdel advokatury. Moscow, 1944.

Veger, V., ed. *Distsiplina i etika.* Moscow, 1925.

————. *Organizatsionnaia rabota i voprosy etiki (s 1 aprelia po 1 oktiabria 1924).* Moscow, 1924.

Ves Kharkiv. Kharkov, 1929.

Ves Petrograd/Ves Leningrad. Petrograd/Leningrad, 1915, 1922, 1923, 1924, 1927, 1928, 1934.

Vserossiiskii s'ezd deiatelei sovetskoi iustitsii IV. Moscow, 1922.

Vserossiiskii s'ezd deiatelei sovetskoi iustitsii V. Moscow, 1924.

Vsia Moskva. Moscow, 1923, 1926, 1928, 1929, 1936.

Vsia Srednaia Aziia na 1926. Tashkent, 1926.

Zashchita (Vestnik soiuza moskovskikh advokatov), no. 1, August 20, 1918. Moscow.

III. BOOKS AND MONOGRAPHS

Abdullaev, A. "Istoriia organizatsii instituta zashchity v azer-baidzhanskoi SSR (1920-1926gg.)", in *Trudy*. NII sudebnoi zashchity: Baku, 1969.

————. "Iz istorii advokatury azerbaidzhanskoi SSR (1927-1930gg.)" in *Trudy II*. NII pravovoi zashchity: Baku, 1970.

Advokat v sovetskom grazhdanskom protsesse. Moscow, 1954.

Advokat v sovetskom ugolovnom protsesse. Moscow, 1954.

Apraksin, K., ed. *Advokatura v SSSR.* Moscow, 1971.

Arkhiv russkoi revoliutsii. Edited by I. Gessen. 22 vols. Berlin, 1922-1937.

Babb, H. *Soviet Legal Philosophy.* Cambridge, Mass., 1951.

Bailes, K. E. *Technology and Society under Lenin and Stalin: Origins of the Soviet Technical Intelligentsia, 1917-1941.* Princeton, N.J., 1978.

Bekeshko, S. "Zashchita v stadii sudebnogo razbiratel'stva v sovetskom ugolovnom protsesse." *Kandidat* dissertation, Minsk, 1954.

Berman, H. *Justice in the USSR: An Interpretation of Soviet Law.* Rev. ed. Cambridge, Mass., 1963.

Bilinsky, A. *Die Organisation der sowjetischen Anwaltschaft.* West Berlin, n.d.

Braude, I. *Zapiski advokata.* Moscow, 1974.

Carr, E. H. *The Bolshevik Revolution, 1917-1923.* 3 vols. London, 1950-1953.

———. *The Interregnum.* London, 1954.

———. *Socialism in One Country.* 3 vols. New York, 1958-1964.

———, and Davies, R. *Foundations of a Planned Economy.* 2 vols. New York, 1969-1971.

Collignon, J. G. *Les juristes en Union sovietique.* Paris, 1977.

Conquest, R. *The Great Terror.* New York, 1968.

Dobrovol'skaia, T. *Verkhovnyi sud SSSR.* Moscow, 1964.

Dubkov, E. "Demokraticheskie osnovy organizatsii sovetskoi advokatury." *Kandidat* dissertation, Moscow, 1964.

Durdyev, B. "Organizatsiia i razvitie sovetskoi advokatury v Turkmenistane." *Kandidat* dissertation, Ashkhabad, 1974.

Eroshkin, N. *Istoriia gosudarstvennykh uchrezhdenii dorevoliutsionnoi Rossii.* Moscow, 1983.

Fediukin, S. *Sovetskaia vlast' i burzhuaznye spetsialisty.* Moscow, 1965.

Fitzpatrick, S. *Education and Social Mobility in the Soviet Union, 1921-1934.* Cambridge, 1979.

———. *The Russian Revolution, 1917-1932.* Oxford, 1982.

———, ed. *Cultural Revolution in Russia, 1928-1931.* Bloomington, Ind., 1978.

Garvi, P. *Professional'nye soiuzy v Rossii v pervye gody revoliutsii 1917-1921*. New York, 1958.

Getty, J. Arch. *Origins of the Great Purges: The Soviet Communist Party Reconsidered, 1933-1938*. Cambridge, 1985.

Ginzburg, G.; Poliak, A.; and Samsonov, V., eds. *Sovetskii advokat*. Moscow, 1968.

Gol'dshtein, M. *Advokatskie portrety*. Paris, 1932.

————. *Rechi i stat'i*. Paris, 1929.

Graham, L. *The Soviet Academy of Sciences and the Communist Party, 1927-1932*. Princeton, N.J., 1967.

Gruzenberg, O. *Ocherki i rechi*. New York, 1944.

Hazard, J. *Law Student Life in Moscow*. Zug, 1978.

————. *Settling Disputes in Soviet Society: The Formative Years of Soviet Legal Institutions*. New York, 1960.

Isaev, M. *Podpol'naia advokatura*. Moscow, 1924.

Istoriia gosudarstva i prava azerbaidzhanskoi SSR, 1920-1934gg. Baku, 1973.

Istoriia russkoi advokatury. 3 vols. Moscow, 1914-1916. Vol. 1 written by I. Gessen; vols. 2 and 3 edited by M. Gernet.

Istoriia sovetskogo gosudarstva i prava. 3 vols. Moscow, 1968.

Iz istorii VChK. Moscow, 1958.

Izmeneniia sotsial'noi struktury sovetskogo obshchestva 1921-seredina 30-kh godov. Moscow, 1979.

Juviler, P. *Revolutionary Law and Order*. New York, 1976.

Kaiser, D. H. *The Growth of the Law in Medieval Russia*. Princeton, N.J., 1980.

Kaminskaya, D. *Final Judgment: My Life as a Soviet Defense Attorney*. New York, 1982.

Katkov, G. *Russia 1917: The February Revolution*. London, 1967.

Kemp-Welch, A. "The Origins and Formative Years of the Writers' Union of the USSR, 1932-1936." Ph.D. dissertation, London School of Economics and Political Science, University of London, 1976.

Kozhevnikov, M. *Istoriia sovetskogo suda 1917-1956*. Moscow, 1957.

————. *Sovetskaia advokatura*. Moscow, 1939.

Krylenko, N. *Za piat' let 1918-1922*. Moscow-Petrograd, 1923.

Kuchemko, N. *Ukreplenie sotsialisticheskoi zakonnosti v Sibiri v pervye gody nepa (1921-1923)*, Novosibirsk, 1981.

Kucherov, S. *Courts, Lawyers, and Trials under the Last Three Tsars*. New York, 1953.

———. *The Organs of Soviet Administration of Justice*. Leiden, 1970.

Kuritsyn, V. *Perekhod k nepu i revoliutsionnaia zakonnost'*. Moscow, 1972.

Kurskii, D. *Izbrannye stat'i i rechi*. Moscow, 1958.

Lapenna, I. *Soviet Penal Policy*. London, 1968.

———. *State and Law: Soviet and Yugoslav Theory*. New Haven, 1964.

Leggett, G. *The Cheka—Lenin's Political Police*. Oxford, 1981.

Lenin o sotsialisticheskoi zakonnosti. Moscow, 1964.

Levin, N. "Zashchita v sovetskom ugolovnom protsesse (v formal'nom smysle)." *Kandidat* dissertation, Leningrad, 1946.

Magnus, J., ed. *Die Rechtsanwaltschaft*. Leipzig, 1929.

Maklakov, V. *Iz vospominanii*. 3d. ed. New York, 1954.

Martinovich, I. *Advokatura v BSSR*. Minsk, 1973.

Medvedev, R. *Let History Judge: The Origins and Consequences of Stalinism*. Edited by David Joravsky and Georges Haupt. New York, 1971.

Mumin, M. "Sozdanie i razvitie advokatury v Uzbekistane." *Kandidat* dissertation, Tashkent, 1975.

Neishtadt, T. *Sovetskii advokat*. Moscow, 1958.

Pashukanis, E. *Law and Marxism: A General Theory*. London, 1978.

Polianskii, N. *Ocherk razvitiia sovetskoi nauki ugolovnogo protsessa*. Moscow, 1960.

———. *Pravda i lozh' v ugolovnoi zashchite*. Moscow, 1927.

Rigby, T. H. *Communist Party Membership in the USSR, 1917-1967*. Princeton, N.J., 1968.

———. *Lenin's Government: Sovnarkom 1917-1922*. Cambridge, 1979.

Rivlin, E. *Sovetskaia advokatura*. Moscow, 1926.

Sarkisiants, G. *Advokatura sovetskogo Uzbekistana*. Tashkent, 1972.

Schapiro, L. *The Communist Party of the Soviet Union*. Rev. ed. New York, 1971.

Schlesinger, R. *Soviet Legal Theory*. London, 1945.

Semenov, N. *Sovetskii sud i karatel'naia politika*. Munich, 1952.

Shalamov, M. *Istoriia sovetskoi advokatury*. Moscow, 1939.

Shmarov, I. "Zashchitnik v sovetskom ugolovnom protsesse." *Kandidat* dissertation, Moscow, 1955.

Simonian, M. *Zhizn' dlia revoliutsii*. Moscow, 1963.

Skripilev, E. "Karatel'naia politika vremennogo pravitel'stva i apparat ee provedeniia." Doctoral dissertation, Moscow, 1970.

Solomon, P. *Soviet Criminologists and Criminal Policy: Specialists in Policy-Making*. London, 1978.

Solzhenitsyn, A. *The Gulag Archipelago*, Vols. 1 and 2. New York, 1973-1974.

Steinberg, I. *In the Workshop of the Revolution*. London, 1955.

Strogovich, M. *Kurs sovetskogo ugolovnogo protsessa*. Moscow, 1958.

Stuchka, P. *Izbrannye proizvedeniia po marksistsko-leninskoi teorii prava*. Riga, 1964.

Sukharev, I. "Organizatsiia i deiatel'nost' advokatury SSSR." *Kandidat* dissertation, Moscow, 1973.

Timasheff, N. *The Great Retreat*. New York, 1946.

Troitskii, N. *Tsarizm pod sudom progressivnoi obshchestvennosti 1866-1895*. Moscow, 1979.

————. *Tsarskie sudy protiv revoliutsionnoi Rossii*. Saratov, 1976.

Tucker, R., ed. *Stalinism: Essays in Historical Interpretation*. New York, 1977.

Valerin, V. *Volch'ia staia—Zapiski chlena kollegii zashchitnikov*. Moscow, 1931.

Vas'kovskii, E. *Budushchee russkoi advokatury*. St. Petersburg, 1893.

————. *Organizatsiia advokatury*. St. Petersburg, 1983.

Volskii, N. [Valentinov, N.]. *The Early Years of Lenin*. Ann Arbor, 1969.

Vyshinsky, A. *K polozheniiu na fronte pravovoi teorii*. Moscow, 1937.

————. *Revoliutsionnaia zakonnost' i zadachi sovetskoi zashchity*. Moscow, 1934.

Waxmonsky, G. "Police and Politics in Soviet Society, 1921-1929." Ph.D. dissertation, Princeton University, 1982.

de Witt, N. *Education and Professional Employment in the USSR*. Washington, 1961.

Wortman, R. *The Development of a Russian Legal Consciousness*. Chicago, 1976.

Zaitsev, Ye., and Poltorak, A. *The Soviet Bar*. Moscow, 1959.

Zelitch, J. *Soviet Administration of Criminal Law*. Philadelphia, 1931.

Index

advocates: definition of, 3n. *See also* Bar; private advocates; underground Bar

Akulov, I., 185n, 194

All-Russian Central Executive Committee (VTsIK), 62, 89-90, 170, 174

Arsenev, K., 22

Bar: legislation on, 12, 25, 32, 42, 44-46, 58, 62-64, 69, 72-73, 85-87, 89, 107, 192-193, 201, 207-208, 215, 220; internal government of, 13-14, 20-21, 27-28, 30, 43-44, 49-50, 57-64, 90-91, 104, 111-112, 117-118, 120, 155-156, 164-165, 200-204, 216-219, 221; external supervision of, 13-14, 20-21, 24-25, 29, 60-62, 70, 84, 86, 90-91, 104, 113, 120-127, 155-156, 164-166, 191-193, 200-210, 218-220; size, 18, 21, 31, 47-48, 61, 64-65, 75, 77-79, 96-99, 160-162, 195-196, 198, 217; geographical distribution of members, 18-21, 99, 217-218; qualification of members, 13-14, 97, 217-218; social backgrounds of members, 13n, 31-32, 95-105, 163, 176-177, 196-199; purges of, 113, 115, 121-123, 152-153, 160-162, 194-195, 198-199, 204, 206-207, 217-218; in Azerbaidzhan, 123, 153; in Baku, 103, 119, 122-123; in Belorussia, 153; in Gul, 138; in Kaluga, 108, 112, 122; in Kazan, 19; in Kharkov, 24, 40, 153, 200-201; in Kiev, 19, 20, 197, 216; in Kirgizia, 198; in Kostroma, 118, 133; in Leningrad, 20, 25, 27, 29-31, 33, 39, 41-43, 47-48, 53, 59-62, 70, 96, 100, 102-103, 108, 110-116, 119, 121-122, 129, 131-132, 135, 148, 150, 156, 188, 196, 200, 202, 219; in Moscow, 18, 20, 26, 31-32, 42-43, 54, 59-61, 64-65, 93, 95-98, 108, 116-120, 122, 124, 134, 136-137, 141, 151-152, 159-160, 162-163, 195-200, 203, 207-208, 213, 218-219; in Nizhnii Novgorod, 121; in Novonikolaevsk, 126, 131; in Novosibirsk, 102; in Odessa, 19; in Omsk, 19, 49, 75, 119, 130, 134; in Pskov, 122; in Rostov, 156n; in Samarkand, 161; in Saratov, 161; in Tashkent, 19, 161; in Tim, 59n; in Turkestan, 64, 97; in Turkmenistan, 121; in the Ukraine, 19, 103, 118, 153-154, 166, 197; in Uzbekistan, 153, 162-163, 195-196, 218; in Vladimir, 108; in Zaporozhe, 153, 162. *See also* advocates; collectivi-

trade unions, 148-149, 161, 174, 199, 206; advocates' exclusion from, 125, 151, 225; legal aid activities of, 132, 141-142, 149; as source of Bar members, 101, 163
TsIK. *See* Central Executive Committee

underground Bar, 19, 65, 81, 84, 95, 101, 133, 135, 155, 226
unions of advocates, 50-52
Uritskii, S., 56

Vinokurov, A., 147
Volodarskii, M., 56

VTsIK. *See* All-Russian Central Executive Committee
vydvizhentsy, 96, 110, 135, 162-163, 177, 198, 217
Vyshinsky, A., 8, 110, 167, 172, 181-194, 201, 212-215, 224

women: in the Bar, 32; as recipients of legal assistance, 128
writers, 104, 181n, 223

Zasulich, V., 22-23
Zelitch, J., 177
Zolotukhin, B., 221

Library of Congress Cataloging-in-Publication Data

Huskey, Eugene, 1952-
    Russian lawyers and the Soviet state.

    Bibliography: p.
    Includes index.
    1. Lawyers—Soviet Union—History. I. Title.
LAW   340'.06'047   85-43288
ISBN 0-691-07706-1 (alk. paper)

Eugene Huskey is Assistant Professor of Government and Legal Studies at
Bowdoin College.